▪ THE MIDDLE YEARS ▪
New Psychoanalytic Perspectives

·THE MIDDLE YEARS·
New Psychoanalytic Perspectives

Edited by

JOHN M. OLDHAM, M.D.

ROBERT S. LIEBERT, M.D.

Yale University Press

New Haven and London

Designed by Sonia L. Scanlon and set in Caslon type by
Tseng Information Systems, Inc., Durham, North Carolina.
Printed in the United States of America by
Vail-Ballou Press, Binghamton, New York.

Library of Congress Cataloging-in-Publication Data
The Middle years : new psychoanalytic perspectives / edited by John M. Oldham and
  Robert S. Liebert.
      p.   cm.
  Consists in part of elaborations of papers originally presented at a symposium held
March 7–8, 1987, in New York City, organized by the Association for Psychoanalytic
Medicine in collaboration with the Columbia University Center for Psychoanalytic
Training and Research.
  Dedicated to the memory of Robert S. Liebert.
  Includes bibliographies and index.
  ISBN 0–300–04418–6 (alk. paper)
    1. Middle age—Psychological aspects—Congresses. 2. Psychoanalysis—
Congresses. 3. Psychotherapy—Congresses. I. Oldham, John M. II. Liebert,
Robert S., 1930– . III. Association for Psychoanalytic Medicine (U.S.)
IV. Columbia University.   Center for Psychoanalytic Training and Research.
BF724.6.M53   1989
155.6'6—dc 20
DNLM/DLC
for Library of Congress   89–8939
                                                                                                            CIP

The paper in this book meets the guidelines for permanence and durability of the
Committee on Production Guidelines for Book Longevity of the
Council on Library Resources.

10   9   8   7   6   5   4   3   2   1

In Memoriam
Robert S. Liebert, M.D.

Robert S. Liebert (1930–1988)

Little did I think as I sat discussing this book with Bob Liebert that, in the short span of time between then and the book's publication date, he would leave us. As he generously gave me his time and his wise counsel about the project, he seemed just as vigorous, energetic, and intellectually vibrant as ever. Of course I knew, we all knew, that Bob had a life-threatening illness. But that fact seemed neither immediately relevant nor real as Bob characteristically plunged ahead, putting adversity aside and involving himself in what intensely interested him and in what he believed in. At or near the top of his list were always the newest developments in psychoanalytic thinking—what was most relevant, useful, and applicable to patients, interesting and stimulating to colleagues in all the healing professions, and intellectually challenging to those in other areas of thinking and creativity.

Still, I look back now and think of the process of writing my own chapter for this volume, which deals with the impact of the death of one's parents and the loss of the illusion of immortality and ends with a quote from *The Death of Ivan Ilych*. I can only marvel at the equanimity that Bob maintained as he helped me revise this manuscript, far more aware of his personal situation than I could let myself be.

Bob was respected, admired, and loved. He helped innumerable patients, educated many students, and was always available and devoted to his family and his friends. He was a leader and tireless faculty member of the Columbia Psychoanalytic Center, where he was a much sought-after teacher, supervisor, and training psychoanalyst. He is and will be sorely missed.

John M. Oldham, M.D.
New York, New York
January 1, 1989

CONTENTS

Titian, *The Three Ages of Man*. Edinburgh, National Gallery of Scotland (on loan from the Duke of Sutherland Collection).

INTRODUCTION
New Psychoanalytic Perspectives

ROBERT S. LIEBERT, M. D.

JOHN M. OLDHAM, M. D.

We introduce our subject of the middle years by briefly referring back in time to Titian's painting of *The Three Ages of Man*. Sharing the joyous foreground are, on the right, two young children innocently cuddling together in sleep, protected by a winged *amorino*. Their idyllic promise is achieved in the next stage of life by the pair of youthful lovers at the left. Here, the young woman offers her lover one of her two flutes so that they may join together in the duet of love. From this Arcadian foreground Titian takes us back to the diminutive figure of an old man contemplating two skulls, absorbed in meditation about death. Whether the skulls represent death in general or Titian himself and his departed life companion, or whether they represent what will inevitably become of the pairs of children and youthful lovers we cannot say. The figure does, however, starkly state the knowledge that time is the devourer of all things.

To us, a striking aspect of *The Three Ages of Man*—and Titian was typical of Renaissance artists in this respect—is that the years between young adulthood and old age are completely disregarded. In contrast, we like to think that the Sphinx, in posing the famous riddle to Oedipus, fully intended, when speaking of "the creature who walks on two feet in the afternoon," that "the afternoon" should span the ages from thirty-five to fifty-five years—roughly the period of life addressed by this volume.

There were those in past centuries who separated the course of life into four stages, six, seven (for example, Jaques in Shakespeare's *As You Like It*), ten, and even twelve stages. But the discipline of psychoanalysis has remained faithful to the spirit of Titian's vision and, with a few notable exceptions, has had nothing to say about the middle years (see Panofsky, 1969).

Psychoanalytic thought originally formulated childhood experience as the basis of adult personality and behavior, with the distinct implication that psychic structure was foreclosed by the end of this period. Then, following World War II, through the contributions principally of Erik Erikson, Anna Freud, and Peter Blos, the importance of adolescence as also formative in psychological development became increas-

1

ingly recognized. Over the past two decades the earlier, more static model has evolved into an epigenetic view of development extending through the stages of the life cycle—and here we are singularly indebted to the contributions of Erikson. With acceptance of this epigenetic view of the life cycle there has been growing recognition that internal change and emergent possibilities are characteristic of many individuals in the middle decades of life.

Although each stage of the life cycle is viewed as having conflicts and resolutions particular to it, remarkably scant attention has been given to the middle years as an entity for psychoanalytic exploration. This relative neglect is striking inasmuch as the majority of patients in psychoanalysis are in their middle years.[1] One exception to this observation is Elliott Jaques's landmark article, "Death and the Mid-life Crisis," published in the *International Journal of Psycho-Analysis* in 1965. This paper is referred to more frequently by the authors in this book than any other single article on the middle years. The continuing presence of Jaques's ideas is reflected in the viewpoint of the majority of the contributors—that intrapsychic change continues during the middle years and that new and heretofore unknown conflicts, fantasies, and self-imagery, along with new defensive organizations and modes of adaptation, emerge and are specific to this period of life. Moreover, this new body of mental life commands special attention—or, to put it more strongly, cannot be overlooked—if clinical work with patients in their middle years is to be successful.

The question lingers—why has so little psychoanalytic thought been devoted to the psychological life of the middle years? We suspect that the elements of waning and loss that are intrinsic to this period—the very things that bring many of our patients into therapy and analysis—have been discordant with the generally optimistic outlook of the field. The issues of waning strength, fading beauty, biological clocks, the aging and death of parents, the departure from home of adolescent children, lost opportunities and renunciation of aspirations, and, perhaps most important, the erosion of one's denial that life is finite and death inevitable are indeed the stressful challenges of the middle years. But,

1. The major studies addressing this period (for example, Levinson, 1978; Vaillant, 1977; and Eichorn et al., 1981) are not, with the exception of Vaillant's study, directly psychoanalytic in orientation, although they are congenial to its concepts. There are, in addition, more general psychiatric books in this area (for example, Howells, ed., 1981). Only one volume, however—that edited by Greenspan and Pollock (1981)—contains articles that address the middle years specifically from a psychoanalytic perspective.

as we shall see in the chapters that follow, the adaptive ingenuity of the middle-aged man or woman operates in a dynamic interaction with these challenges, sometimes triumphing, sometimes faltering.

This volume had its origin in a two-day symposium with the same title organized by the Association for Psychoanalytic Medicine in collaboration with the Columbia University Center for Psychoanalytic Training and Research. About half of the chapters are elaborations of presentations given by the contributors at the symposium. The others were solicited from authors who, we believe, have original contributions to offer to the literature of this subject.

The essays address theoretical, developmental, biological, clinical, and creative aspects of the middle years, all within a psychoanalytic framework. There is more to learn about mid-adulthood, just as there is about the years of later life, from many vantage points in the context of a changing world and man's ever-increasing longevity. From a psychoanalytic point of view in particular, intrapsychic development and interpersonal dynamics continue to evolve throughout the life cycle. Important dimensions of these dynamic processes in the middle years are, we believe, clarified by the contributions in this volume.

REFERENCES

Eichorn, D. A.; Clausen, J. A.; Haan, H.; Honzik, M. D.; and Mussen, P. H. 1981. *Present and past in middle life.* New York: Academic Press.

Greenspan, S. I., and Pollock, G. H., eds. 1981. *The course of life: Psychoanalytic contributions toward understanding personality development.* Vol. 3, *Adulthood and the aging process.* Washington, D.C.: U.S. Government Printing Office.

Howells, J. G., ed. 1981. *Modern perspectives in the psychiatry of middle age.* New York: Brunner-Mazel.

Jaques, E. 1965. Death and the mid-life crisis. *International Journal of Psychoanalysis* 46:502–514.

Levinson, D. 1978. *The seasons of a man's life.* New York: Ballantine Books.

Panofsky, E. 1969. Reflections on time. In *Problems in Titian.* New York: New York University Press.

Vaillant, G. E. 1977. *Adaptation to life.* Boston: Little, Brown.

Part I

Theoretical Papers

· 1 ·

THE DEVELOPMENTAL AND STRUCTURAL VIEWPOINTS
On the Fate of Unconscious Fantasies in Middle Life

MILTON H. HOROWITZ, M.D.

W hen Karl Abraham in 1919 wrote a brief paper about the analysis of patients of "advanced age," he was speaking of those in their thirties and forties. His clinical note suggested that for patients for whom the onset of neuroses was relatively recent, analysis was a feasible procedure even past the age of fifty! To put Abraham's ideas into perspective we must remember that the average life expectancy in the United States in 1920 was *54.1 years* and that the current life expectancy is *74.7 years*. When patients consult us now, middle age is much more likely to mean the fifties and sixties, with their expectations for longevity stretching into the eighties.

Furthermore, although considerable numbers of middle-aged patients come to us complaining of discrete neurotic symptoms, many more consult us because of something that might be characterized as the "wish for a full life." Something seems missing, old ambitions are unfulfilled, personal powers have failed or are failing, physical health is undependable, and romantic and sexual expectations become embroiled in new conflicts. The patients want something more than mere relief of anxiety or depression; they want the fulfillment of old wishes. Often they feel infuriated by the thought that they will be denied the "full life."

Some years ago, a fifty-six-year-old woman, disappointed in her career, her marriage, and her children, consulted me about beginning an analysis. She summed up her needs in a single plaintive query: "I've taken care of everyone; now who will take care of me?" The complaint had a familiar ring. I had heard almost the same words from a number of other patients in middle life. Her poignant and anxious question *was* in fact the beginning of her analysis. It was a rubric or chapter heading which organized a lifelong fantasy of being an unappreciated, unrewarded caretaker and rescuer. Behind this meager surface, seemingly unrelated to her immediate life situation, was an entire autobiography

7

in fantasy. In a manner analagous to the dream work of condensation, her cry for help expressed a central fantasy that had depicted the infantile relation to her parents, revealed an important masturbatory fantasy of adolescence, and described her character structure. The unfolding of the details of a complex structure of interwoven fantasies was the subsequent work of many years.

The central idea presented in this brief communication is that unconscious fantasy is remarkably durable, relatively fixed in structure, variable only in conscious expression and derivatives, and notoriously resistant to alteration. This finding of the durability of patterned behavior has been a consistent one throughout the history of analysis.

It was part of the mythology of the earliest hypotheses of the theory of psychoanalytic therapeutic results that the process of defense could be abrogated. In the 1920s, Franz Alexander (1927), viewing the superego as a "parasitic" organ, thought that it could be *abolished* through analysis. Subsequent analytic work, especially that of Hartmann, Kris, and Loewenstein (1946), demonstrated that the functions of defense were necessary for health and equilibrium and were not the consequence of psychological disorder. Furthermore, the functions of ideals and standards in the superego have been demonstrated as necessary for personal and social coherence. The sense of guilt is quantitatively two-edged—both a source of pain if excessive and guardian of self-esteem if experienced at minimal signal level. The individual capacity for guilt glues the social fabric together and is the unseen backdrop to the joy and pleasure of social coherence. The superego cannot be abolished; it can be analyzed and understood.

Now, too, we can see fantasy and wish as having relative permanence in the life of individuals, either leading to pathology or contributing to subsequent development. Fantasy cannot be analyzed away; its derivatives, however, may be altered. *Nowhere is the issue of the persistence of fantasy more poignant than in the analysis of the middle-aged patient.* Many such patients have the idea that this is their last opportunity to make their wishes come true.

What do psychoanalysts mean by the terms *fantasy* and *unconscious fantasy*? Fenichel (1945) said: "As long as thinking is not followed by action it is called fantasy. There are two types of fantasy: creative fantasy, which prepares some later action, and daydreaming fantasy, the refuge for wishes that cannot be fulfilled." The issue of creative fantasy had been approached earlier by Hartmann (1939), who saw an "auxiliary function of fantasy in the learning process. Though fantasy always implies an initial turning away from a real situation, it can also be a preparation for the reality."

Daydreaming is often visual and pictorial in its form and magical in its representation of wishes and desires as being fulfilled or anxieties as being realized. As early as 1915, Freud had recognized that certain fantasies were not accessible to consciousness but produced derivatives. They were "preliminary stages in the formation both of dreams and of symptoms" (Freud, 1915). From the analysis of dream and symptom we are able to infer the existence of highly organized pictorial and verbal concepts, and representations of self and object and of impulses and wishes in relatively stable structures. Perhaps the most striking evidences of these patterned organizations of wish, self, and object appear in those derivatives we have designated as *transference response*. The patient is given the opportunity in the analytic situation not merely to talk about these derivatives but to experience them in their most peremptory affect-laden forms. The transference situation is the neurosis made *alive* and *present*. It offers a special opportunity to give more accessible form to fantasies that had been unconscious or had been given distorted and unrecognizable form in symptoms.

The simplest way to present the lifelong role of fantasy is by a case illustration from an extended analysis. The patient was a fifty-four-year-old man who had been extremely successful in business but whose personal life was chaotic and painful. He saw himself as having a last desperate chance for the life he had always wanted. A physician friend had suggested to him that he take some mood-alleviating medication and perhaps seek some psychotherapy. Both suggestions were rejected by the patient, who wanted a psychoanalysis with the conscious fantasy that such a procedure "would be a complete overhaul."

He had married shortly after graduation from college. His wife had been a campus beauty queen. He described her in great detail as willowy, long-legged, long-haired, self-possessed, and cool in manner. They came from grossly disparate social backgrounds, he from an upper-class, prestigious, but impecunious family, she from a brutal, alcoholic, rural-poor background. Her great beauty and intelligence had always appealed to teachers, and she had escaped into a world of achievement. She had latched herself onto the patient because she saw him as a "winner." By winning her, he felt victorious over his college rivals and was excessively proud of her good looks. He was pleased to show her off to others, was proud of her talents as a hostess, and saw her as an asset to his business ambitions.

Much of his euphoric pleasure in possessing her came to a crash about a year after their marriage when she confessed to him that her seeming sexual pleasure was an elaborate "act." The act had several consistent elements, central to which was her dressing in black under-clothes, black stockings, and garter belt, all of which had to be worn during the sexual act itself. At first the patient thought this had been *her* interest, but he soon became aware that the costume had obligatory fetishistic meaning to him and that he could not achieve erection with-out her dressing up. After her confession of her sexual anesthesia, he became morose, and she began to drink heavily each evening as they attempted to have some sort of sexual life. He soon took to buying sexual costumes for her. When on business trips, he would buy black underwear and lovingly finger it when he returned to his hotel room, masturbating with the fantasy that he was making love to her. As he told this narrative he recalled that he had masturbated in adolescence while clutching a pair of his mother's silk panties that he had taken from the laundry room at home.

The marriage became more and more painful for both. The birth of a number of children made the internal pressures of the marriage worse. The wife's alcoholism increased; her language became coarse and her behavior violent. She went in and out of institutions to dry out and was euphemistically described as having a "little alcohol problem." The children were sent to boarding schools; the patient missed them. He and his wife lived in a state of sullen misery. He grew increasingly ashamed of her and of himself. He entered a number of brief affairs but found that his potency was absolutely dependent on the fetishistic costume, and it was difficult to secure cooperative partners. As he got older, his sexual interest and abilities underwent a serious decline and he felt hopeless.

A year or so before the consultation he had met a woman who inter-ested him immensely. She had been a childhood friend from a family much like his own. Very plain in appearance, she was somewhat over-weight and had thick legs and ankles. He was astonished that he felt ex-cited by her unprepossessing features. He had many daydreams about living with her but could not bring himself to leave his sick wife.

About a month after the analysis began, to his surprise and mine, he broke down completely and wept uncontrollably, covering his face with his hands and turning to the wall. He said that he was a horrible fraud, that he had been keeping a dread secret from me, and that he felt desperately ashamed. He seemed crushed and spoke in a whisper.

Since he met his old friend something had changed in him that made him feel that he was "going insane." This "something" was a "compulsion" that he tried to put out of his mind. It occurred only while he was on business trips. He could not speak of it for several days and made only elliptical allusions to his shameful compulsion. Finally, in a conspicuous act of courage he told me that he had had an image of his friend in the black underwear and had gone out to buy some for her. He bought the largest size available in the shop, returned to his hotel room, and immediately put it on with an excitement he had never before experienced, masturbating repeatedly for hours. On a subsequent trip he had purchased a dress, a coat, high-heeled shoes, and an expensive wig. In each shop he told the salespeople he was buying the item for his mother. On his last trip, he had dressed himself in the entire costume and made up his face with lipstick and eye shadow. He wanted to appear on the street and be noticed by someone. He went through the same wild excitement. He debated whether he should call for room service and let the waiter see him. He masturbated repeatedly in front of a mirror and fell asleep in a state of complete exhaustion. When he awoke, still costumed, he experienced a strange sense of peace accompanied by the idea that he had lost his mind. This event was the precipitating cause for his seeking the analysis and his wish to "restructure" his personality. This restructuring fantasy was a derivative of the unconscious wish to be made into a phallic woman. Parallel with his conscious wish to change his life was an unconscious wish to undergo another sort of change.

The analytic work was characterized by a deeply ambivalent but clinging transference response. There was extraordinary anxiety at even brief separations, but only if those separations were initiated by me. He had been unaware consciously that separation caused him any distress whatsoever. Well into the analysis, he reported a memory in association to a dream. He saw a child standing in a hospital crib and after a moment of wonder realized that the memory was of a child in the crib next to his own during a hospitalization of many months about the time of his third birthday. He had never remembered anything about this hospitalization, nor was it ever spoken about in his family. He had had a number of bouts of excruciating abdominal pain and fever. What had started as a hospitalization for suspected appendicitis had extended for months until spontaneous resolution of the symptoms. The essential corroborative information for this memory was eventually supplied by the patient's aunt. He was described as not recognizing or responding to his mother when he returned home. But subsequently he became extremely attached and close to her. He was docile and well mannered; his father described him as "too good."

From about his tenth year, he shared an interest in sports with his father. He became an excellent athlete, surpassing the older man in golf and tennis. He imagined that by staying fit he could ward off illness and death. In early puberty he often looked in the bathroom mirror with his penis tucked between his legs imagining what a woman looked like naked. He then surprised himself by letting his erect penis pop out from between his legs. Prominent in his most shame-laden transference wishes were sudden obsessive ideas that I should see him as a woman and be astonished. He wanted an external confirmation that his fantasies could be made real.

It required little in the way of interpretation for this patient to recognize that from early in his life he had had an unconscious fantasy that there was such a creature as a "phallic woman" and that the fantasy had been expressed in several derivatives in object-choice and in behavior. His wife and her long willowy body represented one form of the phallic woman fantasy and his friend with her piano legs represented another form. It did not require much interpretation, either, for him to be aware that the fantasy had helped solve anxiety about separation and about bodily intactness. The most dramatic derivative in the transvestism was that he was safe from separation anxiety; he had become a *self-contained entity*, man and woman, a woman with a penis who needed no one else. He had undone the early infantile separation from his mother, and even when alone in a hotel room, he seemed not alone. The wish to be seen in public, like the transference fantasy, was to confirm that a phallic woman could exist.

The rivalry with other men, the demand for success, the choice of women, the fetishistic compulsions—all exploded in middle life into the dramatic symptom of transvestism. To those familiar with reported cases of the effect of the persistent fantasy of a phallic woman (Fenichel, 1945; Lewin, 1933; Bak, 1939), these events are nothing new. What is so unusual is that they all took place in the same patient at successive stages of his life. The late appearance of transvestism without prior cross-dressing is also remarkable.

Of special interest, too, is that we can trace in this analysis the precipitating events for the shift in each phase of his development. In each, the phallic woman fantasy, which remained unconscious, served as motive power for fresh derivatives in fantasy and behavior. Driving the entire process was the central role of separation anxiety. The early separation experience sensitized this patient to later experiences of anxiety of bodily damage. At each step he attempted to control that anxiety by new methods, but using an old template. When he arrived at the analysis, his "loss" of his wife through her depressive and alcoholic illness, the departure of his children, and the gradually evolving consciousness of his declining powers had pushed his behavior in a regressive direction. He came to be aware that he was not as sharp as he used to be about business issues, and that he had a lesser grasp in remembering names. The small inevitable inroads of age had been denied but had stimulated further regression.

The analysis had a felicitous result. The insight into the role of separation anxiety was the most decisive therapeutic event. The external situation could be altered. He divorced his wife, married the old friend, and decided on a lesser involvement in business. He experienced both his awareness of his declining powers and the end of the analysis with a sense of mourning. His happiness with his new wife and his restored potency, without fetishistic requirements, have given him a more genuine and reliable sense of self-esteem. An unexpected fresh sublimation appeared: he has become deeply immersed in a collection of art which he pursues with the professional élan that once characterized his business life. In the shadow of his collecting is the remnant of his fetishistic interest. Connoisseurship has replaced perversion. He is particularly interested in sculpture and its *tangible* qualities. When I last saw him, he commented that his transvestite symptoms seemed "like a dimly remembered nightmare, all pale and washed out." He had seen a Broadway play about a transvestite; he felt moved and sympathetic, but though he recognized something of himself, it, too, seemed far away. His new wife shares his artistic interests. Their collection can be exhibited by both of them. All the fantasy elements that went into the neurotic and perverse distortions are still there, but they have been rearranged and have led to a very different outcome.

What is the applicability of this dramatic case report to the more general problem of the analysis of patients of middle age? It is simply this: old fantasies and fantasy systems are never extinguished. They have a remarkable persistence, and they may be manifest in a variety of forms throughout the life cycle. More often than not we are accustomed to seeing the persistence of the derivatives themselves. That is to say, we are accustomed to seeing the chronic repetition of symptoms and character traits, and by their clamorous quality these derivatives of the underlying fantasy take our attention. But *symptoms* are not pathogenic. Biological constitution, conflict, disturbance in object ties, alteration of ego functions, and their representations in fantasy are the sources of neurosis. It is the persistence of unconscious fantasy that must constantly claim our attention as analysts. Symptoms and character traits are the consequence of underlying pathogenic predispositions. Fantasy is rooted in the constitution, in bodily and emotional needs, and in the life history. Fantasy is, in fact, the record of that history.

Of all the wide range of potential fantasies, each patient seems to have only a *few* systems of fantasy, and they persist for a lifetime. They manifest themselves in a variety of derivatives and tend to be expressed in the analytic situation in wishes in the transference. Such needs and wishes, rooted in the body and bodily sensations, are the clinical data that underlie those explanatory hypotheses of psychoanalysis which are termed the "drives."

Among the first psychoanalytic views of the persistence of relatively permanent—that is, "structuralized"—fantasy systems resulting in behavior were the concepts of *character* stated by Freud (1909) and elaborated by Abraham (1921). Anna Freud, in a seminal paper (1922), described a beating fantasy carried out over years as if it were a novel. She demonstrated that a basic fantasy could show protean manifestations. Derivatives of unconscious fantasy have subsequently been shown to be manifest in conscious daydreams and masturbatory imagery and in symptom, character, object-choice, and transference manifestation.

The circumstances of middle life, and our opportunity to examine them psychoanalytically, give us a newly discovered mental landscape: *middle age as a developmental phase.* In this phase, a new anxiety is added to the sequence described by Freud, the anxiety of loss of function, decay, and death. In middle age, as in other developmental phases, basic fantasies are reworked in a phase-specific manner leading to certain phase-specific manifestations. The *form* they take is often highly rationalized and presented as seeming reality. For example, a middle-aged woman—fearful of her loss of sexual attractiveness, agitated by her scanty menstrual periods and approaching menopause, frightened of death—had a passionate interest in much younger men. She gave the highly plausible explanation that younger men were more sexually vigorous, had better bodies, made her feel more youthful, and put her in touch with younger people. A sturdy resistance was mounted against any examination of these ideas; they were presented as simple realities.

With reluctance, she examined this view. Behind the seemingly realistic story was a lifelong fantasy of being a boy like her adored younger brother who had always claimed her mother's love. This fantasy had been expressed in a variety of vastly different forms throughout life. A wishful self-image had been transformed into an object-choice. One may tentatively generalize that the manifest form that is taken by underlying fantasy is phase-specific and highly subject to rationalization.

Recent works by Abend (1983) and by Arlow (1969) have presented us with the ideas that theories of cure and theories of pathogenesis have their origin in unconscious fantasies. These concepts have their own phase-specific content in patients of middle life. Although each patient has a unique life experience, unique memories, and unique fantasy systems, culture and society provide some final common pathways of representation and expression. (Heinz Hartmann once said that culture provides a pathway for the discharge of the drives.) The most conspicuous of these modes of representation of the fantasies of pathogenesis, in middle life, is the role given to object relations and the role given to work. Current symptoms are often blamed upon a troubled marriage (or lack of marriage) and upon boring work. Change of lover and change of job may be equated with cure. Cure is seen as taking place in the external world and not in the realm of the mind. As a means of achieving that cure, a very frequent fantasy is the wish for a powerful emotional catharsis in the presence of a loving parent-analyst. Fantasies of rebirth with new parents often stand behind the wish for corrective emotional experience. A culture obsessed with youth will shape the fantasies of the aging.

A special and powerful phase-specific resistance to analysis in the middle-aged patient is the frequent *trivialization* of neurosis. Although such trivialization may take place throughout the life cycle, with the denial of suffering and of serious disorders, middle age provides some special paths of expression. Here, too, insistence is placed upon changing the external reality and minimizing the need for treatment. If treatment is sought, it, too, is trivialized. If analysis is suggested, a frequent response is, "I'm not as sick as all that; all I need is a little help with current problems." It is very frightening for one to turn fifty or sixty and realize that one has not solved a lifetime of trouble. Gently helping such a person to examine a life of fantasy and its consequences is a challenging diagnostic and therapeutic task.

REFERENCES

Abend, S. M. 1983 *Borderline patients*. New York: International Universities Press.

Abraham, K. 1919. The applicability of psycho-analytic treatment to patients at an advanced age. In *Selected papers of Karl Abraham*. New York: Basic Books, 1960.

————. 1921. Contributions to the theory of the anal character. In *On character and libido development*. New York: Basic Books, 1966.

Alexander, F. 1927. The need for punishment and the death instinct. In *The scope of psychoanalysis*. New York: Basic Books, 1961.

Arlow, J. 1969. Unconscious fantasy and disturbances of conscious experience. *Psychoanalytic Quarterly* 38:1–27.

Bak, R. 1939. Regression of ego orientation and libido in schizophrenia. *International Journal of Psychoanalysis* 20:64–71.

Fenichel, O. 1945. *The psychoanalytic theory of neurosis*. New York: W. W. Norton.

Freud, A. 1922. Beating fantasies and daydreams. In *The writings of Anna Freud*, 1:137–157. New York: International Universities Press, 1974.

Freud, S. 1909. Character and anal erotism. In *Standard edition*, 9:167–175.

————. 1915. The unconscious. In *Standard edition*, 14:159–215.

Hartmann, H. 1939. Psychoanalysis and the concept of health. In *Essays in ego psychiatry*. New York: International Universities Press, 1964.

Hartmann, H.; Kris, E.; and Lowenstein, R. M. 1946. Comments on the formation of psychic structure. In *The psychoanalytic study of the child*, 2:11–38. New York: International Universities Press.

Lewin, B. 1933. The body as phallus. *Psychoanalytic Quarterly* 21:23–47.

· 2 ·

OBJECT RELATIONS THEORY
Psychic Aliveness in the Middle Years

ARNOLD H. MODELL, M.D.

I have seen the moment of my greatness flicker,
And I have seen the eternal Footman hold my coat, and
snicker . . .

T. S. Eliot, from "The Love Song of J. Alfred Prufrock"

T. S. Eliot (1962), who wrote this poem in his late twenties, was, I suspect, preternaturally middle-aged. In this condensed imagery Eliot goes to the heart of our subject matter—the loss of self-deceptive illusions and the confrontation with death.

We may not agree on the precise age of the onset of the middle years, but let me arbitrarily claim that it extends from the mid-thirties to the onset of old age. As our increased longevity and changing attitudes toward aging have retarded the onset of old age, for those with normal life expectancies the middle years constitute the longest span of our lives. Childhood and adolescence are but a preparation and old age a postscript. In a certain sense the middle years are life itself, or what living is all about.

Before addressing the specific issue of psychic aliveness in the middle years, I wish first to consider our changing views of the theory of the life cycle. Theories of the life cycle or of adult development are implicitly influenced by contemporary theories of child development, which are in the process of undergoing radical modifications (for example, see Stern, 1985). Although there is no uniformity of opinion, we have unobtrusively modified certain assumptions concerning adult development, assumptions that were implicit in the ego psychology that dominated psychoanalysis twenty-five to thirty years ago. I am thinking especially of the belief of some ego psychologists that maturation is equated with a growing autonomy from the environment achieved by means of internalization. This is, in my opinion, a misplaced biological analogy. Now, it is true that as the child matures it internalizes certain executive and superego functions from its caretakers and in this sense achieves a certain autonomy. But the idea that we as adults are autono-

17

mous from our human environment is obviously false and misleading. We are dependent creatures in childhood and we remain dependent as adults, although, as Fairbairn (1952) noted, we must distinguish and contrast mature and infantile dependency.

The idea that psychic development is orderly and hierarchical is another biological analogy that has been misapplied to theories of human development. Hierarchical assumptions have contributed to the view that developmental epochs, like geological strata, are layered one upon another with comparatively sharp lines of demarcation, such as the division that many consider to exist between the pre-oedipal and oedipal eras. In turn this developmental model influences the way we interpret adult psychopathology. For example, if one believes that maturation is equated with autonomy and that developmental stages are hierarchical, an adult who expresses a wish for a merging union with the therapist may be viewed as undergoing either a serious regression or a significant developmental arrest. This manner of thinking incorporates a developmental or genetic fallacy: if a process has its origins in early development, its appearance in adult life is necessarily a sign of pathology. Further, the earlier and deeper the strata, the more severe the psychopathology.

Our increasing experience with the psychoanalysis of the so-called narcissistic personality will eventually modify our developmental theories and our views of the normative psychology of the middle years, for we can observe that conflicts concerning autonomy and separateness recur throughout the individual's development through each stage in the life cycle. We all have a continuing need for sustaining objects; perhaps it is a biological given. Kohut (1977) has emphasized that adults continue to require self-affirmation as a kind of psychic oxygen. The process of mirroring and the use of transitional objects observed in early development are not relinquished in adult life. Despite their belief in their own autonomy and separateness, most people continue to need the illusion that one's safety in the world is assured by maintaining contiguity with a protective object. Even in a mature love relationship, where the separateness of the loved object is fully affirmed, in another part of the mind that loved one will function as a transitional object.

A hierarchical view of human development assumes an orderly linear progression in accordance with the direction of time's arrow. For example, the pre-oedipal phase has been described by Mahler (1967) as a point of closure. If we base our theory of the life cycle on human or psychic time rather than on linear or objective time, we will not continue to think in terms of points of psychic closure. (I am not ignoring the requirement that some models of child development need to be based upon objective, linear time, such as the predetermined sequence of cognitive development that Piaget has described.) Human time is cyclical or helical. Conflicts recur endlessly and may be worked through at increasingly high levels of mastery, but one can never say that one has outgrown the Oedipus complex or has fully mastered the problems of separation and individuation. Again to quote T. S. Eliot: "Time present and time past / Are both perhaps present in time future, / And time future contained in time past" (from *Four Quartets*, "Burnt Norton").

We need also to remind ourselves that theories of development and of the life cycle occur in specific cultural contexts; one wonders what panelists in a similar conference in China or in Java would say about their middle years. Developmental theory is heavily influenced by cultural assumptions concerning past and future time. Does the past control the present? To what extent is the life cycle molded by the development of the individual, or is it subordinate to the culture?

Ego psychology's equating maturation with autonomy from the environment may be something that is peculiarly American. It reverberates in a certain way with the view of the inner-directed man that Riesman et al. (1950) have described. The term *inner-directed* was defined as characterizing someone who is relatively autonomous from society's traditions. The appearance in 1950 of *The Lonely Crowd* coincided with the flowering of ego psychology in this country. (Parenthetically, we have not taken sufficient note of the implications of the fact that ego psychology has taken root particularly among American psychoanalysts and has not, by and large, among the Europeans.) Riesman and his colleagues had the prescience to note, however, that the inner-directed man was already giving way to a different character type—the other-directed man, someone who conforms and plays the game. That is to say, they predicted a shifting ecology of the neuroses in the direction of the emergence of a narcissistic character type.

It is interesting to note that the title of this volume refers to the middle years rather than to middle age. *Middle years* is a more neutral term, implying that one can occupy the middle years without being or becoming middle-aged. Middle age, then, is a state of mind. Some individuals seem always to have been middle-aged, whereas others remain adolescents until they are overtaken by old age. If one seeks to identify the state of mind that transforms a young adult into a middle-aged person, one thinks of the renunciation of illusions and the acceptance of limitations. For this reason the term *middle age* has for many of us a certain depressive cast, for these lost illusions need to be mourned. Middle age is a time for coming to terms with the limitations of one's self, of one's loved ones, and finally of reality. In youth and young adulthood many share the illusion of immortality; the actuality of one's own death is unthinkable or is postponed to a distant, actually unimaginable, future. This belief in one's immortality may fuel the white heat of creativity, the loss of which may later precipitate a mid-life crisis.

It is here that I must refer to Elliot Jaques's most significant contribution (1965): his recognition that the mid-life crisis that has characterized the lives of so many individuals of genius is precipitated by a growing awareness of the proximity and inevitability of one's own death. It is not entirely by chance that it is a Kleinian psychoanalyst who has most cogently considered the psychology of death. For unlike most psychoanalysts, Melanie Klein believed in Freud's death instinct, but she transformed it into something peculiarly her own. Although I remain unconvinced that there is an instinct for death as such, I think it is plausible that an older infant may experience a sense of impending psychic disintegration, the ultimate terror, the death of the psyche. This fear of disintegration of the self, of which we learn from our sicker patients, may not play a part in the normative psychology of the middle years. The fear of psychic death, however, arises not only from fear of the disintegration of the self but also from the experience of psychic stagnation. Erikson (1959) described the "normative crisis" of the middle years as "generativity versus stagnation." I would interpret this as a crisis of psychic aliveness versus psychic death.

Freudian psychoanalysts may have been inhibited in exploring the psychology of death because of Freud's peculiarly ambivalent attitude toward the subject. Freud firmly believed that death had no mental representation in the unconscious mind (1915). Yet we know from biographical accounts that he was preoccupied with death and that he tried by means of Fliess's numerical tables to prophesy the year of his own death (51 was the number he feared). Nevertheless, he maintained that the unconscious registers castration anxiety but not the fear of death, and never did Freud refer to death anxiety. The French psychoanalyst Pontalis (1981) argues that death was a central but hidden theme in Freud's work. He has gone so far as to say, "In my view the theme of death is basic to Freudian psychoanalysis as is the theme of sexuality. I even believe that the latter was largely accorded a more prominent role in order to conceal the former" (p. 184).

The thesis I propose is that there is a symbolic equivalence between psychic death and actual death; psychic death can symbolize actual death, and the fear of actual death may be mitigated by sustaining a sense of one's psychic aliveness. Death anxiety in the middle years may inhibit creativity, as Jaques observed, but paradoxically it may also inspire a phoenixlike creativity that is life affirming. Periods of barrenness in creative individuals may reinforce death anxiety, which may then lead to a new burst of creativity, so that there is a continuous interplay between these two states. Perhaps for this reason, creative individuals need to be preoccupied with death. Biographical studies of great artists suggest that not only were these individuals preoccupied with death, but their fear of death was transformed into their creations. To cite two examples: Mary Gedo (1983) traces the theme of death in Picasso's paintings of his Blue Period; and the poems of Robert Lowell can be understood as a transformation of the poet's mourning for his lost objects. As one observer put it, "poetic grief was his only defense against psychic nothingness" (Martin, 1983). For Lowell poetry was the alternative to psychic death; in a larger sense all art is transformation. As Stephen Spender (1986) noted, the greatness of the artist consists in his capacity to translate the harsh unpoetic material of the world into poetry.

But what about the ordinary person who is not particularly gifted? As we are considering a normative psychology of the middle years, does the psychology of creativity have a wider applicability? For the ordinary individual there is something analogous in what has been described as creative living, which requires a similar capacity to transform the muck of the world into something better. Here I must refer to the work of Winnicott (1971), who made a particular contribution to this subject. The transformation of the impact of painful reality rests upon psychological processes similar to those underlying creativity, whether or not the individual possesses talent. I am thinking here of his theory of the transitional object, which is essentially a theory of the creative use of illusion. In the presence of a good enough mother who responds intuitively and anticipates the child's wishes, the child's sense of his or her omnipotence will be strengthened in a way that reinforces a positive relation to the world outside the self. This can be considered to be a template for creative transformations of external reality, a capacity to use imagination to transform the experience of the world. Winnicott refers to an intermediate area that belongs neither to the subject nor to the object. This capacity to transform reality through illusion remains as a core within the personality, and for the adult it is a prerequisite for the pleasurable use of the imagination. For those who do not have this core there may be an impairment in the use of symbols, an impairment in the ability to transform the experience of the so-called real world. As clinicians we may observe patients who are unable to form transference illusions, who remain too concrete and literal, experiencing their relation to the therapist as "only" a piece of "reality" (Modell, 1985). The absence of this capacity to transform reality undoubtedly contributes to a sense of the futility of life. Instead of a positive attachment there may be a hatred of reality. This impairment may also be experienced as a psychic deadness, a prefiguration of actual death. Winnicott said, "it is creative apperception more than anything else that makes the individual feel that life is worth living" (1971, p. 65). I understand him to mean that without some illusory overestimation of the object, we are not able to love, and without some illusory overestimation of the self, we are unable to create (see also Pao, 1983).

Yet we think of the middle years as the time when one comes to terms with the limitations of one's self and of reality, a time for the relinquishment of certain illusions, especially the grandiose expectations of adolescence and young adulthood. How can this be reconciled with the need for some illusory overestimation of the self and one's loved objects to foster a positive attachment to reality? Are there good and bad illusions, or is it a question of the use made of illusions and illusioning? The transitional object can be thought of as a paradigm for the creation of illusions, but we remember that the transitional-object concept, as I have noted (Modell, 1984), is a great psychological divide, with its regressive and progressive sides. One needs to create transitional objects—that is, to make use of Winnicott's intermediate space—but transitional objects can also be concretized and enslaving. The latter characterizes certain aspects of the transference of borderline patients. What determines whether illusions can be used creatively or merge into delusion? Mature love contains elements of transitional-object relatedness, but it also presupposes the acceptance of separateness. Similarly, true creativity, whether in art or in science, requires the acceptance of a prior tradition, which stands for the nonself that is transformed by the creative act. Scientific revolutions are never self-created. Greenacre

(1957) noted that there has been an undue emphasis on the narcissistic aspects of creativity. As she viewed it, the artistic product has the character of a "love gift," a "collective love affair with the world." Creative illusions are not solipsistic; they require some form of loving attachment to the world of objects.

We know from our clinical work that for some individuals middle age may be a disaster. These people may be at risk for suicide if their solipsistic grandiosity remains rigid and unyielding when confronted with the limitations of the self and of reality. I am thinking of a man in an interminable psychoanalysis who could be diagnosed as having a severe narcissistic personality disorder. As a child he consciously identified himself with omnipotent figures. He thought he was Superman and was convinced that with sufficient practice he could teach himself to fly; accordingly, he spent hours jumping off small heights, sustained by the hope of future success. The goal of flight was finally relinquished, but only after it was replaced with a series of other omnipotent fantasies that would confirm his uniqueness in the future. It was essential for the preservation of his very existence for him to believe that some day his uniqueness would be apparent to all. This man, although seriously ill, was not delusional in that reality testing was preserved, as the confirmation of his grandiose fantasies was continuously postponed into the future. For him middle age is the period of life when time begins to run out, when the future becomes now.

As I have noted earlier, when we apply a developmental model to the middle years we need to think in terms of psychic as well as objective time. The idea of psychic time is very ancient indeed, perhaps originating in the observations of Saint Augustine (397), who noted that present time has an instantaneous quality and that the past enters into future expectations. He observed essentially the tripartite nature of psychic time. In the middle years future time becomes foreshortened. But psychic time is essentially cyclic, not sequential; fundamental conflicts are continuously reworked in the context of the life cycle. This is especially true with regard to conflicts concerning dependency and autonomy. We never cease to be dependent; therefore we must consider the effect of current object relations on the sense of psychic aliveness.

As the middle years constitute the longest period of our lives, they are also a time when our object ties tend to be more permanent, so that one's partner becomes in a sense a human environment, an inescapable current reality. Current object relations can become the focus of what can be called a "manic defense," a defense that can be considered a major obstacle to creative living. The manic defense, although first observed in manic-depressive illness, is not confined to persons liable to develop mania. Winnicott (1958) understood the manic defense as an inability to give full significance to inner psychic reality. It consists of a flight to external reality, a state in which mourning is postponed or not experienced. In this sense it is ubiquitous defense of everyday life. Winnicott described it further as a denial of deadness, a defense against depressive "death inside" ideas.

The manic defense, then, is an avoidance of deadness by means of a flight into reality, an avoidance of the fear of death at the price of cutting off awareness of inner or psychic reality. We are all familiar with people who fill their lives with activity, who never allow themselves to have moments of contemplation in which they might experience depression and the fear of death. These individuals are cut off from their inner life and appear shallow and superficial. The manic defense thus impedes the interpenetration of inner reality and the external world— the source of creativity and psychic growth.

In reviewing my middle-aged analytic patients I was struck by the extent to which the reality of a painful marriage can become the focus of a manic defense, contributing to a sense of stagnation and an arrest in emotional growth. All therapists are familiar with the defense of externalization, the use of external reality as an escape from psychic reality. But the manic defense includes more than mere externalization, as it leads to a sense of psychic deadness and futility. One's love relations may function as a self-affirming creative muse in the sense that Kohut attributes to self objects. Alternatively, a painful relationship may become the focus of a flight into reality, a flight away from psychic reality. Thus the quality of current object relations makes its contribution to the "aliveness" or "deadness" of the self.

From the perspective of object relations theory I have approached the sense of psychic aliveness in the middle years from two vantage points: that of the internalized object, the core within the self that enables one to transform life experiences creatively, and the actual object in present time. Elliott Jaques (1965, 1981) believes that normative development in the middle years requires the working through of the depressive position. Under constructive circumstances, the created object in mid-life is experienced unconsciously in terms of the good breast, which would moderate the fear component in the fear of dying. My emphasis has been on the interpenetration and transformation of psychic and external reality. These are the preconditions for a sense of psychic aliveness.

Finally we must remind ourselves that as clinicians we are witness to a biased sample of psychopathology. We need to be reminded that for many people the middle years are the best years of their lives. There are those whose capacity for creativity and creative living remains un-diminished and extends into advanced old age.

REFERENCES

Augustine, Saint. 397. *Confessions*. New York: E. P. Dutton, 1939.

Eliot, T. S. 1962. *The complete poems and plays*. New York: Harcourt, Brace & World.

Erikson, E. H. 1959. Identity and the life cycle. *Psychological Issues* 1; no. 1.

Fairbairn, W. R. 1952. *Psychoanalytic studies of the personality*. London: Tavistock Publications.

Freud, S. 1915. Thoughts for the times on war and death. In *Standard edition*, 14:273–300.

Gedo, M. 1983. The archaeology of a painting: A visit to the city of the dead beneath Picasso's *La Vie. Psychoanalytic Inquiry* 3:371–430.

Greenacre, P. 1957. The childhood of the artist. In *The psychoanalytic study of the child*, 12:47–72. New York: International Universities Press.

Jaques, E. 1965. Death and the mid-life crisis. *International Journal of Psycho-analysis* 46:502–514.

———. 1981. The midlife-crisis. In *The course of life*. Ed. S. Greenspan and G. Pollock, 3:1–23. Washington, D.C.: U.S. Department of Health and Human Services.

Kohut, H. 1977. *The restoration of the self*. New York: International Universities Press.

Mahler, M. 1967. On human symbiosis and the vicissitudes of individuation. *Journal of the American Psychoanalytic Association* 15:740–763.

Martin, J. 1983. Grief and nothingness: Loss and mourning in Robert Lowell's poetry. *Psychoanalytic Inquiry* 3:431–484.

Modell, A., ed. 1984. The transitional object and the creative act. In *Psycho-analysis in a new context*. New York: International Universities Press.

———. 1985. Object relations theory. In *Models of the mind*. Ed. A. Rothstein. New York: International Universities Press.

Pao, P-N. 1983. Suspension of the reality principle in adaptation and creativity. *Psychoanalytic Inquiry* 3:431–449.

Pontalis, J-B. 1981. On death-work. In *Frontiers in psychoanalysis*. New York: International Universities Press.

Riesman, D.; Glazer, N.; and Denney, R. 1950. *The lonely crowd*. New Haven: Yale University Press.

Spender, S. 1986. On fame and the writer. *New York Review of Books* 33(20):75.

Stern, D. 1985. *The interpersonal world of the infant*. New York: Basic Books.

Winnicott, D. W. 1958. *Collected papers*. New York: Basic Books.

———. 1971. *Playing and reality*. New York: Basic Books.

· 3 ·

SELF PSYCHOLOGY
The Fate of the Nuclear Self
in the Middle Years

PAUL H. ORNSTEIN, M. D.

Throughout the history of psychoanalysis, clinical necessity, first and foremost, has prompted the repeated expansions as well as the few significant transformations of the field. Thus, psychoanalysis is rightly considered an empirical science—with an updated meaning of the term *empirical*, of course—rather than primarily a theory-based one. This updated meaning recognizes the closely intertwined relationship between practice and theory (or clinical fact and clinical theory)—so closely, in fact, that we find ourselves talking about our empirical observations and their theoretical formulations in the same breath. It is perhaps disconcerting at times that, if we are not deliberately careful, we find it difficult to separate our findings from our theories about our findings.

I therefore think it felicitous that this book and the two-day symposium on which it is based begin with synopses of major contemporary theoretical trends that may be brought to bear on the understanding of the middle years in health and illness. But in the light of the updated meaning of the term *empirical*, it is also fitting that these theoretical frameworks should be presented in terms of their direct clinical relevance and should serve as a backdrop for what is to follow in this book. After all, no psychoanalytic theory can stand alone, without its clinical-empirical referents. My assumption was, as I was preparing my presentation, that our panel was to be *theoretical*-clinical, whereas the remainder of the symposium was to be *clinical*-theoretical, since neither could be just one or the other. For me, this is a matter of emphasis, and the linkage between them is tight.

My task, then, is to present the self psychological *theoretical*-clinical perspective. To do this with the necessary brevity, I shall have to focus on what is new and different in this perspective as compared to other psychoanalytic perspectives; I will have the opportunity to point to historical antecedents or concurrent similarities or divergences only in passing.

I begin with some well-known views on adult development and

27

the middle years; I follow with a brief survey of the development of the "nuclear self"; and finally I trace the fate of the nuclear self in the middle years with a few brushstrokes and the aid of two brief clinical vignettes.

Some Views on Adult Development and the Middle Years

For quite some time young adults were thought to be the ideal candidates for psychoanalysis. Hence psychoanalytic perspectives had little specifically psychoanalytic to offer on the subject of the middle years. It was thought that the potential fluidity of the symptomatically or characterologically bound libido (and aggression) in young adults was a prerequisite for their being freed up and successfully redeployed. In other words, only young adults were thought to be able to attain a healthier orgastic potency upon the resolution of their oedipal conflicts and thereby make their investment in a prolonged analysis worthwhile. But even when the goals and processes of analysis were reconceptualized in terms of ego psychology and object relations theory, this in itself did not seem to extend—on a theoretical level—the domain of psychoanalysis to the middle years and later phases of life. Patients in their middle years (and even older) were, of course, being treated by psychoanalysts with increasing frequency (a practice actually engaged in by Abraham in 1911) but—as far as I could discern—without any understanding as yet of the various developmental phases of adulthood itself (with the notable exception of Jung, 1933).

Psychoanalysis has only slowly come to embrace (clinically as well as theoretically) the entire life cycle—and this embrace is still in its very beginning stage. As is so frequently the case, theoretical formulations have lagged far behind clinical ones. The reasons for this are understandable. Personality development, based on psychoanalytic reconstructions from the transference, appeared, in a fundamental sense, completed with the resolution of the Oedipus complex. The "mind" was essentially formed into a closed system with this resolution, implying that environmental influences could no longer bring about further psychic development. The rest of the life cycle could be characterized from this vantage point (somewhat tongue-in-cheek) as "variations on a theme." At that time even adolescence was thought to be mainly a reworking of the Oedipus complex—a small reopening of the mind for new developmental influences.

From a psychobiological vantage point in psychoanalysis it was Benedek (1950, 1959) who opened up the path of development beyond adolescence and clearly demarcated subsequent phases in adult life with such concepts as "parenthood as a developmental phase," the development of "motherliness" and "fatherliness," and "climacterium as a developmental phase." In her lectures on development she also spoke of "senescence as a developmental phase." Benedek was among those who emphasized early on what is now common knowledge—that adolescence is not merely a reworking of the oedipal conflicts but contains phase-specific new developmental tasks that have to be mastered if a healthy transition to adulthood is to take place.

From a psychosocial vantage point it was Erikson (1959) who opened up the path of development beyond adolescence and clearly demarcated special developmental tasks, achievements, and pathogenetic failures in later life. His well-known "eight ages of man" extended the concept of development throughout the life cycle.

Following Benedek and Erikson, an extensive literature on biological and sociological perspectives on the life cycle has accumulated outside of psychoanalysis. But these biosocial perspectives have yet to become integrated into an overarching theory of human behavior (Neugarten, 1970; Cohler and Boxer, 1984; Offer and Sabshin, 1984). Thus, although ideas regarding the presence of developmental potentialities throughout the life cycle have been around for some time, psychoanalytic thinking remained only marginally influenced by them until very recently—except for the work of some child analysts and analytic developmental researchers. This is most likely due to the fact that these revised ideas did not originate in the recognition of special features or forms of the transference and were thus not derived from psychoanalytic reconstructions. They were garnered from observations outside the clinical situation. Psychoanalysts, with their interpretive eyes riveted on the transference, did not know what to do with this new knowledge imported into the psychoanalytic treatment process.

Kohut's contributions followed closely on the heels of Benedek's and Erikson's extensions of development throughout the life cycle. In stark contrast, however—and sharply demarcated from the psychobiologic approach on the one hand and the psychosocial approach on the other—Kohut derived his ideas on development from reconstruction of the selfobject transferences through introspection and empathy. He thus offered us a psychological theory of development. Linked so directly to the transference, such a developmental theory is immediately useful clinically. This usefulness is related to the following factors: the concept selfobject encompasses the experience of both inner and outer reality; it is a unique vehicle for the study of the environment's influence on development, including the experiencing of the analyst in the analytic situation as well as the precise role he plays in the curative process. The recognition by Kohut that "we live in a matrix of selfobjects from birth to death" (1978 [1980], p. 478) highlights with epigrammatic conciseness the potential for ongoing development throughout the life cycle. It was his recognition of the nature of the selfobject transferences that enabled Kohut to offer a new view of development in which the *lived experience* of the infant and child became of paramount importance. It is this aspect of self psychology that is now being confirmed by infant researchers in their emphasis on the fit between infant and mother.

Self psychology has, through these elements of its clinical and developmental theories, triggered, directly and indirectly, a significant upsurge of psychoanalytic interest in the understanding and treatment of patients in their middle years and later. This increased interest is of relatively recent vintage. It is most clearly reflected in the works of Colarusso and Nemiroff (1979, 1981) and Nemiroff and Colarusso (1984), who have recently offered a comprehensive psychoanalytic (theoretical and clinical) developmental perspective on the entire life cycle, and in a paper by King (1980), who supplied an illustration and discussion of the nature of the transference and its working through in the middle years. Colarusso and Nemiroff brought us to a new stage in the psychoanalytic understanding of adult development through contributions that in important ways converge on some central tenets of self psychology. They also claim that "changes between organism and environment occur *from birth to death*, producing a continuous effect on psychic development. The adult is not a finished product insulated from the environment, but like the child, is in a state of dynamic tension which continually affects and changes him" (Colarusso and Nemiroff, 1979, p. 61; italics added). This is in direct opposition, they say, to the still prevalent psychoanalytic conception of adulthood as a static phase in which no further development takes place. The two optimistically assume that "a conceptual bridge between [these two divergent] viewpoints may be [brought about by] an increased understanding of the *difference* between the developmental processes in the child and in the adult." Although they clearly acknowledge the existence of differences between early and later development, they categorically deny "the *absence* of the developmental process in the adult" (p. 62).

To summarize thus far, the essential dichotomy in present-day psychoanalytic thinking in relation to development is as follows: In one view, development is considered to be restricted to the early years (until the end of adolescence), with no developmental processes occurring after adulthood is reached. A corollary to this view is the notion that there is an openness to environmental influences on the psyche early on, but that the mental apparatus is essentially a closed system once its structuralization is completed.

In the other view, development extends throughout the life cycle, with differences between early and later developmental processes assumed to be present but not yet microscopically delineated. A corollary to this view is the notion that the psyche is an open system throughout the life cycle, but that this openness is decisively affected by the psychic structures that are built up since infancy and childhood and are in a continuous process of development and change as a result of the ongoing exchanges with the environment "from birth to death."

These dichotomies are still at the root of some of the ferment in our field today. They contribute the silent (or not so silent) background against which our deliberations here take place and against which I wish to present Kohut's contributions and the self psychological perspective on the middle years.

On the Development of the Nuclear Self

Self psychology places the bipolar self at the center of the psychological universe. It focuses on the study of the genesis and development of the self, on its bipolar constituents and functions as well as the aims and disturbances of the self—all within the self-selfobject matrix. In this matrix "self and environment constitute an experiential unit; the self cannot be conceptualized without the selfobject environment, nor can the functions of the selfobject be assessed without taking the effect that these functions have on the self into consideration" (Ornstein and Ornstein, 1985, p. 195). I shall take for granted a general familiarity with these formulations of self psychology on development. A cursory review, however, of the genesis and development of the *nuclear self*— the earliest cohesive, core configuration of the self that may be revived in a psychoanalytic situation in the form of an archaic selfobject transference—may be necessary as a reminder of these basic concepts. This should also lead us directly to a consideration of the middle years.

Kohut grappled with the difficult question of the origin of the self and its earliest manifestations in many of his writings (for example, 1974 [1978], 1977, 1984). He assumed that a rudimentary self was present very early in life and noted that "the human environment reacts to even the smallest baby as if it had already formed such a self" (1977, p. 99). He postulated that the primal, rudimentary self originates when and where the parents' hopes, expectations, and anticipatory fantasies about their as yet unborn baby and its innate potentials converge and intersect. These hopes and expectations are later unconsciously conveyed to the child and shape the child's self. If such parental hopes and expectations are conveyed in relation to the child's innate skills and talents, they have structure-building properties; otherwise they do not. "For example, praise and enthusiasm in response to a particular behavior that is not experienced by the child as an expression of his or her nuclear self are not empathic responses; such responses are more likely expressions of the parents' own expectations than an affirmation and validation of the child's own self." Thus, "the environment's responses to the child 'create' experiences that are unique not only to that child but also to that environment. The experiences that become transmutedly internalized and will constitute the relatively independent *tension, affect, and self-esteem* regulating systems of the self are being 'created' between the infant and his emotional environment in an ongoing way" (Ornstein and Ornstein, 1985, p. 195). From a myriad of such experiences through some as yet unknown process of selection, some will be garnered and retained in what is to become the core self, or nuclear self. Kohut says of the nuclear self that it "is the basis of our sense of being an independent center of initiative and perception, integrated with our most central ambitions and ideals and with our experience that our body and mind form a unit in space and a continuum in time. This cohesive and enduring psychic configuration, in connection with a correlated set of [innate] talents and skills, . . . forms the central sector of the personality" (Kohut, 1977, p. 177). Kohut assumed on the basis of his reconstructions that "traces of both ambitions and idealized goals are beginning to be acquired . . . in early infancy, [but] the bulk of nuclear grandiosity consolidates into *nuclear* ambitions in early childhood . . . and the bulk of *nuclear* idealized goal structures are acquired in later childhood."

The consolidation of the nuclear self also means the acquisition of an "action-poised program," an internal ground plan or design, whose fulfillment will henceforth be the central goal of the self. The acquisition of such a well-consolidated nuclear self is a sine qua non for mental health. It is acquired through the empathic mirroring of budding and then expanding ambitions; the availability of alter-ego support for skills and talents; and opportunities for merger with idealized greatness. Mental health means in this context the ability to live out the particular inner design of the nuclear self that was laid down in the center of the self.

I shall not supply the details of how we move developmentally from the acquisition of the nuclear self to the middle years. I shall say only that it is in the middle years, especially in the late middle years, that the nuclear self, whether sturdy or enfeebled, has its greatest impact on mastery versus failure in relation to the phase-specific life tasks of this period. Although each of us may be exposed to the possibility of anxiety and guilt related to unsolvable conflicts at this age, the painful consequences of lowered self-esteem, in connection with failures to fulfill our most central ambitions and to live up to our most cherished ideals, dominate the experiences of this era in our lives. I turn now to a small, highly selected segment of these issues with the aid of two clinical vignettes.

The Nuclear Self and the Middle Years

From whatever perspective (psychobiologic, psychosocial, psychoanalytic) we approach the middle years, there is a remarkable consistency with which certain areas of experience are—at least on the manifest level—considered characteristic of and central to this epoch in the life cycle. Only the explanations of their origins, development, and significance for health and illness vary according to the theoretical framework applied.

Love and marriage, parenthood, and vocational and social-civic activities, mentioned by everyone as continuing from young adulthood, dominate the middle years, with some special characteristics added, especially in the second half of the period: concerns about the prospects of retirement; the increasing loneliness of those who never married or are divorced or widowed; the shadow of illness and the inevitability of death, which also become more consciously perceived threats.

Self psychology still lacks a comprehensive developmental psychology of adulthood which could serve as the basis for encompassing these experiences from a psychoanalytic point of view. But we do have a good general framework, which suggests that we should begin with the study of the specific selfobject functions needed during the middle years. It slowly dawned on Kohut in the mid- to late 1970s that his concept of the archaic, structure-building selfobject had to be expanded to include the selfobject needs from birth to death. He realized that selfobjects *could not* and *need not* be given up but must undergo a transformation from archaic to mature forms. He suggested that one of the central tasks of self psychology in the coming decades would be a detailed mapping out of selfobject needs throughout the life cycle. This project is still in its infancy, with only broad outlines available at present (for example, Tolpin, 1971; Ornstein and Ornstein, 1985).

The mirroring, alter-ego, and idealizing selfobject functions needed for the construction, development, and consolidation of the nuclear self are the very same needs throughout the life cycle with phase-specific changes in quality and configuration. Although they no longer have structure-building functions, they nevertheless make essential contributions to the maintenance of cohesion, vitality, and vigor in the healthy adult self. It is in the middle years that the consolidated nuclear self with its built-in basic life plan and its evolving high-level functions, such as creativity, empathy, humor, wisdom, and the capacity to contemplate one's own transience with equanimity, will stand the middle-aged and older person in good stead. Why?

The answer lies in the assumption that the successful unfolding of this innate program will essentially sustain the self in its ability to respond to the life tasks of the middle years with continued self-esteem, enjoyment, and the pursuit of remaining life goals in keeping with one's values and ideals. The middle years put a particularly severe burden on the self in these regards in the areas of love and marriage, parenthood, and vocational and social-civic activities.

Anna Ornstein and I began studying parenting as a function of the adult self, a function that requires optimal consolidation of the self (Ornstein and Ornstein, 1985). What we consider optimal in a parent is a self capable of empathic attunement to the constantly changing and developing self of the child from infancy through latency and adolescence. Failure in selfobject functions manifests itself in the caretaker's inability to be phase-appropriately responsive to the growing child.

A not uncommon situation is described in the first clinical example that follows.

CLINICAL EXAMPLE OF MRS. SILVER

Mrs. Silver was forty-one years old when she began treatment for symptoms of depression.[1] For about a year she had felt increasingly irritable, slept poorly, lost interest in many of her activities, and found herself more and more concerned about ordinary aches and pains. She eventually had to be hospitalized. During this period she was intensely preoccupied with her oldest son, Danny, who had abruptly left law school and gone to work instead. It was in the course of her treatment that Danny's vital selfobject function for the mother was recognized.

The mother herself had been a promising student but had dropped out of college to marry Danny's father. During her pregnancy she continued her studies but was unable to finish college; she retained a sense of inferiority about herself in having failed to fulfill her scholarly ambitions. She was unaware of her expectations that Danny, the oldest and brightest of her children, would complete her own self-development in this respect. This became clear only when she developed a severe depression following his abandonment of his studies. After her recovery from her depression, Mrs. Silver again returned to college and worked very hard to prove to herself that she could excel academically. Once she had done very well she gave up college and began to look for other avenues through which she could live up to the ideals of her nuclear self.

During treatment, the elucidation of the major acute precipitant for Mrs. Silver's depression led to a focus on the loss of Danny's intellectual-professional aspirations. On the surface this might appear to be a very narrow set of explanations for Mrs. Silver's depression, perhaps simplifying a much more complex web of causative factors. Certainly, her own adverse life experiences and the dynamics of her nuclear family, as well as those of her current family, were multilayered and undoubtedly contributed to the ensuing depression. The treatment process, however, was able to uncover that, for Mrs. Silver, Danny represented the embodiment of the intellectual-professional ideals and aspirations of her own nuclear self—ambitions and ideals she had given up at the time of her marriage. This left her with a vulnerability related to the structural deficit in her self. Essentially, she had failed to fulfill her own ambitions and idealized strivings and attached them to her selfobject son, who was to pursue and attain them for her. When he

---

1. This example was first published in Ornstein and Ornstein (1985).

abruptly turned away from these pursuits, she developed a depressive reaction based on this specific core psychopathology. When she made another major effort to turn again to these earlier abandoned intellectual pursuits, this was only partially successful because it was to repair the enfeebled and fragmentation-prone self rather than express its consolidated ambitions and ideals.

It should be noted that whatever complex set of dynamics might be formulated to have caused or brought about Mrs. Silver's depression, in the subsequent period of her psychotherapy, the importance of her son as a selfobject was understood and interpreted. It was the specificity of these interpretations that resulted in the considerable improvement of her depression.

Another facet of the impact of an insufficiently consolidated nuclear self (both in its pole of ambitions and in its pole of values and ideals) on the middle years of a professional man is illustrated in the next clinical example.

CLINICAL EXAMPLE OF MR. BARNES

Mr. Barnes, a married man in his middle forties, came into analysis for a variety of vague, disturbing feelings and thoughts. He complained that his wife of a few years was a great disappointment to him sexually, but mostly he bemoaned the fact that she was not helpful to him in his various efforts to make a success of himself. This idea of making a success of himself was practically an obsession with him, he said. Although he was quite productive—his coworkers and superiors thought he was good and still growing—he thought it was all empty; he could not really enjoy any of it. In the initial interview, while giving an account of the many professional and civic matters he was currently involved with, Mr. Barnes made a comment that caught my attention as something to be filed away for further exploration. He spoke of just having signed up for an evening course on a serious academic subject he had abandoned in college and always wanted to get back to. As happens so often with these efforts just before applying for treatment, when he returned to begin his analysis a month or so later he did not mention the pursuit of this exciting course at all. It turned out that he had never got as far as starting it. Later we understood that the immediate meaning of his announcement was to impress me with his highbrow cultural pursuits to ensure that he would be accepted for analysis. But later another significant meaning emerged: his announcement was a signal of his "curative fantasy" (Ornstein and Ornstein, 1976), an unconscious wish to pick up an earlier abandoned developmental move forward. It appeared to be a tentative expression of a thwarted need to grow.

He quickly developed an intense idealizing transference, alternating with a generally more hidden and resisted revival of the need to be admired and validated. Initially he seemed to gain from this transference experience considerable energy and enthusiasm for more involvement with various projects; it landed him a significant advancement as well as an important assignment with an obvious potential to enable him to grow professionally, as he had always wished. But although he plunged into his new work, he continued to pile up unfinished project after project, felt harassed, complained of overwork and overcommitment, and could not enjoy the fruit of his work.

To streamline a great variety of complex issues, I shall focus on a single central thread in the transference to make another point regarding the consequences of an insufficiently consolidated nuclear self in the middle years. The working-through process of the transference, especially when it shifted more explicitly and sustainedly into a wish to shine, be admired and valued—both within and outside the transference—brought forth his intense need for prestige from his work. He laughingly said once that he wants and desperately needs the prestige before he has actually earned it. He was constantly preoccupied with the prestige value of his activities. If he could not feel that the job he was doing was prestigious enough, it was a drudgery to perform it and he hated it—yet he could not say no to it. He simply could not organize his life in such a manner that he could feel comfortable with his schedule and allow his performance to garner him some prestige.

Mr. Barnes was able to recover a multitude of memories of having felt "disregarded," "not valued," "not really noticed" for who he was; he had been painfully shunted aside by his father in favor of an artistically talented older sister and an older brother who "was more like Father in his talents and interests and personality." At a particular moment in the analysis, Mr. Barnes had the wishful fantasy "to chuck it all" and become an artist, living freely and doing what he wished without the compulsion to consider its prestige value. As he mused about what it would be like, he recalled a painful early memory that he could not place exactly chronologically. His older sister drew a horse which the father admired greatly. Mr. Barnes also drew one "but it turned out more like a cow" and did not elicit his father's attention. This memory and others that followed in rapid succession led us to recognize one central meaning of many of his frenetic and compulsively pursued un-enjoyable activities. Nothing seemed to fulfill an inner program of his nuclear self—we could at first not even identify such a program clearly. All his activities appeared to be compensatory efforts to attract his childhood father's attention, admiration, and praise—and, of course, the analyst's in the mirror transference.

The course Mr. Barnes wished to take on the highbrow academic subject appeared to be the kind of interest and activity that came closest to expressing his insufficiently consolidated nuclear ambitions and ideals. Here was a middle-aged man who was doing very well by all objective criteria—yet he felt unfulfilled in his work and was desperately searching to recapture the "lost" inner program of his nuclear self.

These two clinical vignettes highlight different facets of Kohut's conception of "Tragic Man"—men and women engaged in a lifelong attempt to fulfill their nuclear ambitions, nuclear skills and talents, and nuclear values and ideals, but never quite making it. When their failure is more than "average expectable," so is their suffering. This suffering is often masked until the middle years—as was the case in both clinical examples. When time begins to run out and the chance for some fulfillment of these ambitions, skills, talents, values, and ideals appears to be less likely, the well known mid-life crisis sets in. I have presented one frame of reference particularly suited for the understanding and treatment of this crisis.

REFERENCES

Abraham, K. 1919. The applicability of psychoanalytic treatment of patients at an advanced age. In *Selected papers on psychoanalysis*, 312–317. New York: Basic Books, 1954.

Benedek, T. 1950. Climacterium: A developmental phase. *Psychoanalytic Quarterly* 19:1–27.

———. 1959. Parenthood as a developmental phase: A contribution to the libido theory. *Journal of the American Psychoanalytic Association* 7:389–417.

Cohler, B. J., and Boxer, A. M. 1984. Middle adulthood: Settling into the world—person, time and context. In *Normality and the life cycle: A critical integration*. Ed. D. Offer and M. Sabshin, 145–203. New York: Basic Books.

Colarusso, C. A., and Nemiroff, R. A. 1979. Some observations and hypotheses about the psychoanalytic theory of adult development. *International Journal of Psychoanalysis* 60:59–71.

————. 1981. *Adult development*. New York: Plenum.

Erikson, E. 1959. *Identity and the life cycle*. Psychological issues, monograph 1. New York: International Universities Press.

Freud, S. 1912. Types of onset of neurosis. In *Standard edition*, 12.

Jung, C. G. 1933. *Modern man in search of a soul*. New York: Harcourt, Brace & World.

King, P. 1980. The life cycle as indicated by the nature of the transference in the psychoanalysis of the middle-aged and elderly. *International Journal of Psychoanalysis* 61:153–169.

Kohut, H. 1971. *The analysis of the self*. New York: International Universities Press.

————. 1974. Remarks about the formation of the self. In *The search for the self*. Ed. P. H. Ornstein, 2:737–770. New York: International Universities Press, 1978.

————. 1977. *The restoration of the self*. New York: International Universities Press.

————. 1978 [1980]. Reflections on advances in self psychology. In *Advances in self psychology*. Ed. A. Goldberg, 473–554. New York: International Universities Press.

————. 1984. *How does analysis cure?* Chicago: University of Chicago Press.

Nemiroff, R. A., and Colarusso, C. A. 1984. *The race against time: Psychotherapy and psychoanalysis in the second half of life*. New York: Plenum.

Neugarten, B. L. 1970. Dynamics of transition from middle age to old age: Adaptation and the life cycle. *Journal of Geriatric Psychology* 4:71–100.

Offer, D., and Sabshin, M., eds. 1984. *Normality and the life cycle*. New York: Basic Books.

Ornstein, A., and Ornstein, P. H. 1985. Parenting as a function of the adult self: A psychoanalytic developmental perspective. In *Parental influences: In health and disease*. Ed. E. J. Anthony and G. Pollock. Boston: Little, Brown.

Ornstein, P. H., and Ornstein, A. 1976. On the continuing evolution of psychoanalytic psychotherapy: Reflections and predictions. In *The annual of psychoanalysis*. Vol 5. New York: International Universities Press.

Tolpin, M. 1971. On the beginnings of a cohesive self. In *The psychoanalytic study of the child*, 26:316–354. New Haven: Yale University Press.

· 4 ·

THE IMPACT OF MIDDLE AGE ON AMBITIONS AND IDEALS

ELIZABETH L. AUCHINCLOSS, M. D.,
AND ROBERT MICHELS, M. D.

Long before Elliott Jaques (1965) coined the term *mid-life crisis* for use by the psychologically minded, observers of the human condition had known that the experience of middle age has an enormous impact on ambitions and ideals. Psychoanalytic clinicians, steeped in a developmental model that stresses the influence of childhood on psychic life, have learned that they must also be mindful of the impact of middle age, particularly in an era in which there is increasing interest in the use of psychoanalytic treatment for the "older" patient. Common among the psychological tasks of middle age is a vigorous and conscious reexamination of life goals. Ideals and ambitions that were formed long ago under the influence of childhood fantasy must be updated in the face of new, overriding realities. The psychoanalyst who participates in such a reexamination has an opportunity to observe the interaction between these age-specific realities and the development of psychic structures; the analyst may also be faced with the opportunity, indeed the necessity, to reexamine the adequacy of his or her own theories. Clearly psychoanalysts have much to learn from the great books, from personal experience, and from common sense as they approach the analysis of the middle-aged person.

But although psychoanalysts have much to learn about psychological development in the middle years, there is more question regarding what they have to contribute. A growing body of literature argues that psychoanalysis has little to add, based on its privileged knowledge, of much importance to general psychology. Many mental processes—for example, the so-called autonomous ego functions—recognized as important determinants of psychic life are best studied by other kinds of psychologists. Many important themes, such as sex and aggression, which can be studied by psychoanalysts as they are reflected in the inner life of any given individual, cannot be understood in terms of their general psychological significance when explored by psychoanalytic methods alone.

Psychoanalysts are experts on personal fantasies that express univer-

sal themes of human experience as well as on the impact of these fantasies on the rest of life. Although these themes, including ambitions and
ideals, are universal, psychoanalysis may have little to contribute to the
understanding of what is universal, generalizable, or normative about
them. Even if the definition of psychoanalysis is limited to the study
of the transformations of these themes in personal fantasies, psychoanalysts would be hard pressed to give a description of a process of
psychic transformation that has general validity, although they are on
better footing here than they would be in discussing other aspects of
general psychology. Furthermore, with regard to the study of specific
epochs of psychological development—a pursuit intimately linked with
the history of psychoanalysis—a review of the epistemological status
of psychoanalytic developmental theories forces us to consider again
whether they may not be on shaky ground when they attempt to make
general statements. This caveat applies particularly to statements about
postadolescent development, since so many developmental ideas in
psychoanalysis are based on genetic reconstructions of childhood and
adolescence in the psychoanalyses of young or middle-aged adults.

Psychoanalysis became interested in psychological development very
early in its history through the surprising discovery that adult psychopathology seemed to be caused by pathogenic thoughts and feelings
that could be traced first to childhood traumas and, later, to childhood
fantasies. The study of these fantasies, as uncovered in the analyses of
adults, led to a genetic psychology that, on the surface, looked very
much like a developmental psychology and was presented as such.
Many writers have pointed out, however, that it is a mistake to confuse psychoanalytic narratives of development with a general theory
of development. As Grossman and Kaplan (1988) say, "One of the
difficulties with such narratives is that they appear to assume that the
discovery of significant nodal points in development is also a discovery
of how they are inevitably transversed and what their weights are in developmental outcome." Whatever the boundaries or limits of any epoch
or theme in psychological experience, psychoanalysis tries to discover
what unique interpretations the individual has selected within those
limits and why. The psychoanalytic method is ideally suited to uncover correlations and links in psychic life, which may be presented as
problems for other psychologists to study and explain.

Freud himself was mindful of the important difference between a
psychoanalytic narrative of events and a general theory of development.
He wrote:

So long as we trace the development from its final outcome backwards, the chain of events appears continuous, and we feel we have gained an insight which is completely satisfactory or even exhaustive. But if we proceed the reverse way, if we start from the premises inferred from the analysis and try to follow these up to the final result, then we no longer get the impression of an inevitable sequence of events which could not have been otherwise determined. We notice at once that there might have been another result, and that we might have been just as well able to understand and explain the latter. From a knowledge of the premises we could not have foretold the nature of the result. (1920, p. 167)

Another complication of the attempt to expand the psychoanalytic theory of development into middle age is the fact that the prototypic psychoanalytic theory of development, the libido theory, is a theory of child development, which, although derived largely from reconstructive genetic data from the study of adults, is focused on biologically rooted drives and patterned after embryologic models from biology (Sulloway, 1979). It is revolutionary as a psychologic developmental theory because it emphasizes biologic maturation, critical periods (rather than gradual change), and repeated transformations, all in contrast to a commonsense understanding of adult psychology. When the characteristics of the developmental model of the libido theory are extrapolated past adolescence into adult development, the model becomes less plausible. The social determinants of development that are so prominent in adult life are less regular and predictable than the biologic determinants of childhood development. As the epigenetic model is stretched, it loses power. We often find it hard even to remember the sequence of themes from critical periods of postadolescence that have been postulated by Erikson and others.

Despite these problems and misgivings, however, with the growth of interest in building psychoanalysis into a general psychology linked to broad social and biologic considerations, there have been ceaseless efforts to extend the psychoanalytic model of development beyond childhood, first through adolescence and later through the middle years and into old age. Depending on one's point of view, these extensions of the psychoanalytic model of development can be seen either as necessary steps toward strengthening the claims of psychoanalysis to be a general psychology or as misguided and somewhat sterile efforts, based on a misunderstanding of the epistemologic status of the psychoanalytic model of development and leading to little more than a translation of commonplace biologic and sociocultural perspectives on human aging with admixtures of psychoanalytic jargon and humanistic prose.

What, then, is the proper relationship between the practicing psychoanalyst and a general theory of psychological development? Should we abandon the subject altogether and confine our work to efforts to reconstruct or construct the "present unconscious" (Sandler, 1986–87) within the limits of our methodology? The answer is obviously no. Psychoanalytic inquiry cannot proceed in isolation from a developmental viewpoint. Human beings inevitably experience themselves in terms of a personal history, in a state of growth and development. There is no personal narrative that is not, in some part, a narrative of the self traveling through time. Even if psychoanalysis cannot construct an adequate model of some prior biosocial reality to account for development, developmental models will always be important guidelines for interpretive strategies as we approach the patient's fantasies and constructions. The psychoanalyst must work with a developmental model whether he wants to or not. Furthermore, the model of development adopted by any given psychoanalyst will inevitably and powerfully affect his work.

Three Models of Mid-Life Development

On close examination, at least three models of mid-life development are suggested in the psychoanalytic discussion of the middle years. The most traditional model sees the development of the core of the personality ending in adolescence or before. Mid-life provides new material to be worked over in light of childhood fantasies, which themselves do not change. Mid-life presents new challenges and adaptive tasks that become opportunities and occasions for the expression of old conflicts. In this model, the experience of mid-life is like the day residue or occasion for a recurrent dream. This view is most closely represented by Horowitz's contribution in this book.

A second model extends the first by stressing that strategies of coping and conflict resolution continue to evolve throughout adult life. Therefore, although infantile fantasies and conflicts persist through the life cycle, new defensive styles and new modes of adaptation may emerge as the individual approaches the challenges of mid-life. This viewpoint is presented most notably in Vaillant's studies of adulthood and may also correspond to that presented by Modell, both also in this book.

The third and most radical model of development in the middle years holds that continuing growth leads to changes in the basic components of conflict and fantasy; it proposes that wishes, fears, and components of self-representation may truly change with time. This viewpoint stresses either continued biologic development, as suggested by Roose and Pardes in this book and by Benedek (1959), or the importance of relationships and experience in shaping core wishes, as Ornstein argues in this book. The most noted exponent of this last point of view with regard to the middle years has been, of course, Elliott Jaques (1965).

It is possible to integrate aspects of all three models into a perspective on the impact of middle age on ambitions and ideals. The psychoanalytic understanding of these phenomena, as of all others, has focused largely on their conflictual origins and their construction from the component wishes, fears, and object relationships of childhood. Every psychoanalysis explores the infantile origins of the superego and the ego ideal, the important structural underpinnings of ambitions and ideals, and their relationship to love, hate, fear, and the images of real and fantasized parents in the minds of young children. Psychoanalysts are always mindful, therefore, of the first model of adult psychological development, which stresses the influence of infantile fantasy on adult ambitions and ideals.

The story of the origins of any mental phenomenon, however, can never be a full description of that phenomenon. An understanding of the ambitions and ideals of adulthood requires more than an understanding of their conflictual roots in childhood. Ideals are late structures, abstracted, decentered, cognitive, and ideational. As late structures, they are highly subject to later transformations and may change more in adult life than do other psychic structures. Changes in function and secondary autonomies also must be taken into account, as well as important changes in basic content. Although an exploration of the roots of ideals in early relationships and primitive experiences may explain much of their force and power, explanations presented solely in terms of oedipal and pre-oedipal dynamics are roughly analogous to explanations of international politics in terms of primate territoriality. We must remain mindful, therefore, of the third model of psychic development, which stresses the possibility that new themes of psychic life may appear in the middle years and become components of conflict and fantasy.

The second model of psychological development, which emphasizes that strategies of conflict resolution continue to evolve throughout adult life, is also crucial to an understanding of the impact of middle age on ambitions. Ambitions are more personal than ideals, less abstract, and more directly influenced by the constraints and opportunities of reality, such as age and situation. Ambitions are closely connected to capacities and coping strategies. The working of the reality principle leads to a modification of ambitions as the capacities of the individual or the constraints of the environment change. Furthermore, as certain realities of middle age affect ambitions, ambitions may in turn influence ideals, at times defensively, but also, under the best of circumstances, creatively and synthetically.

The Reality of Death

What, then, are the overriding realities presented by middle age? There is, of course, at least one recurrent theme of the middle years recognized as paramount by all who have attempted to describe the essential experience of this phase of life. The middle-aged person must come to terms with an increasing awareness of the reality of death. In contrast to the child, the adolescent, or the young adult, the middle-aged person finds himself closer to the end of life than he is to the beginning. In response to an awareness that the time remaining can accommodate less, many life decisions begin to hinge upon the question of which possibilities to discard rather than which to pursue. It often becomes clear that painful conflicts among roles can no longer be set aside. The fact that the time remaining is limited means that to pursue one goal is to relinquish another. A clinical example illustrates the awareness of limits, of finite future time, and of the need to relinquish potentialities that is so characteristic of middle age.

Mrs. A, a professional woman in her thirties, was deeply involved in her work, but in the back of her mind she had always assumed that "someday" she would have a child. The fantasy of "someday," as long as it was not today or tomorrow, served to delay the need to face the issue. An illness that raised questions regarding her ability to bear a child, along with marital conflicts, led her into treatment, however. Mrs. A was acutely aware of the calendar and was distressed to discover that her strongest motive to have a child stemmed from her anxiety that this might be her "last chance." In her analysis, she explored the origins of her ambivalent attitude toward motherhood, the unconscious equation she had made between her career and the envied role of the male father-husband whom she viewed as protected from such choices, and her naïveté regarding the possibility of fulfilling all her ambitions. Throughout this exploration, however, the frame and shape of the analytic dialogue were powerfully delineated by the reality of the patient's age.

Similar themes were important in the analysis of Mr. B, a fifty-year-old married man who sought help when he faced a distressing choice. His wife had discovered his long-standing extramarital affair. Mr. B was passionately in love with a female colleague some years his junior, and they had planned to marry after his adolescent children had grown. While deeply attached to these children and committed to his paternal responsibilities, Mr. B had long experienced his marriage as a "slow emotional death." He had thought that compromise was possible, but his wife's discovery shattered his timeless illusions. She demanded that he make a choice now: give up his romance or end the marriage. He experienced her demand as meaning that he must relinquish one half of his life in order to protect the other. Mr. B was overcome with despair, feeling he had no hope for more than "half a future."

It was a similar choice that led Mrs. C, at the age of thirty-six, to a gradual and painful awarness of the reality of her adult status. She had been married for ten years, but for five years had carried on an affair with a somewhat older colleague. This man had promised to leave his wife, but he had made no serious moves to do so. When his wife suddenly died, Mrs. C's lover demanded that she leave her husband to marry him. Mrs. C, who for years had railed against her lover for his inability to leave his wife, was now confronted with her own uncertainty. She experienced anxiety and depression that surpassed any she had known during her long affair. Mrs. C spent many hours in her treatment exploring her feelings about her lover and her husband. She examined at length their many conscious and unconscious meanings to her in an effort to decide which of them would make her happier. The treatment, however, did not advance; Mrs. C was unable to choose. A change occurred only when her analyst realized that Mrs. C's sustaining fantasy was that treatment would result in a revelation to her of the "best thing to do." Analysis would tell her which of two apparently appropriate men was "Mr. Right." The fact was, she loved them both, and each had many fine qualities. It was choice itself that Mrs. C wished to avoid at all costs. She implored the analyst to give her criteria that would tell her how to proceed. Persistent interpretations of her frightened flight from decisions led her to feel utterly abandoned. In one dramatic session, when Mrs. C was, as usual, engaged in a bitter struggle against the necessity for choice, she blurted out: "This whole problem makes me feel so middle-aged!" For Mrs. C, decision meant not only the abandonment of one of the men she loved but the loss of the illusion of eternal youth, with all future potentials preserved.

The Comforts of Middle Age

These examples have illustrated the relationship between middle age, the awareness of time, and the necessity for painful choice. Such awareness, accompanied by the heavy clang of inexorability, is invariably frightening, and the response to this fear of aging and death will powerfully determine the manner in which middle age affects ambitions and ideals. There is, however, a second set of dominant themes of middle age that can have a somewhat tempering effect. Adult life, in contrast to infancy and childhood, is a period of relative stability (Michels, 1981). Although many of the syndromes of the mid-life crisis may represent efforts to re-create the lost experience of excitement, change, and transformation so characteristic of youth, the stability of the middle years offers comfort and security to many. Several studies using the Holmes and Rahe inventory of life events have demonstrated that between young adulthood and middle age there is a general decrease in the frequency of stressful life events. Furthermore, middle-aged and older respondents rate equivalent stresses as less disruptive than do younger people (Chiriboga, 1981). It seems, therefore, that middle age is not only less eventful but also less stressful than youth. It is reassuring, if ironic, to recognize that as one is confronted in middle age with the awareness of ultimate fear and ultimate loss, this awareness can be faced with the armor of wisdom, experience, and stability.

A second irony of middle age is that although it brings an awareness of the organismic limitations of being, it also brings with it a relative freedom from biologic demands and constraints. The mental life of the mature adult is more independent of the influences of immediate biologic determinants than that of either the child or the older adult (Michels, 1981). Related to this is the fact that for many, mid-life brings the greatest possibility of creativity and generativity which transcends the boundaries of personal experience and offers the hope of symbolic immortality. Biologists have pointed out that information alone, either genetic or cultural, is truly immortal. For most, the opportunity to identify with the transmission of genetic information through parenthood or of cultural information through accomplishment reaches its peak in the middle years.

The case of Mrs. D, a fifty-two-year-old widowed business woman, dramatically illustrates how middle age provides opportunities for creativity and generativity that not only may ease the pain of aging and loss but may dramatically affect ambitions and ideals. Mrs. D came to treatment deeply depressed because she could not find a man who would "take care of things" for her and make her "feel alive." Her husband had died ten years earlier, leaving her to run a locally based community business, which had been in his family for years. Mrs. D had always looked up to her charismatic husband and had relied on him to provide her with security, a sense of fun, and a feeling of specialness. In his absence, she felt enslaved to the business. Although she had excelled as president, greatly expanding production and winning many prizes for community service, she felt no pride or comfort in these accomplishments.

A deeper exploration of Mrs. D's yearning for a man revealed masochistic and hysterical character traits. Her overriding ambition was to shed the role of the wretched Cinderella and dangle on the arm of her ideal prince. Her increasing realization that this fantasy was unrealistic, especially since her ideal was a dazzling man in his mid-forties like her lost husband, plunged Mrs. D into depression. It was clear that guilt over unconscious envy and hostility toward her husband, aggravated by incomplete mourning, had interfered with Mrs. D's experience of satisfaction in her success as a business woman. As these conflicts were worked through, she began to experience joy and pride in her business, particularly in a corporate outreach program she had developed to fund local community projects. Mrs. D also took pride in the company as a training place for young, idealistic business people. As she became more comfortable with her new ambitions, her ideal self-image changed from a "delightful little girl" to a "respected woman, committed to civic life and interested in the young." Analysis of unconscious conflict had facilitated this change, but the opportunities provided by the status of middle age had contributed to making change possible.

The Spanish philosopher Ortega y Gasset (1958) has called the middle-aged the "dominant generation" and maintains that people in this age group are the natural leaders of society. Thus, at one level, middle age is truly the prime of life. Mrs. D made use of new potentialities that emerged in her middle years to alter her ambitions and her image of an ideal self. She demonstrated what research psychologists have shown to be characteristic of middle age. Themes of social purpose and mastery are often prominent in the thinking of middle-aged people, many of whom report feeling effective, competent, and at the peak of their powers (Chiriboga, 1981). These themes appear somewhat later in the mental life of women than they do in men, often emerging as women begin to express the repressed aspects of their personalities, a process that is characteristic of both sexes in middle age. This phenomenon of the balancing of mid-life personality was first stressed by Jung (1933), particularly with regard to the expression of gender roles. As men and women are freed from the constraints of the social roles that are currently typical of family life men often shift toward a more nurturing, sensual, and affective orientation while women, in contrast, begin to explore more "socio-expressive roles" involving assertion and aggression (Chiriboga, 1981). Similar shifts have been described by Person in her work on romantic love (Person, 1988). In this way, the middle years provide an opportunity for the expression of repressed aspects of the ideal self.

Mrs. D also demonstrated other characteristics of the middle years including the development of a new orientation toward the inner world (Chiriboga, 1981) combined with a contrasting interest in the feelings and fate of other people (Michels, 1981). Middle-aged people typically assume responsibility for others, and people of all ages, young and old, turn to those in the middle for advice and aid. Often a 'psychological disengagement" from the emotional impact of the environment is accompanied paradoxically by an increase in actual social engagement and "social competence" (Chiriboga, 1981).

These psychological characteristics of the middle years develop under the impact of the double reality of new fears and new potentials. They are reflected in that most crucial aspect of middle-age ambitions and ideals: the emphasis on what is "possible." For the child, ideals dominate ambitions and the sense of future time is limitless. In adolescence, ideals become even grander and more powerful. By young adulthood, we begin to see some awareness of the boundaries of personal time and a shift of ambition away from "what should be" toward "what might be." In middle age, realized ambitions are important as sources of self-esteem and internal reward. Unrealized ambitions, more clearly unrealizable with each passing year, become the raw material for a subjective sense of finite time. Attention is now focused on potentially realizable but not yet realized ambitions, the shrinking field that defines a personal psychic future. As we have seen, many adults preserve their ideals by detaching them from fantasies of grandiose personal triumph and displacing them onto symbolic extensions of the self—the family, group, nation, church, science, and of course, the child. This shift from self to other preserves the valued internal image of the ideal self and is an essential mechanism for the transformation of infantile narcissism into the mature goals of the normal adult (Michels, 1981).

This shift was illustrated in 1981, when the sixty-two-year-old millionnaire Eugene Lang astonished the sixth-graders at P.S. 121 in Manhattan who were half-listening to his commencement address while daydreaming about their plans for the summer. Midway through his speech, Lang became aware of the absurdity of the idealistic platitudes he was offering his audience of inner-city black and Hispanic twelve-year-olds. Realizing how irrelevant his grand thoughts must seem to a group whose reality bore no resemblance to what he had faced when graduating from the same school years earlier, Lang abandoned his prepared text and announced that he would pay for the education of every student in that class who was accepted into college. His proposal was greeted with shouts and cheers from the parents and students; it was the inauguration of what later became the "I Have a Dream" program now operating in twenty U.S. cities. The dramatic story of Lang's experience at the podium and his subsequent actions is an example of the essence of late middle-aged ambitions and ideals. Ideals that start in childhood with concrete goals become abstract principles in adolescence, and then shift back to the level of generality at which the individual believes his own life might make a difference. Children are concerned with what they can touch and with what directly touches them, adolescents with the most general and ideal of principles, and adults with something in between—they are concerned less with the great abstractions of good and evil and more with what touches the meaning of their lives and the lives of those around them.

Creativity and the Mid-Life Crisis

Elliott Jaques (1965), in "Death and the Mid-Life Crisis," begins his exploration of the psychology of middle age with the observation that the nature of creativity often changes between the ages of thirty and forty. The "hot-from-the-fire," impulsive creativity of youth is transformed in mid-life into the "sculpted," worked-over creativity of mature adulthood. Lyric and descriptive content gives way to tragic, reflective, and philosophical themes. For Jaques, these changes reflect larger psychological themes inherent in the successful resolution of the mid-life crisis, brought on by awareness of the inevitability of death. According to Jaques, this inescapable awareness awakens an ancient infantile fantasy of annihilation and abandonment by the destroyed and persecuting maternal breast and thus presents a secondary opportunity to work through Klein's depressive position. Mid-life terrors can be calmed by "loving grief" and mourning and can be replaced by a deeper, sustaining integration of love and hate in which destruction and envy are mitigated by reparation and gratitude. Jaques feels that "late adolescent and young adult idealism and optimism are accompanied by split-off, projected hate and denial of death. In the mature adult, idealism is given up and supplanted by a more contemplative pessimism."

There is a shift, too, from radical desire and impatience to a more reflective and tolerant conservatism. Beliefs in the inherent goodness of humanity are replaced by a recognition and acceptance of the fact that inherent goodness is accompanied by hate and destructive forces within, which contribute to misery and tragedy. "Acceptance of the facts requires constructive resignation and detachment" and results in a sense of "goodness which is sufficient but not idealized, not subject to hollow perfection." All "creativity takes on new depths and shades of feeling." Under the best of circumstances, the created object is experienced as life-giving and comforting in the face of death. If the crisis of mid-life is not successfully traversed, Jaques feels that the result will be either despair or a reinforcing of manic defenses in the form of "unconscious fantasies of omnipotence and magic immortality."

Jaques considered the greatest hero of the middle years to be Dante, who, "midway in the journey of life," found himself lost in a dark wood. Jaques interprets the *Divine Comedy* as Dante's experience of the mid-life crisis, a "full and worked-through conscious encounter with death." Dante is led through hell and purgatory by his master, Virgil, eventually to find his way, guided by his beloved Beatrice, into paradise. Jaques sees Dante's encounter with the being of God as more than a rapturous and mystical merger experience; he sees it as a "highly organized experience consisting of a vision of supreme love and knowledge, with control of impulse and will, which promulgates the mature life of greater ease and contemplation which follows upon the working-through of primitive anxiety and guilt, and the return to the primal good object." This is no manic defense or denial through magical omnipotence. Reparation has made it possible for loving impulses to become ascendant and the harshness of the superego, expressed in "The Inferno," to be relieved. Jaques quotes the philosopher Croce as saying: "What is not found in the 'Paradiso,' for it is foreign to the spirit of Dante, is flight from the world, absolute refuge in God, asceticism. He does not seek to fly from the world, but to instruct it, correct it, and reform it. . . . he knows the world and its doings and passions." Dante's *Divine Comedy* expresses the tragic sense of life that rejects any thought of defensive disengagement.

In light of Jaques's comments, it is interesting to consider Freud's identifications with various underworld travelers. For the title page of *The Interpretation of Dreams* (1900a), Freud chose the famous passage from Book VII (line 312) of the *Aeneid*: "Flectere si nequeo superos, Acheronta movebo" (If I cannot bend the Higher Powers, I will move the Infernal Regions). Freud explains that these lines from Virgil are "intended to picture the efforts of repressed instinctual impulses" to force their way into consciousness (1900b, p. 608). We may imagine, however, from his decision to place these lines on the title page of his greatest masterpiece, that Freud identified with Juno, the speaker of these bold words. The furious and vengeful goddess, outraged at her inability to wield power on Olympus, vows to enlist the fury of the frightful underworld deity, Allecto, "the maker of grief and war," against her enemy, Aeneas. Earlier, in a letter to Fliess of August 6, 1899, Freud had described the opening chapters of *The Interpretation of Dreams* as follows: "The whole thing is planned on the model of an imaginary walk. At the beginning, the dark forest of authors (who do not see the trees), hopelessly lost on wrong tracks. Then a concealed pass through which I lead the reader—my specimen dream with its peculiarities, details, indiscretions, bad jokes—and then suddenly the high ground and the view and the question: which way do you wish to go now?" (Masson, 1985, p. 365). In this passage, Freud identifies with Aeneas himself, who travels through the underworld with his guide, the Sybil, past Grief, Anxiety, Fear, and Guilty Joys, in search of a last meeting with his dead father. After an arduous journey, Aeneas ascends a final rise and gains a clear view of the "luminous, green plains" below. Here he finds his father, Anchises. In their final conversation, Aeneas learns about the mysteries of reincarnation and the cleansing of souls, the story of his own glorious future, and, interestingly, in his father's parting words, the secret of the interpretation of dreams:

> There are two gates of Sleep: the one is made of horn,
> They say, and affords the outlet for genuine apparitions:
> The other's a gate of brightly shining ivory; this way
> The Shades send up to earth false dreams that impose upon us.
>
> (Virgil, 1952, lines 893–896)

It is important to note, however, that Freud does not adopt the attitude of the pious Aeneas, longingly seeking his father's embrace and advice. In his letter to Fliess, Freud contemptuously discards the words of his forefathers, becomes his own guide, and leads the reader to the high ground himself. He enters the underworld as a conquering hero, more, perhaps, in the spirit of the furious Juno than of Aeneas or Dante. Although Freud wrote that the reminder of his graying hair was a factor in his decision to publish *The Interpretation of Dreams* (1900b, p. 478), this work, published when he was forty-three, a few years after his father's death, most clearly expresses the psychology of a young man actively engaged in a struggle to overthrow his father. Freud identifies both with Aeneas, the child who still needs his father, and with Juno, the adolescent who spurns and defies the father. Psychologically, Freud is not yet middle-aged.

Keeping these speculations in mind, one finds it interesting to turn to another potential source of knowledge about adult development: not the content of clinical psychoanalysis but the structure of psychoanalytic works themselves. Just as the memories and fantasies of childhood reported by adult patients in analysis may tell more about the adult in the present than the child of the past, so may psychoanalytic theories of child development tell us more about the psychology of the theory maker than the psychology of the child. From this viewpoint, psychoanalytic theory reflects the developmental stage of the theorist as well as the epoch of life that is the subject of the theory.

Classical libido theory, for example, emphasizes conflicts, critical periods, and intense emotions. It presents a history of the past that highlights crisis rather than peace and tranquility. Within the subjective sense of future time that characterizes youth, this story of inner conflict is most often a story of passion, desire, anxiety, and fear. In these respects, libido theory differs from theories presented by traditional or nonpsychoanalytic developmental and social psychologists. The most obvious explanation for this difference is that psychoanalysis is designed to look beneath the surface. A second explanation is the possibility that traditional psychoanalytic descriptions of stormy childhood and rebellious adolescence represent the nostalgic wishful fantasies of middle-aged analysts longing for the excitements associated with a youth now past.

A third explanation, suggested above, is that Freud's own youthful psychology lasted well into his mid-forties and resonated powerfully with his intellectual gifts in the brilliant creation of libido psychology, written in the language of desire, fear, and guilt. Although it is always possible to describe conflict in terms of desire and fear, there are other words and images that may be closer to the most common experience of the middle years. Middle-age narratives may emphasize the necessity that one relinquish one good for another rather than the terrifying demand that one renounce pleasure or face disaster. Psychoanalytic explorations of the overwhelming influence of fantasy on human life traditionally have focused on the power of fantasies from the infantile past. However, as one ascends the final rise of middle life and begins to view a sweep of personal time that for the first time appears finite in terms of future as well as past, fantasy becomes influenced by anticipation as much as by memory. The central position of fantasies of infantile relationships and even of the primal events that preceded one's birth is complicated by images of the future, of death, and of what follows death. These themes are prominent, of course, in the termination phase of analysis, when the "timelessness" of the analytic situation is challenged (Michels, 1981).

With these thoughts in mind, one can view the distinction drawn by Kohut between "guilty" and "tragic" man (1977, p. 243) as representing not just the difference between two themes of character or of psychopathology but that between two stages in a developmental sequence that shifts from the psychodynamics of guilt, which expresses the experience of conflict for many who are younger, and the psychodynamics of tragedy, which may be more meaningful to those in the middle or later years. For example, Freud himself changed during the many years that spanned his adult creative life. The young psychoanalyst who struggled vigorously with the power of the father throughout *The Interpretation of Dreams* by 1910 had become the father himself, painfully obsessed with the problem of succession and the future of the psychoanalytic movement (Erikson, 1980). It is almost impossible to recognize the youthful Freud who so openly expressed his boundless grandiosity in *The Interpretation of Dreams* (1900b, pp. 469–470) when we turn to the aging Freud of "Analysis Terminable and Interminable" (1937). A striking example of the change in the nature of Freud's theories during this period may be seen in his theory of humor, first presented in 1905 as a theory of aggression, fear, and disguise. By 1927, his theory of humor is a theory of love—more precisely, of loving comfort of the ego by the superego, like the comforting of a child by a parent, in the face of inevitable death.

Psychoanalytic thought has long taken as its central myth the tragedy of *Oedipus Rex* (Michels, 1986), which Freud interpreted as representing the "fate of all of us, perhaps, to direct our first sexual impulse towards our mother and our first hatred and our first murderous wish against our father" (1900a, p. 262). A forty-year-old humanities professor reread the tragedy of *Oedipus at Colonus* during the termination phase of his analysis, in an effort to learn "what happens next." In this play, second in the Oedipus trilogy but written last, Sophocles tells how the blind Oedipus, after years of wandering with his faithful daughter Antigone, seeks refuge at Colonus, not far from the city of Athens. After making peace with the Furies through sacrifice, the exiled king finds protection at the hands of King Theseus, who prevents Creon from carrying his brother-in-law, Oedipus, and the daughters of Oedipus off to Thebes. At the center of the drama, Oedipus confronts and curses his son Polyneices, who had betrayed him at the time of his exile, but who has now come to Colonus seeking his father's help and forgiveness. In a dramatic ending, a messenger describes how Oedipus, in death, seems to vanish into thin air, as if carried off by "some attendant from the train of Heaven" (Sophocles, 1954, line 1661), a final indication that the aged king has at long last found favor with the gods.

Although the patient found Oedipus recognizable by his characteristic stubborn and vengeful rage, he was impressed by the change in the ambitions of the king, from those of a fearless ruler seeking to be the omniscient "master in everything" (Sophocles, 1954, line 1522) to those of a frightened old man in search of comfort, a home where "I might round out my bitter life conferring benefit on those who received me" (line 91). He saw in the death of Oedipus not only the loss of his analyst, who stood between him and middle age, but also a frightening image of his own death.

Freud interpreted the tragedy of *Oedipus Rex* as consisting not in the classic formulation of a conflict between man and the supreme force of destiny but rather in a conflict between man's adult consciousness and his unconscious infantile wishes. He explicitly stated that the "tragedy of destiny" in *Oedipus Rex* does not carry the emotional impact of the play (1900a, p. 262). Freud vigorously denied the role of fate. The middle-aged person, however, may be more powerfully drawn to the story of *Oedipus at Colonus*, which stresses the impact of aging and death, so important in the psychology of the middle years. Contrary to what Freud said, catharsis may indeed be found in a "tragedy of destiny." In *Oedipus at Colonus*, which focuses on the problems of loss and rage, forgiveness and love, Sophocles teaches that almighty "Time has the power to disquiet all other things" (line 609), yet may also be the "teacher of contentment" (line 6).

REFERENCES

Benedek, T. 1959. Parenthood as a developmental phase: A contribution to the libido theory. *Journal of the American Psychoanalytic Association* 7:389–417.

Chiriboga, D. A. 1981. The developmental psychology of middle age. In *Modern perspectives in the psychiatry of middle age*. Ed. J. Howell, 3–25. New York: Brunner/Mazel.

Erikson, E. H. 1980. Themes of adulthood in the Freud-Jung correspondence. In *Themes of work and love in adulthood*. Ed. N. Smelser and E. Erikson, 43–74. Cambridge: Harvard University Press.

Freud, S. 1900a. *The interpretation of dreams*. In *Standard edition*, 4.

———. 1900b. *The interpretation of dreams*. In *Standard edition*, 5.

———. 1905. *Jokes and their relation to the unconscious*. In *Standard edition*, 8.

———. 1920. The psychogenesis of a case of homosexuality in a woman. In *Standard edition*, 18:145–172.

———. 1927. *Humor*. In *Standard edition*, 21:159–166.

———. 1937. Analysis terminable and interminable. In *Standard edition*, 23:209–253.

Grossman, W. I., and Kaplan, D. M. 1988. Three commentaries on gender in Freud's thought: A prologue on the psychoanalytic theory of sexuality. In *Unconscious fantasy, myth, and reality: Essays in honor of Jacob Arlow*. Ed. H. Blum, Y. Kramer, A. Richards, and A. Richards. Hillsdale, N.J.: Analytic Press.

Jaques, E. 1965. Death and the mid-life crisis. *International Journal of Psychoanalysis* 46:502–514.

Jung, C. G. 1933. *Modern man in search of a soul*. New York: Harcourt, Brace.

Kohut, H. 1977. *The restoration of the self*. New York: International Universities Press.

Masson, J. M. 1985. *The complete letters of Sigmund Freud to Wilhelm Fliess 1887–1904*. Cambridge: Harvard University Press.

Michels, R. 1981. Adulthood. In *The course of life: Psychoanalytic contributions toward understanding personality development.* Vol. 3, *Adulthood and the aging process.* Ed. S. Greenspan and G. Pollock, 25–34. Adelphia, Md.: National Institute of Mental Health (Mental Health Study Center).

———. 1986. Oedipus and insight. *Psychoanalytic Quarterly* 55(4):599–617. Also in *The Oedipus papers.* Ed. G. H. Pollock and J. M. Ross. New York: International Universities Press, 1988.

Ortega y Gasset, J. 1958. *Man and crisis.* New York: Norton.

Person, E. S. 1988. *Dreams of love and fateful encounters: The power of romantic passion.* New York: W. W. Norton.

Sandler, J. 1986–87. The past unconscious and the present unconscious: Toward a development of a theory of psychoanalytic technique. Reported by Elizabeth L. Auchincloss. *Bulletin* (Association for Psychoanalytic Medicine) 26:22–29.

Sophocles. 1954. *Oedipus at Colonus.* Trans. R. Fitzgerald. *Oedipus, the king.* Trans. D. Grene. In *The complete Greek tragedies.* Chicago: University of Chicago Press.

Sulloway, F. 1979. *Freud, biologist of the mind: Beyond the psychoanalytic legend.* New York: Basic Books.

Virgil. 1952. *The Aeneid of Virgil.* Trans. C. D. Lewis. Garden City, N.Y.: Doubleday.

· 5 ·

THE EVOLUTION OF
DEFENSE MECHANISMS
DURING THE MIDDLE YEARS

GEORGE E. VAILLANT, M. D.

Fifty years ago Anna Freud observed that "the chronology of psychic processes [defenses] is still one of the most obscure fields of analytical theory" (1937, p. 57), but she had no doubt that such a chronology existed. Over the years, several writers have offered developmental hierarchies for the maturation of defenses. The hierarchy that I will use in this chapter (see table 1) was modified from one proposed by Elvin Semrad (Semrad et al., 1973; Vaillant, 1971) and is the hierarchy for which the greatest empirical evidence has been generated (Vaillant, 1976, 1977, 1986; Vaillant et al., 1986).

Ego development is distinct from—if parallel to—psychosocial development as described by Erikson (1950). Like biologic and cognitive development, ego development is dependent upon development from *within*. In contrast, psychosocial development depends more on the interpersonal environment, development from without. Put still differently, psychosocial development reflects the step-by-step negotiation of the neo-Freudian or Eriksonian life cycle. The steps of this model are often labeled by psychosexual metaphor (oral, anal, phallic, latent, pubertal, and genital). The goal of this model is the achievement of mutual loving relationships with other people (for example, Kernberg in this book). In contrast, models of ego development reflect a more Jungian or Piagetian concept of maturation. They reflect unfolding patterns of mastering and making sense of our own inner experience. Jane Loevinger (1976) provides the most differentiated explication of this point of view.

Psychiatrists often regard personality disorders as reflecting some indelible defect in character, from which remissions are as miraculous as spontaneous recovery from cancer. But psychoanalysis allows us to regard personality disorder as more than a deficit state. Such "disorder" may actually reflect an ordered, if unconscious, effort at mastery through an aggregate of immature defense mechanisms. If this viewpoint is true, then prospective study should reveal lawful improvements in psychopathology over the life span. The ego and its defenses should manifest the same maturation during adult life as research by Kohlberg (Colby et al., 1983) suggests holds true for moral development.

Jack Block (1971) and Norma Haan (1972) contrasted prospectively studied adolescents to the same subjects as thirty-year-old and forty-five-year-old men and women. They observed that, over time, behaviors reflecting reaction formation and fantasy declined, but those reflecting altruism and suppression increased. They observed that compared to themselves at thirty, forty-five-year-olds were seen as "more sympathetic, giving, productive, and dependable" (Block, 1971).

The pooled data from the Study of Adult Development at Harvard and Dartmouth have supported Haan's and Block's observations. With the passage of time, mature defenses were used with relatively greater frequency (Vaillant, 1977). In other words, the middle years of the adult life cycle revealed not only deepening career commitment and generative responsibility for others, as predicted by Erikson's psychosocial model, but also a progressive maturation of adaptive modes, as suggested by table 1. To illustrate the kind of development I am suggesting, consider as one example of conflict resolution the predictable changes in the jokes enjoyed at different ages. The sadomasochistic pratfall and the hilarious thumbtack in the chair (passive aggression) enjoyed by the first-grader later evolves into the displaced aggression of cartoons, *Mad* magazine, and puns; then into the more sophisticated displacement of parody and political lampoons; and then into the subtle mitigation of reality present in the adult humor of the *Punch* or *New Yorker* cartoon. Adults do not find thumbtacks funny and children may be baffled by *New Yorker* wit.

We can build on this idea by examining the evolution of defense mechanisms during the middle years. Our research sample was drawn from 268 college sophomores selected for mental health in the 1940s and followed until the present time. As adolescents, these men were twice as likely to use immature defenses as mature ones; but as young adults they were twice as likely to use mature mechanisms as immature ones; and, finally, in middle life they were four times as likely to use mature defenses. (Such findings are consistent with the work of Roose and Pardes reported in this book.)

Let me begin by illustrating the evolution from psychotic distortion, to acting out, to intellectualization and reaction formation. When in middle life some criminals burn out, they replace their seemingly mindless delinquent acts with intellectualization and become jailhouse

Table I
A Theoretical Hierarchy of Defense Mechanisms

I. Psychotic Defenses
  1. Delusional Projection
  2. Psychotic denial
  3. Distortion

II. Immature Defenses
  4. Projection
  5. Schizoid fantasy
  6. Hypochondriasis
  7. Turning against the self (passive aggression)
  8. Acting out

III. Neurotic Defenses
  9. Dissociation (Neurotic Denial)
  10. Isolation (Intellectualization)
  11. Repression
  12. Displacement
  13. Reaction formation

IV. Mature Defenses
  14. Altruism
  15. Humor
  16. Suppression
  17. Anticipation
  18. Sublimation

a. The image-distorting defenses (for example, splitting, idealization, projection identification) elucidated by Melanie Klein may be included here and encompass much the same phenomena as the terms that I have borrowed from Anna Freud. In part, our present-day semantic confusion stems from the fact that Freud and Klein refused to borrow from each other.

b. Theoretically, dissociation belongs with the neurotic defenses; its empirical association with psychopathology (Vaillant et al., 1986) would militate for placing it with the immature defenses.

lawyers. When in middle life some addicts and delinquents recover, their subsequent lives may appear restricted through reaction formation. Thus, my first example is a recovery from sociopathy, but since our study's somewhat Victorian selection process was designed to exclude the undersocialized, Robert Hood's presence in the study never ceased to amaze the staff. He had been a child who found the giants and witches in fairy tales so real that he believed they actually entered his room. These "delusions" occurred after Hood, unlike any other study subject, had been repeatedly separated from his childish, inconsistent mother by her three-month vacations.

As he grew older, impulsive acting out protected Hood from feeling. Although he came from an upper-class home, he behaved like a street urchin. He started smoking at twelve and was addicted by fifteen. In boarding school he was in chronic danger of expulsion. By his freshman year in college, he was an extremely heavy drinker who boasted of drinking a quart of whiskey before 5:00 P.M. every day. During the time that Hood was violating school rules and engaging in reckless, almost suicidal driving, his mother was being openly courted by her next husband and was suing Hood's father—who was suicidally depressed and in the hospital—for divorce. Yet the study internist could write of Hood: "Robert doesn't see any concrete problems to ask anyone about and sees himself as happy." The study staff called him "psychopathic"— without sadness, remorse, or anxiety.

During World War II, Hood was a severe disciplinary problem; he was one of two study subjects to be broken in rank. After his marriage, he was chronically unfaithful and came perilously close to becoming a child batterer. Hood flew into rages against his hapless child because, he said, "The prospect of vicariously reliving the years of my boyhood is quite intolerable." But Hood's military demotion for disorderly conduct, extreme promiscuity, and possible child battery occurred during a period when he himself was in the throes of divorce. After his divorce, he never saw his child again, his severe drinking and promiscuity waned, and his military career became successful.

At thirty-two, Hood finally admitted to the study, "From age eighteen, I had the belief that my life would necessarily be terminated by suicide." And had he not escaped through acting out, Hood might well have become as dangerously depressed as his father. But by age thirty-five Hood's earlier Grant Study diagnosis of psychopathic personality was no longer applicable. Instead of acting on his emotions without thinking or feeling them, Hood thought about his emotions without feeling or acting—in short, he substituted intellectualization and re-action formation. In his early thirties, when he was asked what his philosophy was during rough spots, Hood replied, "I always have had a great deal of faith in the integrity and excellence of my own mind." Instead of binge drinking, he now worked as a psychologist in a cancer center and *studied* the pharmacological relief of human pain. When Hood was in middle life, instead of being politically active in support of his right-wing views, he contented himself with reading racist tracts.

At forty-five, Robert Hood had not only solved his binge drinking through total abstinence but, after four divorces and multiple affairs, finally achieved a stable if constricted marriage with total abstinence from coitus. As Sigmund Freud once quipped, "A young whore makes an old nun."

Let me next examine recovery from hypochondriasis. When Freud first described hypochondriasis as a defense he pointed out that it contained "covert reproach" (1896). Since then psychiatrists have sometimes forgotten that the goal of hypochondriasis is rarely "secondary gain" and that the hypochondriac who transforms covert rage into complaints of pain is incapable of comfort. Like the Ancient Mariner, the hypochondriac seems driven to let others know the most excruciating details of his agony and is relieved only when the observer acknowledges that the pain is the worst since the world began. Often, rather than reproach others who in the past have failed to care for him, the hypochondriac berates his doctor. Thus, to the unwitting observer the hypochondriac is a chronic help-devaluing complainer.

Not surprisingly, when hypochondriacs are transferred from a medical to a psychiatric context, they are often rediagnosed as "borderline." In selecting John Hart to illustrate recovery from hypochondriasis I choose a very tame example. John Hart was good at doing things for himself and tried to use reason rather than complaint. He was a man who could read blueprints before he could read books and was always better with numbers and symbols than with words. He became one of the most brilliant mathematicians his university had ever seen. Until his graduation from college, he enjoyed excellent health and, unlike some subjects, had exhibited no particular concerns about his heart.

In September 1944, John Hart's father, who had had angina for many years, died of a coronary thrombosis. That year, Hart first noted the onset of his own chest pain. Two years later, after a friend had a heart attack, Hart's chest pains became more severe. Finally, after six years of visiting doctors' offices, he read an article in the popular science press on "imaginary" heart disease. Later that year he wrote the following letter to the study internist:

> I have been having some difficulties over the past few years in which I thought you might be interested. You may remember that my father died of heart trouble in 1944. During the next year or so I felt occasional pains in my chest and suffered several dizzy spells which became more frequent, until finally—I think in 1947—I had a physical examination and was assured by the doctor that there was nothing wrong with my heart. He asked me whether the pains were comparable to someone crushing my chest; I said no. I had no more attacks for about six months. Then, they began again, this time accompanied by a crushing feeling, like a muscle cramp in the chest. I tried to tell myself it was all imaginary, but that didn't seem to help. Finally, after a very severe attack in which my heart rate rose so fast I could not count it, I became really frightened. I went to see another doctor again, and I described my symptoms. He said it certainly was not heart trouble—probably a spasm of the stomach valve— and asked if I had pains in my arms, which I did not have. After all of this, I was fairly convinced that my difficulties were psychosomatic. . . . About a month later, I began having the same sort of attacks again, for no apparent reason. This time they lasted all night, with pains in my arms. . . . I returned to the doctor and had another electrocardiogram and chest X-ray, both negative. I was particularly disturbed to discover that even after being convinced that the symptoms were psychosomatic, I still could not make them disappear permanently.

Indeed, Hart told me much later, when a doctor indicated that a sign of real cardiac trouble would be edema of the ankles, shortly afterward he developed ankle swelling for the first and only time in his life. But the next year—1952—Hart wrote his confessional letter to his college doctor and never had any further symptoms or pain related to his heart. At forty-seven he described his biggest health problem as "dandruff and boils," and at age sixty-five he remained in excellent health.

When Hart was reinterviewed in 1967 at age forty-six years, I asked him about his cardiac symptoms. He seemed surprised and did not remember his long confessional letter to the internist. Even more amazing, this brilliant mathematician could not remember the year or even

the season of the year when his father died. Hart did remember, however, that at his father's funeral "I had wondered what was expected
of me emotionally"; then he admitted that he had felt somewhat inadequate and "inclined not to show grief." He related that until he had
read the article on "imaginary heart disease" he had made no conscious
connection between his father's death and the onset of his own cardiac
symptoms.

We can only speculate about why his cardiac symptoms vanished.
But certainly, two things happened to this man in 1952 that had not
happened before. This brilliant logician did what none of his physicians
had done. First, he consciously connected the ungrieved death of his
father with the beginning of his symptoms. Second, he then wrote the
entire story in great detail to another person in whom he had trust, a
trust that was justified because the physician to whom he described his
symptoms wrote back that in such cases he was convinced the cardiac
pain was real and not imaginary or located somewhere other than the
heart.

The lives of three women with severe personality disorders in youth
—Mary Baker Eddy, the founder of Christian Science, Florence Night-
ingale, the founder of modern nursing, and Bertha Pappenheim (a.k.a.
Anna O. in Breur and Freud's case history), a leader of the German
women's movement—offer more dramatic examples of recovery. These
women's lives also serve to illustrate how the mechanism of hypochondriasis is used as a profoundly irritating means of containing hostility
and/or grief.

In his descent into and recovery from alcoholism, a Grant Study
economist, James O'Neill, illustrated the developmental linkages
among the three ego mechanisms of passive aggression (masochism,
in the language of psychoanalysis), reaction formation, and altruism.
O'Neill had been strictly brought up by warm but abstemious parents.
Although he once went so far as to label his upbringing "Prussian,"
in 1972 a child psychiatrist—with no knowledge of the eighteen-year-
old O'Neill's future—considered his childhood environment and his
psychological soundness in college well above average for this college
sample. Ten years after O'Neill's graduation, the director of his college health services summarized the data that the Grant Study had
gathered up to that time as follows: "A sufficiently straightforward,
decent, honest fellow . . . should be a good bet in any community."
O'Neill's adaptive style could be most consistently characterized by the

neurotic, albeit normal, mechanisms of reaction formation and intellec-tualization. "I deal with ideas," he said; "I love ideas." And so O'Neill was faithfully married to his high school sweetheart and helped pio-neer the statistical and actuarial techniques now used in the economic management of large corporations.

By age thirty, however, James O'Neill had lost control of his ability to drink socially. Drawing upon his excellent intelligence, he wrote a creditable Ph.D. thesis and obtained lucrative industrial employment. Nevertheless, much of his day from morning to night involved secret drinking in bars.

Chronic intoxication diffusely impairs brain function, and impaired brain function leads to less mature styles of defense. Thus, O'Neill's case record for the years after thirty provided ample evidence of passive aggression, projection, and acting out. This once straitlaced man was repeatedly and senselessly unfaithful to his wife. Yet during his motel trysts he did nothing to hide his identity. This shrewd mathematician compulsively borrowed funds so that he could masochistically reinvest them at parimutuel windows. This "decent, honest fellow" was caught stealing equipment from his employer to finance his drinking bouts. For this last misbehavior he was fired, then hospitalized, and finally diagnosed as an "inadequate character" by his physician. James O'Neill read psychiatric textbooks and rediagnosed himself as a "psychopath."

Eight years later, O'Neill was again hospitalized. This time the functioning of his brain had been further compromised by the acute withdrawal of alcohol. The resulting mental disorganization led to his manifestation of more primitive defense mechanisms—distortion and delusional projection. Since he was a Ph.D. on chronic welfare, he was incorrectly diagnosed a schizophrenic by his psychiatrists. (With hindsight, delirium tremens would have been a more accurate label.) A year later a wiser physician, instead of renewing his prescription for chlorpromazine, introduced him to Alcoholics Anonymous. When I first met Dr. O'Neill in 1973 he had been sober for three years. Intellec-tualization was once more a dominant defense, and his former reaction formation now facilitated his passionate espousal of sobriety.

After three years spent within the socially supportive network of Alcoholics Anonymous, O'Neill had deployed two additional adaptive styles: sublimation and altruism. Unlike neurotic mechanisms, these mature defenses introduced some pleasure into the life of this recov-ered thief and philanderer. His old addiction to gambling was now sublimated into the considerably more remunerative task of serving as consultant to his state's lottery commission. He was proud that his current job no longer used his analytic talents to help commercial industry and the military establishment plan global warfare; instead, he now performed actuarial analysis for a major foundation concerned with population control. Modestly religious in adolescence, utterly nonreligious during his two decades of alcoholism, he now took an active role in his church. Within Alcoholics Anonymous, he was positively addicted to helping other people. As both Loevinger and Kohlberg have documented, morality and ego development are inextricably linked.

The life of Francis DeMille illustrates the evolution of a histrionic character disorder into a symptom-free community leader and shows how repression and dissociation can evolve into sublimation and suppression. In 1940, Francis DeMille had impressed the Grant Study staff with his charm. Throughout college, DeMille never dated, totally denied sexual tension, and blandly observed, "I am anything but aggressive." He discussed his interest in the theater with a cultivated animation and struck several observers as rather effeminate. The psychiatrist marveled that "DeMille has not yet begun to think of sexual experience"; the staff noted that his dreams were not well remembered; the subject noticed that "distressing emotional reactions fade quickly."

Francis took an active and enjoyable part in college dramatics. Like many people who use repression as a major defense, he reported that he preferred "emotional thinking to rational thought"; and on one occasion he told the study, "I worked up a beautiful case of hysteria." Indeed, like many histrionic actors, DeMille was a master of dissociation. For example, he found it "revitalizing to free myself from inhibitions by venting my emotions on someone else in a play." Christian Science greatly appealed to him, and despite the fact that the staff worried about his inner unhappiness, during psychiatric interviews he seemed "constantly imbued with a cheerful affect."

Francis DeMille had grown up in suburban Hartford. He had never known his father, a businessman who left home before his birth and died shortly thereafter. His father's relatives played no part in his upbringing, and the DeMille household consisted only of his mother and two maiden aunts. Francis spent his first ten years in an utterly female ménage. He was encouraged to play by himself in a well-equipped playroom, and his mother proudly reported to the study that he "never played with other boys." During his adolescence, she boasted, "Francis would take me to a nightclub as a man does a woman." Even during

World War II, naval lieutenant Francis DeMille managed to remain emotionally and geographically at his mother's side. The study internist feared that he would become a lifelong neurotic, fixated on his mother.

It was in the navy, however, that with continued maturation De-Mille's repression began to fail. He became conscious of his lack of sexual interest and fearful of possible homosexuality. Discussing this problem with the study, he made a revealing slip of the pen, as do many people who use repression: "I don't know whether homosexuality is psychiological [*sic*] or psychological in origin." As it turned out, De-Mille's unconscious was right; there was nothing *physiologically* wrong with his masculinity.

In manageable doses, however, anxiety promotes maturation, and it was in the navy that Francis began to replace dissociation with sublimation. He wrote to the study that he was always "rebelling" against the navy, always standing up for his own individuality and that of his men. Had we not had access to his military efficiency records as well as his own report, his behavior might have been labeled "passive-aggressive." Objective evaluation of his behavior, however, revealed that he had received his highest officer efficiency rating in "moral courage" and "cooperation." In short, this timid man had made his military rebellion well appreciated, a veritable work of art.

By twenty-seven, DeMille's worried letters about possible homosexuality were replaced by his joyful announcement, "I enjoy working with girls!" He had found a job teaching dramatics at a women's college. By managing the move from Hartford, he had also gratified the "great necessity I feel for breaking away from home." Three years later, he shattered maternal domination still further by marrying an actress whom he had formerly directed.

After marriage, DeMille's repression became still further transformed. In reply to a questionnaire that asked about his marital adjustment, he wrote, "I must have a mental block on the questionnaire. My reluctance to return seems to be much more than ordinary procrastination." He was in conflict over his sexual adjustment, and finally, he consciously recognized this conflict. With insight, however, comes resistance, and that was the last the study heard of DeMille for seven years. During this time, he never saw a psychiatrist. Instead, in keeping with his fresh capacity for sublimation, he wrote a successful comedy called "Help Me, Carl Jung, I Am Drowning."

Then DeMille returned to the study. Although he had vowed that he would never associate himself with the "specter of American business," he became a very special corporate success story. Despite his theatrical interests, he succeeded as an executive in Hartford, where insurance was king. In an industry not known for its opportunities for individual expression, DeMille crafted a niche in an advertising department where he had autonomy, high occupational status, and a chance to exercise his artistic flair. He took pains, however, to assure me that his success threatened no one and that he was not "overly aggressive." As he put it, "The ability to stay alive in a large corporation took all the craftiness I have." Only in his community theater group could he unashamedly enjoy playing aggressive roles.

Without psychotherapy, DeMille's earlier repression of important masculine figures in his life had given way at age forty-six to his vivid recollection of a hypermasculine uncle who, during Francis's adolescence, had been an important, if previously unacknowledged, source of identification. Five years after our interview, DeMille further elaborated on his uncle as "the only consistent male influence—very dominant—a male figure that earlier I had rejected." But not entirely, for behind his pipe, tweed jacket, and leather study furniture, the middle-aged DeMille now rather resembled this uncle. The charming emotional outpourings of his adolescence were gone; he now hid emotions behind lists, orderliness, and a gruff, bulldog, over-forty exterior. "In college," he mused, "I was in a Bohemian fringe; but I've changed since twenty-five years ago. Maybe some clockwork ticked inside me and made me go down this route." Perhaps that explained why, a few years before, he had given up his mother's religion and was "suddenly smitten" with his father's Baptist beliefs.

After retirement at age sixty-five, he has become a leader in the Berkshire town to which he retired. Aggressively he helped transform the town. His creativity no longer expressed itself in the illusionary worlds of advertising and theater. Now he directly affected how his town runs and the nature of its institutions. He is one of the best-adjusted retirees in the study and remains happily married.

The progression from a schizoid character disorder to a courageous obsessional adjustment is illustrated by the life of Herman Crabbe. Herman had grown up in a small mining town in West Virginia, and the Crabbe yearly income rarely exceeded a thousand dollars. In high school, his towering achievement had been a remarkable collection of moths—a collection that, if it did not bring him friends, won him statewide recognition and a full scholarship to college.

Herman Crabbe had suffered perhaps the most pathological mother in the entire study. Mrs. Crabbe was a paranoid woman who, on the one hand, accused her crippled husband of going out with other women and disparaged him to his son and, on the other hand, capitalized on her husband's old back injury to keep him unemployed and an invalid. During Herman's childhood she had shopped around until she found a doctor who could hear her son's "heart murmur" and helped her keep him from any kind of athletic or independent social activity. As a child, Herman had been as adept at fantasy as DeMille had been at dissociation. In contrast to DeMille, Crabbe knew that his mother was clinging to him, but he could not muster the appropriate emotion. Instead, he withdrew into the safety of his own head and spent time with his moths, not people.

In high school Herman had identified with his paranoid mother and believed that the other children were out to get him. In college, he was bizarre. The study staff called him "solitary, stammery, unkempt, and ill-bred. . . . He looked no one in the eye, but wore a chip on his shoulder." At nineteen, he summed up his philosophy: "Everyone is out to get as much as he can. . . . It doesn't pay to pay much attention to the other fellow." He lied to his parents and had no friends. Wearing a T-shirt full of holes, he avoided people and worked in the chemistry laboratory until 9:00 P.M.

After college, because he had dared to marry the one close friend he had had in high school, the twenty-three-year-old Crabbe imagined that his university would persecute him for getting married without telling the authorities. His fears of retaliation reflected his real guilt about escaping from his mother's possession. Until age thirty, isolation, fantasy, and projection were his dominant modes of survival. At thirty, Herman Crabbe still resembled a village eccentric or a very young child. The social anthropologist commented that Herman was preoccupied with his own inferiority: "He seems to lack basic courtesy; he does not see people as they are psychologically but rather in terms of whether or not they provide support, whether they make demands or leave you." At least two observers diagnosed Crabbe as schizoid.

At last Herman's mother died. Instead of devastation, both Herman and his father enjoyed a sudden burst of health. Herman renewed his relationship with his rejuvenated father, cut back on his compulsive research, and for the first time began to move toward people. The study internist commented that Crabbe "appears more confident and happier than I have ever seen him." Herman bought a boxer dog and wrote the study, "I enjoy dealing with people to an extent I did not anticipate." His marriage prospered. In short, contrary to common psychoanalytic assumption, events in adult life as well as in childhood can exert a significant effect on personality.

The year after his mother died, Herman received psychological testing as part of the study. The clinical psychologist, without information besides Crabbe's Thematic Apperception Test, wrote: "His mother is seen as parasitically wanting her son for herself because of her own frustration in marriage. . . . In his fantasy world, ignorant armies clash by night. . . . some eccentricities may be present due to occasional intrusion of fantasy into a well-wrought obsessive-compulsive surface. Unlikely that this would reach schizoid proportions."

At fifty, the change in Crabbe had gone further. He no longer used daydreams for comfort. Instead, he wrote, "I react to events with a good deal of feeling." Although Crabbe's jokes were still a little adolescent, he maintained eye contact throughout our interview. As our time together passed, there was a progressive thawing of his demeanor. He was now the director of a research team of twelve Ph.D.s and was repeatedly cited for superior achievement. At nineteen he had stated flatly that he preferred "things" to humans; but at fifty he told me, "I don't think I'm worth much working with things. I would prefer to work through other people." He still put in a sixty-hour week, but it was not for his own sake. "I am not a great scientist," he wrote, "but I'm good at guiding others."

In his own words, he wrote, "It's a hell of a note to graduate summa cum laude at 22 and grow up and feel secure and confident in your own ability only after 50. . . . At 52 I have more ambition, more confidence, and more good ideas for work than ever before." This boast was not fantasy; his ideas led to millions of dollars' worth of new business for his company. But reliance on fantasy had been replaced by reliance on intellectualization. Crabbe lived his life according to a strict schedule. Each event of the day was ritualized, and he conducted all his social relationships either at work or with his wife. Although he was reserved, I was impressed as we talked by the intellectualized candor with which he discussed his own psychological workings. He described sexual problems graphically but without emotion. Perhaps as a legacy from living so long within his own mind, he understood how he felt. Intellectualization has advantages as well as drawbacks.

To conclude, what are the steps that account for recovery from personality disorder? What allows a world of fantasy to evolve into a world of creative ideas? What allows the ego to grow in maturity?

First, to an enormous, if uncharted, extent, the human ego is a precipitate of the people it has experienced. But as we saw with De-Mille, these introjects can lie dormant for long periods. Callous as it may sound, Crabbe benefited from the death of his mother; he was at last free from his mother's psychopathology. He benefited also from his subsequent rediscovery of his father. Crabbe's shift in adaptive style paralleled their renewed relationship.

Second, psychotherapy—or, more broadly defined, interpersonal healing relationships—allows rigid defenses to be abandoned and replaced by more flexible means of coping. Dr. O'Neill's membership in Alcoholics Anonymous is one example; Herman Crabbe's remarkably supportive marriage is another. After twenty-five years Crabbe wrote to the study, "I have the same wife, and am getting more attached to her all the time." If the ego shapes our relationships, it is also shaped by them.

Third, as suggested in the chapter in this book by Roose and Pardes and by the work of Yakovlev and Lecours (1967) and Denny-Brown (1962), the brain is dynamic. The "embryological" unfolding of the human brain certainly is not complete at five, and its neurobiological development may well continue into mid-life. If we are to elucidate the phenomena of adult maturation over the next half century, neurobiology and psychoanalysis must join hands.

REFERENCES

Block, J. 1971. *Lives through time*. Berkeley, Calif.: Bancroft.

Colby, A.; Kohlberg, L.; Gibbs, J.; and Lieberman, M. 1983. A longitudinal study of moral judgment. *Monographs of the Society for Research in Child Development* 48:1–124.

Denny-Brown, D. 1962. *The basic ganglia and their relation to disorders of movement*. Oxford: Oxford University Press.

Erikson, E. H. 1950. *Childhood and society*. New York: Norton.

———. 1976. Reflections on Dr. Borg's life cycle. *Daedalus* (Proceedings of the American Academy of Arts and Sciences) 105(2).

Freud, A. 1937. *Ego and the mechanisms of defense*. London: Hogarth Press.

Freud, S. 1894. The neuropsychoses of defense In *Standard edition*, 3:45–61.

———. 1896. Further remarks on the neuropsychoses of defense. In *Standard edition*, 3:162–185.

Haan, N. 1972. Personality development from adolescence to adulthood in the Oakland growth and guidance studies. *Seminars in Psychiatry* 4:399–414.

Hartmann, H. 1960. *Psychoanalysis and moral values*. New York: International Universities Press.

Loevinger, J. 1976. *Ego development*. San Francisco: Jossey Bass.

Semrad, E. V., Grinspoon, L., and Feinberg, S. E. 1973. Development of an ego profile scale. *Archives of General Psychiatry* 28:70–77.

Vaillant, G. E. 1971. Theoretical hierarchy of adaptive ego mechanisms. *Archives of General Psychiatry* 24:107–118.

———. 1976. Natural history of male psychological health, V: Relation of choice ego mechanisms of defense to adult adjustment. *Archives of General Psychiatry* 33:535–545.

———. 1977. *Adaptation to life*. Boston: Little, Brown.

———, ed. 1986. *Empirical studies of ego mechanisms of defense*. Washington, D.C.: American Psychiatric Press.

Vaillant, G. E., Bond, M., and Vaillant, C. O. 1986. Empirical evidence for a hierarchy of defense mechanisms. *Archives of General Psychiatry* 43:786–794.

Weinstock, A. 1967. Longitudinal study of social class and defense preferences. *Journal of Consulting and Clinical Psychology* 31:539–541.

Yakovlev, P. I., and Lecours, A. R. 1967. The myelogenetic cycles of regional maturation of the brain. In *Regional development of the brain in early life*. Ed. A. Minkowski. Oxford: Blackwell Scientific Publications.

Part II

Special Groups

· 6 ·

THE IMPACT OF TEENAGED CHILDREN ON PARENTS

HELEN MEYERS, M.D.

The middle years bring with them a number of new issues, one of them the parenting of adolescents. Rearing and guiding the teenaged child, a major task of these years, constitutes a powerful force in the parent's life. Erikson, indeed, called these years the stage when the psychosocial task is the establishment of generativity. According to him, this represents a new psychosocial primacy in which the earlier developmental attainments are not only fully represented but also transcended:

> The ability to lose oneself in the meeting of bodies and minds (i.e., in the previous stage of intimacy) leads to a gradual expression of ego interests and of libidinal cathexes over that which has been thus generated and accepted as a responsibility. Generating is primarily the interest in establishing and guiding the next generation or whatever in a given case may become the absorbing object of a parental kind of responsibility. (Erikson, 1950)

"Stagnation" represents a failure at this task. This approach implies successive phases of development in the progression from infancy to childhood, adolescence, and adulthood. Changes should reflect the new problems of inner organization and object relationships posed by each advance in development.

Others since Erikson have proposed the idea of continued psychic development throughout the life cycle. Benedek (1959) specifically elaborated on parenthood as a developmental phase, and more recently various authors (for example, Caloruso and Cath) have written on definitive adult developmental phases with normative crises, such as fatherhood. In a manner that anticipates the issues of parenting adolescent children, D. Pines (1982) has defined pregnancy and motherhood as a specific developmental phase. She called it a third separation-individuation phase, which includes regression to the early mother/child dyad. The pregnant woman is postulated as identifying with both the "mother of her own infancy" and "the child within her as the child she was herself within mother." Thus pregnancy, representing

75

symbiotic union, and having the child, representing separateness and identification with the nurturing mother, will revive strong unconscious conflicts in these connections.

Similarly, intense involvement with the adolescent child characteristically leads to middle-aged parents' regression to their own unconscious resolved and unresolved adolescent conflicts. This includes both concordant identifications with the teenager, as the teenager once was, and complementary identifications with the adolescent's objects, one's own parents.

But there is even more to be understood about parental regression. In adolescence itself we find two kinds of regression, basically different from each other. We are familiar with regression as a defense mechanism. The other regression, however, is not defensive but functions in the service of the ego (E. Kris, 1952), a developmental detour that makes growing up feasible and workable. This kind of regression enables the advanced and relatively competent adolescent ego to get in touch once more with the unfinished business of childhood. Thus adolescence offers a second chance, predicated on coming to terms, through regression, with the developmental and conflictual residue from an earlier period of life. To a lesser degree this process is repeated for middle-aged adults, who in intimate contact with their adolescent offspring, are getting in touch once again with the unfinished business of their own adolescence. This regression may lead to a damaging breakdown of working compromises or may, with regression in the service of the ego, provide another chance for a better solution.

Developmental Phase or Impact?

Whether we can apply the terms *developmental phase* or *normative developmental crisis* to any phase or event after adolescence depends on our definition of the terms. If we define them simply as periods or events that *can* result in intrapsychic structural change, they would indeed be applicable, since such changes would seem possible throughout life, following trauma, psychoanalysis, and other important life events. If, on the other hand, we limit these terms to phases or crises *essential* for structure building with a specific internal task necessary for structure *completion*, the application of these terms after adolescence is more questionable. The two conceptualizations are quite different. Having a baby, for example, can obviously have great impact on a woman's sense of femaleness, maternal ego ideal identifications, and sense of fulfillment, but we doubt that the experience is necessary for completion of a woman's sense of mature feminine *identity*. In our second definition, then, pregnancy and childbirth would be highly significant but would not be considered a *developmental crisis*. The difference between the early years of structure building and the later years of modification is reflected in the rate of change, the extent of the change, and the intensity of the stimulus required—that is, the degree of trauma or assault to the existing structure necessary to effect change.

The middle-aged adult has an integrated psychic structure and character built during the formative early years of childhood and consolidated in late adolescence. Nevertheless, adolescent children, with their struggles and successes, challenges and opportunities, will have an impact on mothers and fathers in their middle years. This impact may indeed be profound, for it both involves the reaction to the adolescent and affects the structure of the parent's personality itself. The kind and degree of impact will, of course, depend on the nature of the adult's psychic structure, its content, solidity, and flexibility, and its success in functioning. It will be influenced by the reality situation of the adult —the fulfillment of ambitions and ideals, the concordance of his life situation and his ego ideal and superego—and by the real interaction with and reality situation of the particular teenaged child. The impact will be determined by the degree of assault on the established structure, the parent's stereotypic attitude about adolescence, and his own unresolved adolescent conflicts. And finally, the impact will relate to the level of organization not only of the parent but of the child in different stages of the adolescent process. The impact varies, then, with whether the teenaged child is struggling with the tasks of early, late, or mid-adolescence.

And, of course, although I use the general term *parent*, it is to be understood that mothers and fathers will differ in their reactions, and in the adolescent's impact on them, according to their individual character, which includes different gender identities, gender roles, and gender-related problems. Further, the triadic dynamics among mother, father, and adolescent potentiates the different parental reactions. In a two-child family, one adolescent, boy or girl, may bring out the best in one parent and the worst in the other, whereas the other child may have the reverse effect. This leads to issues of same-gender and opposite-gender parent-child vicissitudes once adolescence is reached. This will be touched on later in the clinical vignettes.

Tasks of the Middle Years

Mid-life brings with it certain general issues that every adult must deal with, regardless of the presence or absence of a teenaged child. It is a time for productivity, creativity, and generativity in the larger sense. One may have reached the height of one's career and of relationships, both marital and with friends. It is the age when one can become president or can see one's options narrowing. Choices become more nearly final. Success and failure assume more meaning and reality. One's responsibility, as a member of the generation in charge, takes center stage. And yet the decline of the preceding generation, the loss of one's parents, the beginning awareness of one's own finiteness, and the waning of physical powers and youthful vigor are disturbing.

The relationship with the teenaged child informs all these issues, intensifying problems, enhancing satisfaction, and offering new solutions. Gratification or dissatisfaction in the parent will determine whether he or she can take joy in the adolescent's growth as a separate person, or whether the parent needs to live through the offspring's successes or, paradoxically, needs the adolescent to fail. Will the parent experience pride or envy in relation to the adolescent's freedom and burgeoning prowess? If the middle-aged parent is disappointed in relation to his own ambitions and ideals, he may look to the adolescent for fulfillment of his own frustrated goals, investing the youngster with unrealistic expectations that can lead only to disillusionment. When losing or threatened with the loss of his or her own parental figures, the parent may respond to the increasing autonomy of the adolescent child with fear and loneliness.

Adolescent Tasks and Their Impact

What are the tasks, challenges, and opportunities of adolescence that the parent in his middle years can react or regress to? The parent may react to the adolescent as the adolescent's object (complementary position) or may regress to unresolved conflicts (concordant position). Thus the parent can be caught again in the adolescent turmoil, leading to

a breakdown of working compromise formations or providing another
chance to work through conflicts to a more successful solution with a
now fully mature ego. How does this impact manifest itself? In order to
understand these processes in parents it may be useful to review briefly
some adolescent tasks and stages.

Adolescence is often referred to as the period of the second individuation (Blos, 1967), a struggle between dependence and independence; a time of apparent contradictions, of upheaval and achievement.
Yet curiously, some adolescents seem to traverse this period relatively
calmly and easily (Offer, 1969). Intellectual (Piaget, 1969), physical,
and sexual maturation leap forward; experimentation and intense and
labile feelings are characteristic. Yet all this must be assimilated into the
tasks of socialization, identity formation, and consolidation of internal
structures—of superego and ego reformulation and character formation.

In early adolescence (ages twelve through fourteen), the youngster
struggles internally with the upsurge of instinctual urges and the need
for internal object removal. Externally he needs to separate from the
incestuous objects and turns first inward and then outward to peers.
This is apt to stir up early fears of loss and abandonment and beginning
fears of loss of control in the parent who is vulnerable because of his
or her own early problems in the mother-child dyad and problems of
internal controls.

Mid-adolescence, or adolescence proper (fifteen through seventeen),
is the time of greatest turmoil, of loosening of ego controls in the service
of new ego integration, and of formation of social and sexual identity.
Externally it is a time of experimentation, both acting out and action in
the service of the ego, rapid shifts and emotionality. In the parent, it
is apt to rouse all the old conflicts around sexuality and aggression, the
fears and guilt over instinctual wishes, as well as the fascinated envy
of the adolescent's increasing sexual and physical powers, freedom,
gratifications, and narcissism. This may disequilibrate established compromise solutions within the vulnerable parent, resulting in anxiety,
depression, or acting out. It can lead to subtle and not so subtle encouragement of the adolescent to act out for the parent or to implicit
or explicit frightened or competitive and envious prohibitions (Meyers,
1971). It is the time when adolescents are likened to "fast moving express trains" (A. Freud, 1958) or "erupting volcanoes" (Geleerd, 1957)
and adult stereotypes of adolescents (Anthony, 1969) are applied. The
adolescent may be experienced as a dangerous or endangered object;
as a sexual object—rampant or frightened; as an object of envy for his

freedom in sexuality, action, and choices or as an object of pity for his suffering, confusion, and maladjustment; as a sadly lost object or one to be gotten rid of as soon as possible. These stereotypes are set up by society but are adopted by the parent whose conflicts revolve around these same issues, whose inner world of self and objects is in accord with these images.

Major internal tasks of late adolescence (seventeen through twenty-one) are character formation and superego and ego-ideal consolidation. Character has been defined (Moore and Fine, 1968) as the habitual mode of bringing into harmony the tasks presented by internal demands and those set by the external world—the habitual way of achieving intrapsychic synthesis and integration. Although largely originating in conflict, character is removed from conflict by its codification of con-

flict solution and patterned fixity, a fixity manifested by distinctive traits or qualities and by typical ways of conducting oneself. Its func-

tion involves the maintenance of psychosomatic homeostasis, patterned self-esteem regulation, stabilization of ego identity, and automatization of threshold levels (Blos, 1968). Clearly character formation marks the final achievement of the second individuation process, the consolidation of ego identity, the beginning of the adolescent's defining himself in relation to society and entering a stage of true intimacy with people other than his parents.

The parent is now confronted with a separate person—individual, different, and apart. He or she may react to this with a sense of loss and estrangement, mourning the loss of the "child." The parent may try to cling to the lost object or try to "parentify" the adolescent in a reversal of roles at a time when the parent may be losing a parent as well. Confronted with an individual who is now his or her own person, the parent may take genuine pride and pleasure in the adolescent's achievement; or the parent who tried to undo his or her own disappointments by living through the offspring may find these hopes permanently dashed. The idealism of the late adolescent, the depersonified abstract ideals that now arise out of earlier depersonalized idealizations, may sweep the parent along in a new burst of enthusiasm. Or the middle-aged parent, sadly confronted with his own lost ideals, and with his offspring's deidealization of *his* parent, may find himself defensively in a painful, often bitter battle with the idealistic youth.

Positive Impact

Most parents in their middle years and their teenaged offspring pass through these stages with mutual pleasure and pride, resulting in satisfaction and growth for both. The adolescent identifies with his parents, yet individuates satisfactorily. His role with respect to the adult has a special and satisfying quality to it that was not present in his dependent status as a child and will not be present in his ultimate status as an adult. In some ways, it can be viewed as a learning experience in which the adolescent is practicing the adult role under the experienced tutelage of a friendly and encouraging adult (Anthony, 1969). The relationship is regarded as basically helpful and trustworthy. In these parents, rigid and stereotypic responses are minimal. Their reactions are relatively free of irrational influences from the past and include an element of sympathy toward the adolescent, originating in the parents' relatively satisfactory adolescent experiences—experiences that were not free from conflict, but in which conflicts have principally been accepted and resolved.

For most parents the opportunities outweigh the problems. The opportunities are threefold: guiding the adolescents, sharing in their experience, and further developing themselves.

There can be great satisfaction in the generative task of guiding and establishing the next generation. These parents want their children to do better than they have done, to be happier and more accomplished, and to live in a better world. This is part of their parental ego ideal and enhances their sense of self-worth. There are pride and gratification in one's part in this endeavor, in one's tutorial success. There is also joy for the other in his growth and success. This positive parental outcome involves true object love of the child as a separate other, as well as some degree of healthy narcissistic investment in someone who is like oneself or was once part of oneself (S. Freud, 1914). This mixture is, I believe, the key to the intensity and indestructibility of parental love. Parental difficulties emerge if the narcissistic component becomes dominant and the parent lives through the child, the child becoming the bearer of the parent's needs and satisfactions.

Adolescence is an exciting time, and the mature parent can share in this intellectual ferment, optimism, and experimentation with feelings and relationships. Sharing will enhance the adult's experience as long as it is empathic, a temporary identification while maintaining awareness of separateness. It will be destructive, however, if the boundaries are lost—if the parent becomes overidentified, every success of the adolescent becoming the parent's success, every failure his failure. In this psychological climate the stage is set for the parent to act out regressively.

The proper balance of identification and separateness may yield another felicitous result. The parent can let go of her own residual youthful turmoil and struggles, the adolescent part of herself—so disturbing and yet so precious—and hand over the mantle of Sturm und Drang to her adolescent child, separate yet related, confident that these important battles will continue to be fought by someone who is appropriately qualified. This will result in releasing the parent and freeing her to concentrate on her mid-life tasks with greater calm and flexibility.

Let us take this a step further. The adolescent, raised by the parent, is apt to share the parent's value system. Often, in late adolescence, if he is not in revolt, he will turn to interests or beginning career choices that derive from his parent's interest—both explicit and more dormant. This may be acting out, but often it is not; rather, it is the adolescent's own interest developed out of true identification with his internalized representations of his parents. If this interest coincides with a parent's overt interest, the parent, if not too competitive or needy, can appreciate this shared interest without co-opting it. If this interest coincides with a more hidden ambition of the parent, the parent may be able finally to relinquish this fantasy—now safely delegated to his offspring —and find more satisfaction in his present life.

The opportunities offered to the parent by the interaction with his or her adolescent child go beyond the satisfaction of generativity and the pleasure of shared experience. It provides a new chance to work through some lingering problems, opening closed doors to new horizons within the parent himself.

I will illustrate with some typical examples. These brief vignettes have been purposefully simplified. No attempt is made to present these people, their past and present, in their psychodynamic and genetic complexity. I am merely teasing out one small theme to make my point.

A successful lawyer had conscientiously but narrowly pursued his career to the exclusion of all other intellectual interests. As his son's *intellect* blossomed while he was studying philosophy and literature at a fine college, the father began to get involved in his son's studies, reading and even attending some classes—first, to share his son's experience and excitement and, to a limited extent, to compete with him.

Soon, however, it became the father's own interest, one that he continued to pursue with great pleasure and enthusiasm long after his son had grown. He had gotten in touch with his own thwarted potential, his own early intellectual curiosity, which had been suppressed by his obsessive-compulsive character structure and his single-minded need to succeed. Now, under the impetus of his son's intellectual freedom, and in the greater security of his mid-life achievements, he was able to again expand his intellectual horizon. He felt that a whole new and richer world had opened up to him.

Another man reared in a conservative, restrictive environment, unconsciously afraid to revolt, had obediently followed his father and grandfather into the expected banking career. In his middle years, he was a bank president, unsatisfied with his career choice and unhappy with the people he associated with in his business. It was, however, only after two of his adolescent children had *experimented* successfully with the pursuits of photography and architecture, perhaps even acting out for him but with no dire results, that he dared to act himself after much soul-searching and permitted himself to return to his early love of art. He changed careers and became a quite successful painter and director of an art institute, utilizing his very real talents both as an artist and as an organizer—and became a much happier man.

Another couple, who in their youth were quite idealistic and ardently involved in causes, had become more conservative or indifferent, even cynical in their middle years, caught up in the business of everyday life and whatever fears might have had a constraining influence on them. When their adolescent son became a leader in a liberal cause—probably in actual identification with them—they experienced both fear and pride. They were now faced with a reexamination of their own value system, but stimulated by their son's *idealism*, they were able to rekindle their own. Returning to some age-appropriate activity, more in accord with their own ego ideal, they felt increased pride and new hope for the future.

A final example: A mother in her early forties, with lifelong oedipal guilt and resulting sexual inhibitions, had ceased having sexual relations with her husband for some years. When her daughter reached sixteen and her *sexuality* blossomed, the mother reacted with expectable fear, envy, and fascination, leading to attempted prohibition as well as subtle encouragement of the daughter's activities. Having some awareness of and distance from this, however, the mother was able to keep destructive action to a minimum and even take some tentative pleasure in her daughter's blooming sexuality, which seemed to have no ill effects. Her own sexual interest was powerfully rearoused in identification and competition with her daughter and could no longer be denied. Between this pressure and the partial reassurance she perceived in her daughter's survival, and after much difficulty, the mother—with a now somewhat more mature ego—was able to rework her previous solution of sexual inhibition and turn to her husband for sexual gratification.

Negative Impact

Now let us return to some of the problems. These tend to be what we see in clinical practice and are, therefore, what we often are aware of and concerned with as clinicians. Throughout this chapter, I have pointed out explicitly and implicitly that the impact of the teenaged child on the parent in the middle years can also be painful and damaging. The greater the external pressure, the more strain there is on any system. The more vulnerable the system, the less stress is required to disturb it. A trauma in the life of the adolescent—an illness, a hurt, a failure—will cause pain to any loving parent and stimulate a response. But a *mutative* impact on the parent's own *personality* resulting from this or from the more ordinary struggles of adolescence—whether the parent's functioning or structure will be damaged or his ability to help the adolescent be interfered with—will depend on such factors as the nature of the parent's psychic structure, his unresolved conflicts from earlier periods including adolescence, and the reality situation of the particular parent and adolescent.

Let me illustrate with some typical examples, again simplified and reduced to a single theme for our purpose.

LOSS AND EARLY ADOLESCENCE

Early adolescence often stirs up in the vulnerable parent early separation problems, fears of loss of control, and fears of inability to cope with the adolescent struggles. For example, a mother in her mid-forties, with a poor mothering experience herself and somewhat fragile internal object relations, had dealt reasonably well with life and her children while they were small, although with a tendency toward anxiety and social isolation. When her daughter entered adolescence, she became panicked and depressed, frightened of losing her child and, as she experienced it, of her daughter's impending loss of impulse control and inability to cope with the social tasks of adolescence. She herself had had a fairly painful adolescence. In an unconscious effort to hold tighter to her daughter and keep her a child, she moved to a more rural area, which only increased her isolation and depression.

SEXUALITY AND MID-ADOLESCENCE

The adolescent's blossoming sexuality may stir up the middle-aged parent's earlier unresolved conflicts around sexuality—envy, competition, fear, guilt—and may lead to guilty and competitive prohibitions, fascinated encouragement, and acting out on everybody's part.

The mother of a fifteen-year-old girl became preoccupied with her daughter's sexual maturity. She bragged about it, dressed her provocatively and encouraged her popularity, but also restricted the girl's activities arbitrarily and sometimes punitively and lived in constant panic with fantasies of the girl's promiscuity. At the same time, the mother began to dress more provocatively herself and to compete with her daughter for the young men who came to visit. The competition culminated in a party at which the mother flirted with and triumphantly danced off with a waiter who had tried to seduce the daughter. In a panic about the feelings the episode stirred up, both mother and daughter entered treatment.

The impact of the adolescent's sexuality on the opposite-gender parent is also notable. In most situations, this leads only to appreciation and admiration of the youngster and revives the parent's pleasure in sexuality. But the impact may be profound on other parents, whose resolution of their own conflicts in this area is unsatisfactory, who perhaps have some inadequacy in their current marital relations, or who fear waning sexual power and attractiveness. Fathers of teenaged daughters, stirred up by their daughters' fresh sexuality, often deal with their fear and guilt about these incestuous longings by repression and projection into fantasies about their daughters' sexual activities and their boyfriends' dangerous desires. They may react with outward anger and increased restrictions and prohibitions. Others go further and act out their unacceptable wishes by displacing them onto affairs with women "young enough to be their daughters." Some even leave their wives to marry younger women. Such stories are, of course, commonplace.

Mothers of teenaged boys also, stirred up by their sons' sexuality, nowadays increasingly become involved with younger men. I say "nowadays" because this has become a more viable option in today's culture, formerly too frowned upon by society to be an acceptable displaced "solution." More often, however, this unacceptable desire becomes overtly desexualized as these mothers turn to their sons as substitute husbands in every way other than sexual.

One woman, for example, with much oedipal difficulty and attachment to her father, resulting in guilty sexual and other inhibitions, married a man with mirroring difficulties. Yet they managed a reasonably comfortable marriage. As their son, however, proceeded through adolescence, she began to let her relationship with her husband deteriorate, and to concentrate on her son. She spent time talking to him alone, taking him to dinner, taking trips with him—all to the exclusion of her husband. As the son reached late adolescence, she seduced him into entering her profession, using him as her assistant, critic, and confidant. When the son, after considerable difficulty, finally started to relate to other women, the mother became possessive and jealous and tried subtly to undermine each relationship. The son resisted and withdrew, and the mother became depressed, experiencing a sense of loneliness and emptiness, as she was now unable to reestablish a relationship with her alienated husband.

LOSS AND DISAPPOINTMENT

The above example, of course, involved a problem of object loss as much as it represented sexual conflicts. In this mother, her own separation-individuation issues played an important role. Like other parents with such pre-oedipal problems, she needed to hold onto her offspring as a substitute parent as well as "lover." She needed him to live out her own frustrated professional ambitions as well, an area in which she had done well but had not reached the top of the ladder. She had hoped to achieve through him the success she felt had eluded her. His leaving thus meant a loss of these hopes as well. Other parents who try to live through their adolescent child may use the adolescent for narcissistic repair in other areas—social, sexual, or intellectual—where they feel they themselves failed in adolescence and may push the youngster to achieve in those areas against his or her will or talent, often with sad results for all concerned. The loss and disappointment experienced by such a parent, as the late adolescent leaves or fails or turns to other interests, may then be threefold: the loss of the object needed for completion or repair, the crushing pain of adolescent failure once again, and the loss of potential narcissistic supplies, hopes to be given up forever.

Competition

A final word about the impact of the inevitable competition. The adolescent competes with the parent, the parent with the adolescent. This may be friendly and enhance growth, or it may be more destructive. As some of the middle-aged parent's powers are beginning to wane, some of his choices to narrow, the adolescent is on the rise physically, sexually, intellectually. He may play better tennis, run faster, read more widely, be more popular than his parent. The insecure parent may envy the adolescent's youth and vigor, his freedom and narcissism. To maintain his threatened superiority, yet afraid of being overthrown by the primal horde, this parent may try to compete to crush the young Turk, either succeeding in undermining the youngster or failing himself in the competition. This may lead to lowered self-esteem, impotent anger, and depression. And if the middle-aged parent cannot come to terms with this, it may add to despair rather than wisdom in the stages of life yet to come.

The impact of the teenaged child on mothers and fathers will depend on the nature of the parents' psychic structure, on their unresolved conflicts from earlier periods, including adolescence, and on the reality situation of the particular parent and adolescent involved. The impact may be mild or profound, temporary or permanent. It may be both good and bad, involving conflicts of pride and envy, disappointment and fulfillment, loneliness and separation, or it may lead to further growth.

REFERENCES

Anthony, J. 1969. The reactions of adults to adolescents and their behavior. In *Adolescence: Psychosocial perspectives*. Ed. G. Caplan and S. Lebovici, 54–78. New York: Basic Books.
Benedek, T. 1959. Parenthood as a developmental phase: A contribution to the libido theory. *Journal of the American Psychoanalytic Association* 7:389–391.

Blos, P. 1967. The second individuation process of adolescence. In *The psychoanalytic study of the child*, 22:162–186. New York: International Universities Press.

———. 1968. Character formation in adolescence. In *The psychoanalytic study of the child*, 23:245–263. New York: International Universities Press.

Erikson, E. 1950. *Childhood and society*. New York: W. W. Norton.

Freud, A. 1958. Adolescence. In *The psychoanalytic study of the child*, 13:255–278. New York: International Universities Press.

Freud, S. 1914. On narcissism. In *Standard edition*, 14:73–102.

Geleerd, E. R. 1957. Some aspects of psychoanalytic technique in adolescents. In *The psychoanalytic study of the child*, 12:262–283. New York: International Universities Press.

Kris, A. 1982. *Free association: Method and process*. New Haven: Yale University Press.

Kris, E. 1952. *Psychoanalytic explorations in art*. New York: International Universities Press.

Meyers, H. 1971. The therapist's response to today's adolescent. *Psychosocial Process* 2:38–46.

Moore, B., and Fine, B. 1968. *A glossary of psychoanalytic terms and concepts*. New York: American Psychoanalytic Association.

Offer, D. 1969. *The psychological world of the teenager*. New York: Basic Books.

Piaget, J. 1969. The intellectual development of the adolescent. In *Adolescence: Psychosocial perspectives*. Ed. G. Caplan and S. Lebovici, 22–26. New York: Basic Books.

Pines, D. 1982. The relevance of early psychic development to pregnancy and abortion. *International Journal of Psychoanalysis* 63:311–319.

· 7 ·

THE THIRD INDIVIDUATION
Middle-aged Children and Their Parents

JOHN M. OLDHAM, M. D.

In the psychoanalytic literature, the term *individuation* most often refers to the developmental process occurring in the first few years of life and normally culminating with the establishment of basic trust and object constancy. In 1967, Peter Blos coined the phrase "the second individuation," by which he meant an intrapsychic restructuring process occurring in adolescence and reflecting the "changes that accompany the emotional disengagement from internalized infantile objects" (p. 164). In this chapter, I will suggest that a third individuation occurs in mid-life, which, though unique, shares many characteristics of the second individuation. In particular, I will suggest that in the middle years there is a process of intrapsychic structural change that centrally relates to the involution and death of one's parents. Like both earlier individuations, the third can be stressful and emotionally turbulent, but it is also a "normal" process. Moreover, as in adolescence, the third individuation can reactivate unresolved conflicts and precipitate pathological or maladaptive behavior.

In addition to the intrapsychic process proposed here, the cascade of events in becoming a parent to one's parents involves many reality factors, such as the provision of medical care, rearrangement of living quarters and finances, and the like. These changes in life circumstances between parent and son or daughter are often stressful, but they can also be rewarding, involving renewed mutual love and appreciation. Mid-life individuation in the child, however, more crucially relates to internal reactions to the decline and death of the parents. Those reactions will be strongly influenced by the nature of one's previous relationships with the parents, especially, perhaps, during the first two individuations.

In what follows, I will review some aspects of the third individuation as a normal process which, as in adolescence, involves development and leads to a more mature sense of self. I will then comment on some problems associated with special situations, and, finally, I will touch on certain aspects of the third individuation when psychopathology is involved.

89

The Third Individuation as a Normal Process

Blos (1967) described the adolescent individuation process as a psychic restructuring and an emotional disengagement from internalized infantile objects. As a result of this process, self-esteem and mood can be more constant and not, as previously, so heavily reliant on external sources. The loosening of infantile object ties also makes way for age-adequate relationships. Continuity remains in the relationship with the actual parents after the infantile character of the relationships is given up, and a more contemporary version of parental object representations is adopted.

Emotional turbulence characterizes this adolescent process. There is depression, which is due to loss of the infantile object, and there are periods of ego weakness, which are due to a combination of increased drive strength and disengagement from parental ego support. Episodes of limited regression are essential components of the process. The ways in which the adolescent copes with those alterations in ego state, in both its normal and its pathological forms, are well known and need not be reviewed here.

It is remarkable how many parallels can be drawn between the individuation process of adolescence and the particular aspect of middle age that involves the dependency, illness, and death of one's parents. For example, just as the adolescent process involves psychic restructuring secondary to disengagement from parental ego support, mid-life development involves intrapsychic change secondary to the death of the parents.

Vaillant (1977) has described a continuing process during adult development of intrapsychic structural change and maturation of defense mechanisms. He suggests that the ability of middle-aged adults to tolerate parental loss is largely a function of the internalization processes that have occurred. Whereas at adolescence biologic and social maturation demands relinquishing the infantile version of one's parents, in middle age the actual physical and mental impoverishment and involution of one's parents require relinquishing continued reliance on them for guidance, comfort, and help. In fact, the adolescent process is never a total one, and residues of infantile attitudes toward one's parents remain. What is the nature of the "new" relationship to one's parents that emerges from adolescence? It is, of course, one that still involves parent as parent. It is this relationship, often an enduring, meaningful, and rewarding one, that nevertheless must be relinquished. The psychic restructuring that follows involves mainly coming to terms with one's own mortality—a process often referred to as the central task of the middle years.

A second parallel between the two individuations is the presence of emotional turbulence characterized by depression and regression. In adulthood, the transformation of one's parents from sources of advice, strength, and comfort to a reverse arrangement in which one becomes the care giver is often turbulent indeed. Depressive reactions to this loss are common, and regressive episodes of behavior have been widely described. Whereas the adolescent faces adulthood with all its challenges and imponderables, he does not face it alone, since, whether he asks them or not, his parents are available to help. In the middle years, the loss of the parents and their generation leaves no one older to turn to. A significant psychological adjustment is usually required for this reality to sink in. Central to this adjustment is the inescapable confrontation with one's own mortality. As the adolescent deals with his emerging conflicts in an emotionally turbulent way, so may the middle-aged adult. Often there is protest, acting out, regressive self-centeredness, and adolescentlike behavior.

A third parallel between adolescent and mid-life individuation involves the replacement of previous parental object representations with more contemporary ones. Emerging from adolescence into young adulthood involves replacing infantile object representations with more contemporary ones; that is, the internal parent becomes less magically omnipotent. These new internal objects remain relatively stable, although they undergo continual revision as the young adult interacts with the real parents from a more independent vantage point, seeing them increasingly as they really are. In mid-life, there is a curious reversal of this process, since it becomes increasingly difficult to internalize the parents as they really are when that reality is one of diminishment and loss. Instead, the unconscious internalized parent may remain robust and even once again become omnipotent and immortal, in marked contrast to the real one. Only after the death of the parent does the final version of the internalized parent become consolidated. Parents are gradually forgiven for their shortcomings, since one can no longer secretly hope for them to change or make amends for earlier mistakes. What is relinquished in the mid-life process is the continued and reactivated residue of the infantile omnipotent parent. The final parental object representations are usually ones with which the mid-life "child" can comfortably identify—loving parents who did the best they could, largely forgiven for their real limitations and mistakes. And with that identification comes the hope that ultimately one's own children will be able to understand and forgive in like fashion.

LOSS OF THE ILLUSION OF IMMORTALITY

I will now move beyond direct comparison of the mid-life and adolescent individuation processes in order to focus more extensively on the various ways in which the process of becoming a parent to, and ultimately losing, one's parents can affect the middle years. Authors from divergent professional backgrounds have addressed this issue, and the conclusion that is repeated most frequently is that the major developmental task involving parental loss is coming to terms with the concomitant loss of the illusion of immortality. Freud (1915), in his paper "Our Attitude towards Death," described our readiness "to maintain that death was the necessary outcome of life," yet our tendency to behave as if it were not so. Freud added, "No-one believes in his own death. . . . In the unconscious everyone is convinced of his own immortality" (p. 289). Yet there is a mid-life collision between this wish for immortality and the growing awareness of the fact of mortality, heightened not only by the retirement, illness, dependency, and death of one's parents, but also by the gradual deterioration in one's own physical capabilities. It is ironic that during the years when parents are most likely to become seriously physically disabled and needy, their middle-aged children must not only provide help for the parents' needs but also cope with their own loss of physical youthfulness.

A patient of mine began analysis in his late thirties because of a chronic sense of dissatisfaction in his life, characterized by a severe work inhibition, emotional isolation, and an almost obligatory pattern of compliance to authority combined with secret rage and resentment. Athletic and youthful in appearance, he constantly felt "like a kid." His mother had died when he was young, and his father, an often intolerant taskmaster, a few years later. Subsequently the patient and his four siblings lived with and were treated harshly by various relatives. Only after several years of analysis did he begin to realize the impact of these early events on his current life. Essentially, after he had been unable to join the adult world, as demonstrated by a failed career and an inability to marry, he had unconsciously, regressively, rejoined his dead mother, adopting an attitude of compliance to the outside world, a world that had no significance to him. As he became aware of these patterns, he became depressed and aware of his self-imposed loneliness. In the fourth year of analysis, when he was aged forty-two, an unusually large number of family members in his parents' generation died. He said, "It seems like there has been a lot of death in my family in the past year. It makes me think about myself. Sometimes I feel more adultlike, but not in the way I want to feel more adult. I'm suddenly aware of all of the older generation dying off. And I'm aware of all the things that can go wrong. My brother was talking about my sister having arthritis. And he has a heart problem. All of these things are reminders of aging. Of getting ill—things that can go wrong. Things I prefer not to think about. As if I've skipped over all the things I wanted to be as an adult, and I just think about all of the unpleasant aspects of it." Eventually, however, in middle age, he was able to mourn and relinquish his idealized internalized mother and he was able to recover longings for the good aspects of his father. As a result he began to experience some enjoyable aspects of being an adult in his own right.

The unconscious conviction of one's immortality is challenged by the decline and death of one's parents. For the first time in one's life, one can no longer secretly cling to the belief that it is still someone else's turn to die. It could be argued that, in the service of defense, one could attempt to maintain a sense of immortality by transferring the role of the parent onto others who are significant in one's life. Indeed, I suspect that we all do this to some degree, and certainly in analysis this is an essential aspect of the transference. For the termination process to be effective, it must include thorough analysis and working through of the transferential recapitulation of the loss of the parents and of the illusion of one's immortality.

THE WINDOW OF AUTONOMY

We may ask, when does one develop a "true" sense of autonomy? Although the term generally connotes successful completion of the second individuation process, I would suggest that so-called true autonomy cannot be achieved until the third individuation occurs. Only after the death of the parents does one become more nearly psychologically autonomous, and this state is not always comfortable. Under the best of circumstances, mid-life adults only gradually say good-bye to their parents as parents. They accept the responsibility to care for the parents as strange versions of new children—paradoxically strange because they still are their parents, yet their needs have become increasingly childlike. Stranger still, because these needs, though reminiscent of the needs of one's children—to be fed, clothed, gently advised or admonished, or even to be bathed and diapered—occur in the context of increasingly imminent death rather than growth and fulfillment.

Even in close, caring families, where the adult children are highly motivated to repay their parents gratefully for all that they have received from them, the process can be emotionally and financially draining, and it can be the source of resentment, death wishes, and an impulse to withdraw. It can severely hamper one's autonomy, since spare time and vacation time can be consumed by new caretaking burdens. The parents during this period may express worry about being a burden. And the children, though willing to be so burdened, increasingly anticipate the future liberation that will be brought about by the parents' death. Wishes of this sort, though inevitable, produce guilt and may reactivate earlier guilt feelings over angry adolescent acts of rageful rebellion in the service of being free and separate. The pendulum may swing back and forth from careworn resentfulness to oversolicitous self-denial. My emphasis, however, is on the concept of freedom or liberation, which occurs in a more fully realized sense than ever before only after the death of the parents. A time-limited process of mourning occurs and with it a reworking of internal object representations leading to a sense of fulfillment in becoming one of the elders, who provides wisdom and guidance to others.

Sometimes unconscious expiation of guilt can interfere with this sense of fulfillment. One can be acutely aware that the days of one's liberation are numbered. It may seem not too far in the future until one's own retirement, failing health, and increasing reliance on one's own children—indeed, until one becomes the object of one's children's resentful and ambivalent attitudes. Such anticipation of being no longer independent lends a certain urgency to this period. There can be phases of sadness over the dwindling years, interspersed with bursts of denial and age-inappropriate behavior. In most cases, however, the mourning process is eventually completed and a new, more mature state is achieved.

The California longitudinal study reported by Eichorn et al. (1981) provided evidence for the development, in mid-life, of previously unexpressed aspects of the self. In particular, these investigators examined the use of the adolescent past by their middle-aged subjects. They found, instead of a reduced meaningfulness of the past, a strengthening of relationships with the past, especially with adolescence, although it varied with the age, gender, and family stage of the mid-life adult. It surely is true that during the years of greatest psychological autonomy, such internalized early experiences, values, and object representations are called upon, since it is now not the living parent but the internal and remembered one whom one consults for guidance.

Common Variations in the Third Individuation Process

At this point I will shift my focus to look at the complexities produced by special situations during the third individuation and at some of the problems in the process when significant psychopathology is present in parent or child. Before doing so, however, I would like to emphasize an implication of what I have said so far. Although the third individuation is stressful, it is also a process of growth and maturation, leading to a new equilibrium which can be quite rewarding. Long-standing tensions with the older generation are put to rest, and greater enjoyment of one's own parental role can develop—a role that involves being supportive and available, but not intrusive. New career opportunities emerge, and enriching experiences with family and friends commonly occur during these years. I mention this here so that my subsequent remarks do not obscure this essential point.

THE UNEMPTIABLE NEST SYNDROME

The well-known phrase "the empty nest syndrome" refers, of course, to the loss and grief experienced after all the children have grown up and moved away from home. More often, however, the term is used to apply to the woman who has inordinately dedicated her life to her children, to the exclusion of her own personal and career interests. In this sense, the term describes a pathological syndrome reflecting inadequate individuation on the part of the woman.

In contrast to a syndrome reflecting unresolved problems in the mid-life adult is another situation that has been underemphasized: the inhibiting effect on normal adult development imposed by prolonged caretaking of elderly parents in the home. I call this the "unemptiable nest syndrome." The popular phrase "the sandwich generation" refers to the mid-life adult caught between responding to the needs of his or her children, on the one hand, and to those of the aging parents, on the other. When, as is usual, there is a gap of several years or longer between the departure of the children and the dependency of the parents, the mid-life adult has a much needed breather. This might be called "the empty nest respite." It is under these circumstances that "second honeymoons" and a renewed sense of intimacy with one's spouse can occur, along with greater freedom to enjoy expanding careers. This period can be thought of as a third version of the "practicing" subphase described by Mahler (Mahler et al., 1975), the second of which occurs in adolescence. This third version precedes the stage of autonomy I have just referred to—that following the death of the parents. Here, the parents are still very much alive, still in a state of reasonably intact independence, yet clearly approaching their decline. Until that time, all kinds of illusions of their, and hence one's own, immortality can be maintained. And the attendant sense of independence can have a wonderful resemblance to the excitement of adolescence, enhanced by the absence of all the agonizing insecurities of the adolescent period.

When sudden illness or incapacity of the parents prematurely interrupts this respite, or when there is no relief from major caretaking responsibilities (for example, when disabled or chronically ill parents move into the home), the toll on the mid-life adult can be heavy. Strong resentment or a sense of the unfairness of it all sometimes leads to denial of the seriousness of the parents' needs, which may be compounded by a parallel denial process in the parents themselves. As a result, the decision that a parent must move into a medically supervised living arrangement or into the home of the child may be inappropriately delayed. In such cases, it may be only when the parent incurs some frightening event, such as an automobile accident or the eruption of a neglected medical condition, that the situation becomes clear. When the needs of the parent make the nest unemptiable, similar patterns of denial or resentment may occur, and reactivation of unconscious patterns from the past may develop. In a sense, a curious sort of transference reaction can take place—the unconscious transference onto one's elderly parents of attitudes and expectations deriving from these same parents in *their* middle years. These processes can be either direct unconscious reactivations of expected behavior from the parent of former times, or they can reflect identification with the former parent, leading to replication of earlier parent-child interactions, but in reverse.

As an example of the latter, a patient kept finding himself annoyed and irritated when he arrived home from work to find that his elderly father had remained sitting for hours watching television, with the dirty dishes untouched in the sink. The father, in fact, had drastically diminished powers of concentration, found television a diverting way to pass time without feeling so solitary, yet had lost any capacity to be a responsible participant in maintaining the household environment. However obvious these severe limitations in the parent might have been to an outside observer, the patient's vision was blinded by a transference distortion stemming from many "unconsciously remembered" reprimands and stern accusations of laziness and lack of ambition from his father to him when he was an adolescent.

In particular cases in which the wife's role has been primarily that of housewife and mother, the burden of caring for an elderly parent in the home falls especially on her. If the parent is her in-law, tensions between husband and wife may be greatly intensified. Long-postponed plans for her own personal or career development may be indefinitely delayed, causing bitterness and resentment. Even if the parent is her own, such resentment may be virtually inevitable. And other tensions may arise from the reactivation of old sibling rivalries, especially if there are siblings who could accommodate the needy parent but are unwilling to do so. Even in situations in which it is financially feasible to have all the help one could wish, this can be an emotionally complicated period for all involved.

PREMATURE PARENTAL LOSS

If parents die prematurely, before the children reach middle age, profound alterations can take place in the adult developmental process. At adolescence, should a parent die during the child's defiant and rebellious efforts to separate, guilt and depression may occur, sometimes followed by a type of developmental arrest, so that the normal resolution of the adolescent rebellion does not occur or is delayed, as was the case with the patient mentioned earlier.

Another patient of mine was determined to marry in his late adolescence, outside of his family's religious faith, and in spite of his father's repeated exhortations that this would cause the father's death. On the wedding day, the father in fact dropped dead, and the son developed an acute depression requiring hospitalization. The patient recovered from his depression, but difficulties in his marriage and a certain aimlessness that hampered his effectiveness in professional graduate school led him to seek treatment.

In this patient's situation, his guilt related not only to his unconscious wish to be rid of his overbearing father in order to gain the autonomy of a young adult, but also to his wish to be rid of his oedipal rival. His oedipal strivings had been reactivated during adolescence, and his father's death on the day he claimed the forbidden woman unconsciously represented the oedipal triumph. His subsequent marital difficulties reflected a struggle between his love for his wife and his unconscious efforts, by pushing her away, to appease his internalized father. Working through the transference allowed him to understand these issues and to gain considerable relief. But only later, when, as a middle-aged man, he returned for a brief period of follow-up treatment, was he able to come to terms with his internal father and to realize how deeply he missed his guidance and advice, in spite of his controlling and intolerant style.

In cases in which both parents die, a strong sense of discontinuity usually occurs, and the inner resources of the child are put to a tough test. Frequently, a new equilibrium is established, often unconscious, that involves transferring the parental role to surrogates either inside or outside the family to a much greater extent than is realized. Grandparents, uncles, aunts, and in-laws, if available, may willingly assume this role as an explicit arrangement, but if they are unavailable, admired figures outside the family may be invested with parental authority. There is, at the age-appropriate mid-life stage, protest enough under ordinary circumstances against becoming the older generation, the generation whose turn is next. Thus many times, when parents die prematurely, there is a strong unconscious drive to re-create a surrogate equilibrium in order to preserve one's illusion of immortality. This drive is, of course, especially strong in such cases because of the assault on this illusion produced by the death of the parents. Interestingly, it frequently seems to happen that even if parents are lost when one is young, a comparable individuation and consolidation process takes place when middle age is reached, as if the parents had been unconsciously, almost magically, kept alive until then.

DELAYED PARENTAL LOSS

Rita Gavin (1986) began a *New York Times* article entitled "What Are We Going to Do about Mother?" by quoting her ninety-three-year-old mother, who said:

"I've died a thousand deaths this week. Every day I ask God why my children have abandoned me." "Do you want to come live with me, mother?" her daughter asks. "I don't want to live with any of my children," she begins. The tears are not far behind and begin in earnest with the next statement. "Your father wanted me to stay in this house as long as I lived." "We all do, mother. That's what the money he left you is for—to make that possible. You don't want to leave your home, your children don't want to leave theirs, you can't stay home alone and yet you refuse to allow us to find a companion for you. What is the answer? You tell me." I can hear my voice beginning to rise. In the living room my husband hears it also and lowers the sound on the evening news. He is anticipating the moment I sink into the couch beside him and ask, as I always do after calling Maine, "What are we going to do about Mother?" He will ask as he always asks, "And what are we going to do about her guilt-ridden children?"

In our culture, the older generation is living longer, and forecasts predict a continuation of this trend. Retirement age comes later, and middle-aged to older-aged offspring may feel relegated to the role of a child for much of their adult lives. The "window of autonomy" may seem never to open. Parents who remain strong and in robust health into their seventies and eighties, although often providing many sources of pleasure and strength to their children, may be unaware of the periodic frustrations their aging children feel. Sometimes imperceptably, the elderly parent, so amazing and strong and for so long a source of pride to his or her children, may begin to regress, and this regression may lead the parent to treat the adult child as if the "child" were suddenly again an adolescent. Reactivated moody and unpleasant power struggles may develop, and until the children appreciate the inappropriateness of the parent's behavior, they may respond with reactivated irritation, resentful of being lectured to or not listened to. This resentment sometimes intensifies in direct proportion to the longevity of the parent, becoming, as it were, an overdose of being parented.

During an extended period such as this, when the middle-aged child is often preoccupied with a growing family and increasing financial concerns, an arena in which tremendous tensions frequently develop is that of the inheritance. Elderly parents may become frightened about their dwindling resources and may worry about mounting medical expenses. They may fear being prematurely "put away" in a nursing home unless they retain control over their finances. The children, on the other hand, may view these concerns as exaggerated, or they may feel that the parents do not trust them. Yet the financially burdened children may guiltily catch themselves musing about how much of the inheritance might be received if the parents were to die. Guilt on their part, and fear on the part of the parents, may lead to an almost phobic avoidance of the topic, and, as a result, important practical decisions may not get made.

The Third Individuation as a Pathological Process

MELANCHOLIA INSTEAD OF MOURNING

Freud's well-known formulation (1917) of pathological mourning in response to the death of a loved one, produced by unconscious ambivalence toward the deceased, certainly can occur during mid-life as a reaction to the loss of a parent. In cases in which there is evidence of serious psychopathology in the parent, an abnormally prolonged mourning process in the middle-aged child may protect him or her from guilt arising from intensely destructive feelings toward the parent and serving as well to fend off awareness of unconscious identification with the hated aspects of the parent. In other words, a prolonged worshipful stance toward the lost parent attempts to preserve reverence and idealization of the parent and hence to preserve a secret view of the self as loving and as a younger version of the ideal parent. Depression and self-denigration then represent a way of fending off awareness of one's own potential to be angry and destructive toward others, like the real, not the idealized, parent.

PATHOLOGICAL ATTACHMENT

Patients at risk for the development of the prolonged, pathological grief just described may demonstrate guilt-driven solicitude or slavish devotion to the parent prior to the parent's death. This may lead to stunted adult growth, so that the middle-aged child develops no independent family. Dependency, though an official DSM III personality disorder, is a generic trait encompassing many different forms of character pathology. This type of pathology has been often portrayed in popular fiction as the affliction of the lonely "spinster" who becomes companion and nurse to her elderly mother, forgoing opportunities to marry and have children of her own. Although less obvious, the man who has many extramarital affairs yet never considers divorce often has an intensely dependent transference attachment to his wife.

These forms of dependency, of course, commonly appear as transference and resistance in psychoanalysis, and they can pose difficult and at times insurmountable obstacles interfering with successful outcomes. It may not be until efforts are made to reach the termination phase of analysis, but the analysis seems interminable, that the depth of such needs may be appreciated. What may have appeared as a successful resolution of pathological dependency on parents or parent-figures as a result of psychoanalytic work may reappear as an equally intense investment in the analyst, leading to inability to successfully terminate the treatment. Patients of this sort may be like those described by Freud, in "Analysis Terminable and Interminable" (1937), as those with "a certain amount of psychical inertia. . . . all the mental processes, relationships and distributions of force are unchangeable, fixed and rigid" (p. 242). Such patients may be among those who are unable to successfully undergo the third individuation.

PATHOLOGICAL AVOIDANCE

An alternative result of psychopathology in the parent-child relationship is the pattern of geographical avoidance of the parent by the middle-aged child. At times, such avoidance can be adaptive, if the pathology in the parent is so severe that the emotional equilibrium of the child can be maintained only at a distance. Such situations are poignant at best and tragic at worst; often they perpetuate an illusion that the child is more psychologically free of the influence of the parent than is the case. It is as if there are powerful externalized defenses that are reinforced by keeping actual contact with the disturbed parent at a minimum.

When the parent becomes enfeebled or dependent, resurgences of old conflicts may occur, compounded by bitterness in the parent for years of (in his or her view) neglect by the child. When the parent dies, the child may consciously experience only relief or indifference and not normal mourning. But the unresolved internalized rage at the parent will persist, intensified by guilt over the real neglect during the parent's terminal years. Pathological states may then emerge, such as depressive reactions or self-defeating behavior. Psychoanalytic work can often enable such a middle-aged patient to work through the anger and disappointment in the parent, thus becoming free to mourn the loss of the valued aspects of the parent.

SIBLING RIVALRY

During the third individuation intense sibling rivalry can be reactivated. Long-forgotten jealousies and rivalries among siblings can resurface in the course of events during the parents' illness and death. Notions of favoritism emerge again. Adolescent or even childish fights break out among the children over how to distribute the tasks of caring for the needy parent. Bitter battles over the inheritance often reflect unresolved sibling rivalry. Greed can erupt as a reaction to a long-repressed sense of being loved less or as a reactivated competitive need to "get the biggest portion." Although milder versions of these rivalries inevitably occur during the normal third individuation process, they can be particularly disruptive in disturbed families, leading to bitterness and sometimes lengthy estrangements.

Conclusions

I have described a third individuation that occurs in middle age, analogous to the second individuation at adolescence. Central to this third process is the intrapsychic re-equilibration that accompanies the involution and death of the parents. Although it involves mourning and loss, the process results in a new level of psychological and emotional maturity.

Ivan Ilych, in Tolstoy's eloquent parable on death, was tortured most by the deception and lie that his family, for some reason,

> all accepted, that he was not dying but was simply ill, and that he only need keep quiet and undergo a treatment and then something very good would result. He however knew, that do what they would, nothing would come of it, only still more agonizing suffering and death. This deception tortured him—their not wishing to admit what they all knew and what he knew, but wanting to lie to him concerning his terrible condition, and wishing and forcing him to participate in that lie. . . . Apart from this lying, or because of it, what most tormented Ivan Ilych was that

no one pitied him as he wished to be pitied. At certain moments after prolonged suffering he wished most of all (though he would have been ashamed to confess it) for someone to pity him as a sick child is pitied. He longed to be petted and comforted. He knew he was an important functionary, that he had a beard turning grey, and that therefore what he longed for was impossible, but still he longed for it. (1960, pp. 137, 138)

Although he was not an elderly parent, the words of Ivan Ilych seem ageless, and they seem eminently suited to represent a few of the needs of elderly parents as they become infirm, ill, in pain, and dependent.

The challenge presented to the middle-aged child to try to meet those needs is a difficult one. Might it not be better to maintain a certain deception? Isn't a little optimism a better approach? When does one cross the line when it becomes appropriate for everybody to admit that the end is near? What if you do so and are wrong? And how can one know what secret wishes one's dying parent may be feeling? Especially if, even if one could guess accurately, providing parentlike care and comfort to a dying parent either might prove impossible or might be rejected by the parent out of pride or embarrassment. The questions are endless. And once it's all over, was everything really done that could have been done? These aspects of the process, which occur within conscious awareness, are complicated enough, and they are compounded, of course, by the unconscious intrapsychic processes that have been described here.

The *third individuation* has been proposed as a term to address this complex process of saying the final good-bye to one's parents and of taking their place. It resembles the first individuation, during childhood, in that it is a growth process and involves movement away from the parents, yet a process of internalizing them at the same time. Even more, it resembles the second individuation, at adolescence, because it is an emotionally turbulent time involving loss, depression, regression, and a process of intrapsychic change that leads to replacement of a previous internal version of one's parents with a contemporary one. It is a time when unresolved parent-child problems inevitably resurface and when the work of psychoanalysis can be quite beneficial in many cases to resolve these reactivated conflicts—conflicts that interfere with the development of the fullest and most enriched and rewarding autonomy achievable during the middle years.

REFERENCES

Blos, P. 1967. The second individuation process of adolescence. In *The psychoanalytic study of the child*, 22:162–186. New York: International Universities Press.

Eichorn, D. A.; Clausen, J. A.; Haan, H.; Honzik, M. P.; and Mussen, P. H. 1981. *Present and past in middle life*. New York: Academic Press.

Freud, S. 1915. Thoughts for the times on war and death. II: Our attitude towards death. In *Standard edition*, 14:289–300.

———. 1917. Mourning and melancholia. In *Standard edition*, 14:243–258.

———. 1937. Analysis terminable and interminable. In *Standard edition*, 23:216–253.

Gavin, R. 1986. "What are we going to do about mother?" is the refrain. *New York Times*, October 19, p. 28.

Mahler, M. S.; Pine, F.; and Bergman, A. 1975. *The psychological birth of the human infant*. New York: Basic Books.

Tolstoy, L. 1960. *The death of Ivan Ilych*. New York: Signet.

Vaillant, G. E. 1977. *Adaptation to life*. Boston: Little, Brown.

· 8 ·

ISSUES IN THE ANALYSES
OF SINGLE WOMEN IN THEIR
THIRTIES AND FORTIES

CAROL C. NADELSON, M. D.

Psychoanalysts often see single women approaching their middle years who press for analysis with the fantasy that it will "cure" them—that is, enable them to find a partner or have a child. This outcome expectation can create substantial resistance in the analytic process, particularly if the uncovering of unconscious fantasy and conflict leads in another direction or if the woman finds that reality precludes some life choices and experiences. The patient's giving up the fantasy of a specific outcome from her analysis can be her resolution of early conflicts and can lead to a new generativity.

This chapter will focus on the conflict generated in many heterosexual women in their thirties and forties who have not married and are childless. Their major presenting concerns involve the demands and pressures of their careers, the integration of career and family, and the need to resolve the issues of mid-life, which for them include childlessness. In order to put these issues in a theoretical perspective I will also briefly consider emerging views in related psychoanalytic areas, including the pre-oedipal determinants of gender identity, the role of relationships in women's lives, dependency in women, the implications of success for women, reproduction and femininity, and menopause.

Presenting Issues: Conscious and Unconscious

Despite changes in contemporary society, for women, the idea that marriage, career, and children may not be compatible reflects the belief that marriage and childbearing continue to be their central adult roles. Other activities are often regarded as temporary and subordinate to and contingent on future family functions (Bernard, 1975; Douvan and Adelson, 1960; Erikson, 1959; Meissner, 1978; Nadelson and Notman, 1981a). In prior generations, women generally have maintained some degree of tentativeness in the evolution of their personal identity, waiting until marriage establishes the context of their lives (Douvan and

Adelson, 1960; Erikson, 1968). A reflection of long-standing societal ambivalence toward career women can be found in the familiar literary and folklore theme of the ambitious woman who is punished by harm coming to her child, who could be taken away by death or illness in retribution for maternal neglect (Moulton, 1986).

Many women who are now in their thirties and forties have made a deliberate decision not to marry because they believe that this choice will afford them greater professional opportunity and autonomy, free them from family responsibility, and allow them the time for solitude and self-reflection. Many have found the experience gratifying and the choice adaptive. Recent societal views of the unmarried state also have been supportive of this position. In the past, however, those who did not marry were often seen as hostile, dependent, unattractive, unwilling or unable to assume responsibility, or socially inadequate (Kuhn, 1955).

For many of those who are motivated not to marry, however, the experience of social isolation, loneliness, and frustration in attempts at intimacy can become a source of conflict. These women may experience anxiety about their ability to make commitments or establish and maintain intimate relationships, because of unresolved intrapsychic conflict that may be developmental or related to early life experiences —for example, child abuse. For some, including those with fragile ego structures, remaining single can be their best adaptation.

Just as unconscious and neurotic factors influence the choice to remain unmarried, so too they influence the conscious choice to marry. Strong dependency needs, failure to develop a secure self-image, or an intolerable fear of isolation or loneliness may be the unconscious motivation. Although changing societal relational patterns have made it possible to fulfill needs for intimate relationships regardless of whether an individual marries, intrapsychic conflict may not be resolved (Nadelson, 1978; Nadelson and Notman, 1981a).

Conscious and unconscious factors also influence the decision to have or not to have children. Those who choose to remain childless may state that they fear pregnancy or have little interest in children or parental roles; they may maximize or exaggerate the responsibilities of these roles and believe that they cannot be good parents. They may, however, be defending against low self-esteem or unresolved dependency wishes, and they may not be aware of their own unconscious struggles with ambivalent parental relationships.

Regardless of career or other goals and expectations, however, from early in life women attend to their ticking biological clock. For a woman, the periodicity of her menses is a constant reminder of the integrity of her body and of its future promise. It contributes to her body image and is part of her feminine identity, whether or not she bears children. The knowledge that possibilities for child bearing are limited and that the biological clock will probably run out in her forties makes a woman aware of the finiteness of life and of her options in a way that men do not share.

Both men and women must come to terms with their own mortality, their limitations, and the loss of dreams and wishes, but they differ with regard to the biological timetable. A woman's identity continues to be closely associated with reproductive potential and function. She can, however, never know if she will regret reproductive decisions until it is too late. For those who expect and hope to have children but do not, a shift in self-image and identity must occur, and the loss of the fantasied family must be mourned. Thus, for many childless women, approaching age forty can lead to symptoms and the decision to seek treatment.

Jaques (1965) suggested that at this time of life both men and women must again work through the infantile depressive position in order to achieve a more reflective and philosophical sense of life as opposed to the optimistic and idealistic views held earlier. If grieving is done and one becomes resigned to one's imperfections, reparations can be made and new generative relationships can be established. The issue of generativity as it involves the approaching end of the capacity to reproduce must be resolved in order to adapt successfully in the second half of life. Marmor (1974) has indicated that successful resolution depends on the integrative capacity of the ego, the nature of interpersonal relationships, the sense of continuing usefulness, and the breadth of outside interests.

Pre-Oedipal Determinants of Gender Identity

The historian Peter Gay has suggested that the roots of patriarchy may be found in a primitive fear that men experience in the presence of female power: "Women's equality represents the intimidating power of their mothers, and men do what they can to control, contain and suppress that threat" (1984, p. 192). This magical power and omnipotence is both threatening and comforting. The pervasiveness of this ambivalence can be seen in the many rituals that require men to cleanse and purge themselves of their mothers' power and influence in order to assume masculine identities. The Lidzes (1986) elaborate on the terrifying puberty rites of New Guinea, which attest to the strength and power of maternal influence.

Since mothers are still the primary caretakers of their infants, attention to pre-oedipal as well as oedipal influence is critical. The range of affects and the ambivalence generated in the pre-oedipal relationship includes fear, awe, love, envy, and admiration. The developmental implications of the necessity to resolve and integrate these affects were elucidated somewhat in the early theoretical and clinical literature (Jones, 1935; Klein, 1932), but they began to be more intricately developed in the 1950s. Bibring (1953) indicated that sons who saw their mothers as hostile and domineering and blamed them for contributing to their fears of inadequacy did not actually have mothers who were as they described them. It was their fathers' authority and connectedness that was missing, leaving the sons overinvolved with their mothers and unable to establish a masculine identification.

Although psychoanalytic writers speak of the importance of early nonconflictual identification of children with *both* parents, the concept of different, asymmetric roles of the mother and father has recently been accorded more attention (Abelin, 1975; Tyson, 1984). Distortion and overidealization can occur when the parent who is not the primary caretaker, most often the father, is influential more by his absence than by his presence. This allows for the development of elaborate fantasy relationships (Chodorow, 1978; Dinnerstein, 1976).

Research concerning gender-related differences in parent-child relationships has provided additional evidence that a parent's relationship with a same-sex child has special significance in regard to mothers and daughters (Brunswick, 1940; Riviere, 1936). Girls experience sameness and boys experience difference (Schafer, 1968a, 1968b), sameness in this context referring to gender identity, not necessarily to self-object differentiation (Clower, 1976; Notman et al., 1986).

It has been suggested that a mother perceives and relates to her infant daughter as a reflection of her own self-image, her internalized relationship with her own mother, and her identification with this daughter. This awakens recognition as well as ambivalence. Thus, a girl's sameness, "reflected back to her by mother's mirroring, reinforces the blurring of self boundaries, and self and object boundaries," and women "cannot achieve the distance from their origins in the same way that men can, and continue to develop as nurturing mothers" (Bernstein, 1983).

This formulation can be tied with our understanding of the fate of early identifications and attachments as they relate to the development of gender identity. The process of attainment of individuality and autonomy implies a degree of differentiation from early objects. Psychoanalysts have differed regarding the process of separation for boys and for girls, the degree of difficulty it entails, and the relevance of these differences, particularly later in life.

If we accept that girls do not relinquish infantile attachments to the extent that boys do, it is necessary to recognize that there are implications of these developmental differences. These include the greater fluidity that girls are said to have between infantile attachment to both parents and adult personality consolidation (Blos, 1980). In terms of the developmental process, Greenacre (1958) and Jacobson (1964) suggested that the boy must "renounce the pleasure and security-giving closeness that identifying with the mothering person affords, and he must form an identification with the less accessible father." Greenson (1966) conceptualized this as a process of disidentification, implying that for boys the early closeness must be relinquished with some distancing from the mother. Stoller (1976) further suggested that the boy must overcome his identification with his mother to achieve masculinity. vs basic femininity

This view rests on a concept of basic masculinity as differentiated from basic femininity, with pre-oedipal nonconflictually determined origins. More than that, it implies the primacy of the closeness and relatedness of the early experience with a mothering person. It suggests that the movement toward separation and individuation can have a defensive component for boys, and perhaps that separation-individuation should be conceptualized differently for boys and girls.

Chodorow (1978) has argued that the process of separation from the mother can be understood as more difficult for the girl than for the boy because her mother experiences her as a narcissistic self-extension. The girl's turning to her father, then, can be seen as a way of separating from her mother. Thus, it appears that the term *separation* may not be an accurate reflection of the early developmental process for either girls or boys. For boys, separation, which is based on turning away from a vital relationship, has been seen as crucial to the consolidation of gender identity. Obviously, it is not the same for girls (Nadelson et al., 1982).

That the process of separation-individuation is intrinsically problematic for both boys and girls was suggested by Person and Ovesey (1983), who integrated the constructs that had been proposed and stated that this process generated intense separation anxiety for both, but was resolved differently, thus contributing to gender differences, particularly with regard to object relationships.

The Role of Relationships in Women's Lives

The central role of relationships in women's lives can be seen to be the result of the resolution of the process described above. For girls, identification with the mother enhances gender identity early in life. There is less pressure to separate and perhaps either greater difficulty in separation or less need to do so. For boys, the need to give up the important primary relational tie can lead to a defensive disavowal of relational needs and can be seen as a factor in the differences between men and women in orientation to relationships.

Person (1982) and Clower (1976) have emphasized the importance for women of the lifelong fear of loss of love. This has its origins in the fear of abandonment by the mother and has pre-oedipal as well as oedipal components. Since the girl's oedipal rival is also her source of dependency gratification, she risks retaliation in separating as well as loss of her source of nurturance. The boy does not share the same experience of loss, since he does not risk loss of his primary love object. For the girl, then, this process can lead to fear of loss of love, a fear that can then be displaced from mother to subsequent love objects. Person (1982) has suggested that this is why many women avoid competition in other areas as well, and it can also explain the formation of other symptoms seen in women, such as work inhibition and sexual conflict.

This formulation contrasts with the classical view of the oedipal resolution. In emphasizing the impact of the close, early pre-oedipal mother-daughter tie, it suggests that girls have more to lose in separating, distancing, or being different from their mothers. It is the ambivalence about endangering the mother-daughter relationship, then, not penis envy, that may be seen as central to the pervasive fear of loss of love that women experience. The need to separate or be different from an ambivalently held mother can fuel the choice for childlessness.

Clower (1976) also underscored the importance of conflict between the loss of the intense tie with the mother and the developmental thrust toward autonomy. She indicated that a girl's vulnerability to anxiety is greater than a boy's and is related to her mother's separateness, since identification with the mother is strengthened at the time that the girl must find her own identity. Thus, she must simultaneously differentiate and remain close. This, Clower noted, can lead to a heightened sensitivity to approval and disapproval, especially by her mother.

Recently interpersonal theorists have focused on an aspect of the girl's early identification with her mother as a caretaker and nurturer. Out of this experience, they suggest that she evolves a "sense of self" which is encompassing of others and can be characterized as a "self-in-relation" (Jordan and Surrey, 1986; Jordan et al., 1982; Miller, 1983; Stiver, 1983). Although they focus on the mother-daughter identification, we can hypothesize that an early self-in-relation may exist for boys, too. Since the boy needs to defend against his maternal identification in order to develop and preserve a masculine self-image, he must give up the self-in-relation to his mother and assume the distance in relationships that has been observed in boys and men.

Dependency in Women

The term *dependency* has been used in many different ways to delineate normal and pathological processes (Nemiah, 1963). It has special meaning for women since it is often used in contrast to independence, and it derives from a model of male development. The meaning as it relates to the feminine developmental model is more relational, and it can be conceptualized as related to an attachment phenomenon.

Conflict related to dependency issues has particular relevance for single women in their thirties and forties, since it must be worked through in order for women to care for themselves in the second half of their lives. Earlier, the fantasy of being cared for by mother, father, and then husband can be sustaining. The realization of singleness and potential childlessness, however, reevokes early conflict around maternal attachment and loss.

Dependency needs are a universal aspect of human experience, and the struggle to achieve a healthy integration of passive, dependent longings and active, autonomous strivings constitutes a lifelong developmental task for both men and women. Lerner (1983) suggested that men may not need to acknowledge their dependency overtly because they go from mother to "mother" again in marriage. Women, on the other hand, in taking on the role of mother, may have to give up *being* mothered and seek gratification of these dependency needs through providing for others. This is also internalized as a component of their self-esteem.

For women who do not become mothers other sources of dependency gratification can be an adaptive sublimation—for example, the nurturance and mentoring of others. This fits with Stiver's (1984) concept of "interacting interdependence" and Fairbairn's (1946) understanding of "mature dependence," both of which reinterpret the concept of dependency (Fairbairn, 1952, 1954). But nurturant needs may also find neurotic fulfillment in inappropriate caretaking behavior in situations where other behaviors are indicated. This can be seen particularly in women approaching middle life who have not worked through the issue of childlessness. They may, for example, take on the mother's role at work, nurturing and caretaking, but often failing to recognize the negative transferential responses of colleagues.

An important aspect of the dynamics of dependency involves maternal ambivalence regarding a daughter's achievement. A mother blocked from her own self-development may feel angry, competitive, or threatened by what she experiences as the loss of her daughter through her daughter's success. This is especially problematic if the daughter achieves success both as a mother and in a career (Notman, Nadelson, and Bennett, 1978). The mother may consciously wish for her daughter's success, but unconsciously she may also experience sadness, since this success may imply rejection. The recrudescence of her own early conflict can engender these feelings of competitiveness and anger. Thus the mother, because of her own dependency needs, may prolong a symbiotic relationship with her daughter, may attempt to prevent separation, or may even force a rejection (Greenbaum, 1981). As a result, a daughter who succeeds may experience profound anxiety and guilt because she risks losing her mother (Nadelson, Notman, and Bennett, 1978). This can be especially painful if her mother is elderly or ill, and she recognizes that she will, in fact, lose her. The decision to remain childless may be a way to expiate her guilt and to remain compliant, dependent, and noncompetitive.

Pre-oedipal conflict around dependency has many manifestations. It may lead a daughter away from maternal identification; it may be expressed as rage toward the mother; or the dependency conflict may force a daughter to separate more definitively from a symbiotic tie. The daughter may also struggle with the mother whom she sees as powerless and inadequate, as a manifestation of her unresolved oedipal conflict or on the basis of her real-life experience of her mother. Thus, often in the analyses of women in their thirties and forties, it is not only singleness or the loss of parenthood that must be worked through but conflictual pre-oedipal and oedipal relationships as well.

Fear of dependency and merger with the mother not only can lead to disavowal of maternal identification but can make the integration of feminine identity difficult (Menaker, 1982). This can be a determinant of the decision to remain childless, and it can also lead to identification with the father. As a manifestation of this paternal identification, the woman may be driven relentlessly and unremittingly to search for success at all costs, especially at the cost of relationships with men other than her father or transference father. This is particularly likely if the daughter sees her mother as unsuccessful and powerless. The daughter may associate femininity with weakness and may fear that becoming a mother would inevitably draw her back to a dependent or regressive position. This is especially likely if the father devalued feminine roles and also devalued the mother. This solution may overtly appear to be successful, but in analysis emptiness and depression are apparent.

The outcome of the struggle with the mother depends a great deal on the strength of the original bond, the daughter's innate ego strength, and the opportunities, experiences, and supports for her autonomous development in the world outside of her family. The current generation of career women is struggling to consolidate a feminine identity that is different from that of many of their mothers, but without losing their mothers in the process.

The Implications of Success for Women

"Success," as Moulton (1986) notes, "has always presented a problem for both men and women, due to the universal conflict between the drive for mastery and self-assertion on one hand, and the wish for security and protection on the other. . . . Success and achievement are sources of anxiety because they threaten to disrupt the fulfillment of hidden dependency needs." For women, success can violate both societal norms and intrapsychic expectations. It can threaten separation from the mother and loss of love, it can cause conflict with nurturant and relational needs, and it can also be viewed as an aggressive act, particularly against the mother (Nadelson et al., 1982).

Schechter (1981), in elucidating the psychoanalytic concept of fear of success, has taken issue with the assumption that it derives from oedipal guilt. She argues that pre-oedipal guilt, related to intense envy of maternal omnipotence, underlies masochistic defenses in women with fear of success. She believes that these women experience intense envy of their mothers' omnipotence and feel impotent by contrast. The urge to replace mother, then, can be seen in pre-oedipal terms as related to fantasies of maternal omnipotence rather than to oedipal wishes. Schechter suggests that for some women who present their options as polarized between career and marriage, the unconscious meaning may be conflict between career and mother.

The mother is seen by the daughter both as devalued and as omnipotent. The fathers of these daughters are often outwardly successful but exceedingly dependent upon their wives, thus reinforcing the ambiguity. The daughters may appear to be identified with their fathers, but they may be more closely identified with their mother's negative self-perception, and they are self-rejecting. Thus they appear to be independent, but the façade masks enormous dependent strivings and low self-esteem. As indicated above, low self-esteem is derived in part from "an unconscious identification with a maternal figure viewed as worthless" (Person, 1982). This constellation is prominent in women who fear failure, and it can inhibit achievement behavior (Applegarth, 1976). It is especially strong in women who appear to be successful but plateau early and cannot advance in their careers as they might have consciously expected.

An aspect of the façade of self-sufficiency may be the girl's positive response to her father's support (Moulton, 1986). She may, however, experience oedipal guilt as a result and continue to be vulnerable to female disapproval and to the envy of female bosses and peers. Frequently, she believes that her success is fraudulent, undeserved, and transient and that it will be taken from her. Since it is achieved at the expense of her mother, with the collusion of her father, she experiences it as not rightfully hers.

Moulton (1986) has stated that "for many women to be successful means that they are unfeminine and unlovable. Without male support, their success is experienced as being either empty or dangerous." She suggests that autonomy is more difficult for women to achieve and that it takes more ego strength to support it, since it may elicit criticism from parents and male partners, and envy from friends and competitors.

In the clinical situation, many single women in their thirties and forties experience their relational ties and needs as oppositional to their achievement orientation. They cannot "aggress against" other women (mother) and be good and loved; and they fear that they will lose men (father) if they are too aggressive. On the other hand, they feel that they must be more aggressive in order to succeed—and, indeed, this may be the reality. Many of these women report that they have been criticized by their bosses for their lack of aggressiveness, competitiveness, or self-assertion.

Many women who are successful and achieving, however, present with problems around low self-esteem. They attribute their success to external events rather than to their own efforts. Since they experience success as an aggressive act against their mothers, and derivatively against anyone they compete with, they defensively externalize instead of failing. If they succeed, they feel they have damaged someone. This can lead to lowered risk-taking behavior, failure to take initiative or to build on previous successes, or self-defeating behavior. Thus the inhibition of achievement-oriented behavior can be seen as the price for preserving relationships (Nadelson et al., 1982; Notman, Nadelson, and Bennett, 1978). In fact, Schuker (1985) has observed that women who are creative often fail to credit themselves with their own ideas. They are frequently seen in psychoanalysis as they approach mid-life, especially if they are childless, because they find that their careers are not evolving as they had hoped and they fear for the future.

On the other hand, by the time most women reach their thirties, Lebe (1982) suggests, they have usually had numerous opportunities to experience their mothers as both weak and strong, and the internal object representation of the omnipotent mother has been modulated. (Similarly, men also are neither idealized nor rejected.) Most women have achieved in a number of areas of life, which reinforces their self-esteem. Since women can be more autonomous and achieving if they are not bound with internal conflict, Lebe believes that as they enter careers earlier and marry later, they may work out individuation from their mothers earlier rather than automatically transferring their dependency onto men in early marriages.

Reproduction and Femininity

Freud's (1933) view of the reproductive wish as substitutive has been countered by other psychoanalysts who have emphasized that motherhood was the primary, not the secondary or substitutive, organizer of a woman's sexual drive and her personality (Nadelson and Notman, 1981b, 1981c). Benedek (1970) viewed identification with the mother as an important determinant of a woman's attitude toward motherhood and of her mothering behavior. She did not, however, focus on the role of pre-oedipal identification with the mother as much as on the biological or instinctual origins of mothering behavior and female drive organization. She hypothesized that the affects associated with pregnancy and motherhood were based primarily on the fluctuations of the female endocrine cycle.

Kestenberg (1956) took a less biologically deterministic position and described the development of maternal feelings as an integral part of the development of female sexuality. She saw motherly feelings as arising from an awareness of the vagina, thus emphasizing the importance of a body concept or image.

The tie between motherhood and self-concept was elucidated early by Klein (1932), who, in her emerging object relations constructs, stated that the wish to procreate stemmed from a sense of self as well as from relationships. This was extended in Kohut's (1975) emphasis on the wish for a child as an aspect of self-expression and relatedness.

Recently, other psychoanalysts (Chasseguet-Smirgel, 1970; Clower, 1976; Stoller, 1976) have suggested, as did Horney (1926) and Thompson (1950) earlier, that the wish for childbearing has its origin in a primary feminine identity. This concept of primary femininity based on a female, not a male, developmental model implies separate and different pre-oedipal developmental experiences and intrapsychic representations. Deutsch (1945a) noted that an important aspect of the internalized concept of femininity included an awareness of the biological capacity for childbearing, whether or not this was fulfilled, but she did not connect this view with the idea of separate developmental lines. She adhered to Freud's formulations that gender identity evolved through the oedipal conflict.

Another aspect of the evolution of concepts of feminine identity as they involve reproduction can be seen in Benedek's (1952) emphasis on women's growth and maturation through motherhood. She stated, "Women have a better chance to achieve completion of their physical and emotional maturation through motherhood than they have if motherhood is denied them." Although she did not explicitly assume that it was the only route, Bibring (1953) felt that the gratifying experience of successful mothering established self-confidence. Erikson

(1959), in a similar vein, spoke of the developmental significance of "generativity," implying that actual procreation was necessary for true maturation. He later modified this view and expanded the concept of generativity so that procreation was not an essential component.

The assumption of a link between femininity and motherhood has more recently given way to the view that feminine identity is not inextricably linked with procreation. In fact, despite earlier views to the contrary, there is no evidence that healthy women who have not borne children necessarily suffer lifelong feelings of loss or deprivation. Most often, consciously or unconsciously, choice or circumstances have led to their situation, and these women adapt and attain successes in their lives without sorrow or lingering regret (McBroom, 1986).

Menopause

A consideration of pregnancy and reproductive potential must inevitably include the loss of this potential. Menopause can be defined as a developmental crisis with characteristics similar to those of other such crises. Early conflicts from all developmental levels are rearoused, and the balance between drives and defenses is threatened. Pre-oedipal and narcissistic issues related to body image and self-esteem are often involved (Tyson, 1984).

Approaching menopause has been conceptualized by psychoanalytic theoreticians largely in terms of loss (Notman, 1979). Deutsch (1945b) spoke of "a narcissistic mortification that is difficult to overcome" and stated that "the mastering of the physiologic reaction to the organic decline is one of the most difficult tasks of a woman's life." She saw it as a narcissistic blow so real that psychoanalysis could not offer much to make up for it. This derived from the view that femininity is essentially tied to sexuality and reproductive potential. Likewise, since self-esteem for women has also been seen as closely tied to reproduction, the end of the reproductive period has been understood as inevitably leading to low self-esteem and depression (Notman and Nadelson, 1977).

Early psychoanalysts predicted that childless women would be most likely to have difficulties during menopause and that regret about a previous abortion might emerge at that time, but there are no data to support these views. Women who are childless do appear to work through the loss of this possibility in menopause and to grieve. Those women who experience the most distress at menopause seem to be those who rely most on their childbearing role as a source of self-esteem and status (Nadelson and Notman, 1981b, 1981c). Moreover, depression does not appear to be as clearly associated with the physical changes of menopause as it does with the mid-life issues of this period (Weisman and Klerman, 1977). In fact, cross-cultural studies indicate that in those societies where women at mid-life have an improved status, women have a greater feeling of well-being and less depression (Bart and Grossman, 1978).

Conclusion

Many women who are childless and single in their thirties and forties find themselves freer to be creative and seek new directions, including some they previously considered unrealistic. Others struggle with the recognition that many of their needs and wishes will not be satisfied and that they must give these up. Some women seek psychoanalysis in this life phase when they experience the recrudescence of conflict related to self-image, self-esteem, or fear of loss of love. The single woman, pushed to achieve in order to survive, must struggle with internalized prohibitions that can prevent her from reaching a new stage of generativity.

Freud wrote: "A man of about 30 strikes us as a youthful, somewhat unformed individual we expect to make powerful use of the possibilities for development opened up to him by analysis. A woman of the same age, however, often frightens us by her psychical rigidity and unchangeability." This view presents a picture of limited possibilities for women that contemporary psychoanalysts cannot support. The insight that development is an ongoing process throughout the life cycle and the experience that growth and change through psychotherapeutic and psychoanalytic techniques can be productive counter Freud's pessimistic view. The working through of loss, physical or psychic, at mid-life must emerge from the perspective of limits of time and possibility, but human creativity and adaptability make this resolution a part of our daily clinical experience.

REFERENCES

Abelin, E. 1975. Some further observations and comments on the earliest role of the father. *International Journal of Psychoanalysis* 56:293–302.

Applegarth, A. 1976. Some observations on work inhibitions in women. *Journal of the American Psychoanalytic Association* 24:251–268.

Bart, P., and Grossman, M. 1978. Menopause. In *The woman patient*. Vol. 1, *Sexual and reproductive aspects of women's health care*. Ed. M. Notman and C. Nadelson. New York: Plenum Press.

Benedek, T. 1952. *Psychosexual functions in women*. New York: Ronald Press.

———. 1970. The psychobiology of pregnancy. In *Parenthood: Its psychology and psychopathology*. Ed. E. J. Anthony and T. Benedek. Boston: Little, Brown.

Bernard, J. 1975. *Women, wives, mothers: Values and options*. Chicago: Aldine Publishing.

Bernstein, D. 1983. The female superego: A different perspective. *International Journal of Psychoanalysis* 64:187–201.

Bibring, E. 1953. The mechanism of depression. In *Affective disorders*. Ed. P. Greenacre. New York: International Universities Press.

Bibring, G. 1959. Some considerations of the psychological processes in pregnancy. *Psychoanalytic study of the child* 14:113–121. New York: International Universities Press.

Blos, P. 1980. Modifications in the traditional psychoanalytic theory of female adolescent development. In *Adolescent psychiatry*. Vol. 8. Ed. S. Feinstein. Chicago: University of Chicago Press.

Brunswick, R. 1940. The pre-oedipal phase of the libido development. *Psychoanalytic Quarterly* 9:293–319.

Chasseguet-Smirgel, J. 1970. *Female sexuality*. Ann Arbor: University of Michigan Press.

Chodorow, N. 1978. *The reproduction of mothering: Psychoanalysis and the sociology of gender*. Berkeley: University of California Press.

Clower, V. L. 1976. Theoretical implications on current views of masturbation in latency girls. *Journal of the American Psychoanalytic Association*. Supp. Female psychology. 24(5):109–125.

Deutsch, H. 1945a. *The psychology of women*. Vol. 1. New York: Grune and Stratton.

———. 1945b. *The psychology of women*. Vol. 2, *Motherhood*. New York: Grune and Stratton.

Dinnerstein, D. 1976. *The mermaid and the minotaur: Sexual arrangements and human malaise*. New York: Harper and Row.

Douvan, E., and Adelson, J. 1960. *The adolescent experience*. New York: John Wiley.

Erikson, E. 1959. *Identity and the life cycle: Selected papers. Psychological Issues*, Monograph 1. New York: International Universities Press.

————. 1963. *Childhood and society*. 2d ed. New York: W. W. Norton.

————. 1968. Womanhood and the inner space. In *Identity, youth and crisis*. Ed. E. Erikson, 261–294. New York: W. W. Norton.

Fairbairn, W. R. D. 1946. Object-relationships and dynamic structure. In *An object relations theory of the personality*. New York: Basic Books.

————. 1952. *The psychoanalytic studies of personality*. London: Tavistock.

————. 1954. *An object relations theory of the personality*. New York: Basic Books.

Freud, S. 1933. *Femininity*. In *Standard edition*, 22:112–135.

Gay, P. 1984. *The bourgeois experience*. Vol. 1, *Education of the senses*. New York: Oxford University Press.

Greenacre, P. 1958. Early physical determinants in the development of the sense of identity. *Journal of the American Psychoanalytic Association* 6:612–627.

Greenbaum, E. 1981. An aspect of masochism in women—fear of success: Some intrapsychic dimensions in therapeutic implications. In *Changing concepts in psychoanalysis*. Ed. S. Klebanow. New York: Gardner Press.

Greenson, R. 1966. A transvestite boy and a hypothesis. *International Journal of Psychoanalysis* 47:396–403.

Horney, K. 1926. The flight from womanhood. *International Journal of Psychoanalysis* 7:324–339.

Jacobson, E. 1964. *The self and the object world*. New York: International Universities Press.

Jaques, E. 1965. Death and the mid-life crisis. *International Journal of Psychoanalysis* 46:502–524.

Jones, E. 1935. Early female sexuality. *International Journal of Psychoanalysis* 6: 263–273.

Jordan, J. V., and Surrey, J. L. 1986. The self-in-relation: Empathy and the mother-daughter relationship. In *The psychology of today's woman: New psychoanalytic visions*. Ed. T. Bernay and D. W. Cantor, 81–104. Hillsdale, N.J.: Analytic Press.

Jordan, J. V.; Surrey, J. L.; and Kaplan, A. 1982. *Women and empathy*. Work in Progress, No. 82:02. Wellesley, Mass.: Stone Center for Developmental Services and Studies, Wellesley College.

Kestenberg, J. 1956. Vicissitudes of female sexuality. *Journal of the American Psychoanalytic Association* 4:453–476.

Klein, M. 1932. The effects of early anxiety situations on the sexual development of the girl. In *The psychoanalysis of children*. Trans. A. Strachey. New York: Delacorte Press, 1975.

Kohut, H. 1975. *A note on female sexuality*. In *The search for the self: The selected writings of Heinz Kohut, 1950–1978*. Vol. 2. Ed. P. Ornstein. New York: International Universities Press.

Kuhn, M. 1955. How mates are sorted. In *Family, marriage and parenthood*. Ed. H. Becker and R. Hill. Boston: D. C. Heath.

Lebe, D. 1982. Individuation of women. *Psychoanalytic Review* 69(1):63–73.

Lerner, H. 1983. Female dependency in context: Some theoretical and technical considerations. *American Journal of Orthopsychiatry* 53(4):697–705.

Lidz, T., and Lidz, R. W. 1986. Turning women things into men: Masculinization in Papua New Guinea. *Psychosexual Review* 73(4):117–135.

Marmor, J. 1974. The crisis of middle age. In *Psychiatry in transition*. Ed. J. Marmor, 71–76. New York: Brunner/Mazel.

McBroom, P. 1986. *The third sex*. New York: William Morrow.

Meissner, W. W. 1978. The conceptualization of marriage and family dynamics from a psychoanalytic perspective. In *Marriage and marital therapy: Psychoanalytic, behavioral and systems theory perspectives*. Ed. T. J. Paolino, Jr., and B. S. McCrady, 25–88. New York: Brunner/Mazel.

Menaker, E. 1982. Female identity in psychosexual perspective. *Psychoanalytic Review* 69(1):75–83.

Miller, J. 1983. *The development of women's sense of self*. Conference on Women's Emerging Identity. New York: American Academy of Psychoanalysis.

Moulton, R. 1986. Professional success: A conflict for women. In *Psychoanalysis and women: Contemporary reappraisals*. Ed. J. Alpert, 161–181. Hillsdale, N.J.: Analytic Press.

Nadelson, C. 1978. Marital therapy from a behavioral perspective. In *Marriage and marital therapy: Psychoanalytic, behavioral and systems theory perspectives*. Ed. T. J. Paolino, Jr., and B. S. McCrady, 89–164. New York: Brunner/Mazel.

Nadelson, C., and Notman, M. 1981a. To marry or not to marry: A choice. *American Journal of Psychiatry* 138(10):1352–1356.

———. 1981b. Women, work and children. *Journal of the American Academy of Child Psychiatry* 20:863–875.

———. 1981c. Changing views of femininity and childbearing. *Hillside Journal of Clinical Psychiatry* 3(2):187–202.

Nadelson, C.; Notman, M.; Baker-Miller, J.; and Zilbach, J. 1982. Aggression in women: Conceptual issues and clinical impressions. In *The woman patient*. Vol. 3. Ed. M. Notman and C. Nadelson, 17–28. New York: Plenum Press.

Nadelson, C.; Notman, M.; and Bennett, M. 1978. Success or failure: Psychotherapeutic considerations for women in conflict. *American Journal of Psychiatry* 135(9):1092–1096.

Nemiah, J. 1963. Dependency: Normal and pathological. *Journal of the Kentucky State Medical Association* 61:415–419.

Notman, M. T. 1979. Midlife concerns of women: Implications of the menopause. *American Journal of Psychiatry* 136:1270–1274.

Notman, M., and Nadelson, C. 1977. Conflicts in identity and self-esteem for women. *McLean Hospital Journal* 2(1):14–23.

Notman, M., Nadelson, C., and Bennett, M. 1978. Achievement conflict in women: Psychotherapeutic considerations. *Psychotherapy and Psychosomatics* 29:203–213.

Notman, M.; Zilbach, J.; Baker-Miller, J.; and Nadelson, C. 1986. Themes in psychoanalytic understanding of women: Some reconsiderations of autonomy and affiliation. *Journal of the American Academy of Psychoanalysis* 14(2):241–253.

Person, E. S. 1982. Women working: Fears of failure, deviance and success. *Journal of the American Academy of Psychoanalysis* 10:11, 67–84.

Person, E., and Ovesey, L. 1983. Psychoanalytic theories of gender and identity. *Journal of the American Academy of Psychoanalysis* 22:2, 103–226.

Riviere, J. 1936. On the genesis of psychical conflicts in early infancy. *International Journal of Psychoanalysis* 17:395–422.

Schafer, R. 1968a. *Aspects of internalization.* New York: International Universities Press.

———. 1968b. On the theoretical and technical conceptualization of activity and passivity. *Psychoanalytic Quarterly* 37.

Schechter, D. 1981. Masochism in women: A psychodynamic analysis. In *Changing concepts in psychoanalysis.* Ed. S. Klebanow, 169–182. New York: Gardner Press.

Schuker, E. 1985. Creative productivity in women analysts. *Journal of the American Academy of Psychoanalysis* 13(1):51–75.

Stiver, I. P. 1983. *Work inhibitions in women,* Work in Progress, No. 82-03. Wellesley, Mass.: Stone Center for Developmental Services and Studies, Wellesley College.

Stiver, L. 1984. *The meanings of "dependency" in female-male relationships.* Wellesley, Mass.: Stone Center for Developmental Services and Studies, Wellesley College.

Stoller, R. 1976. Primary femininity. *Journal of the American Psychoanalytic Association* 24:59–78.

Thompson, C. 1950. Some effects of the derogatory attitude towards female sexuality. *Psychiatry* 13:349–354.

Tyson, P. 1984. A developmental line of gender identity, gender role, and choice of love object. *Journal of the American Psychoanalytic Association* 30:61–86.

Weisman, M., and Klerman, G. 1977. Sex differences and the epidemiology of depression. *Archives of General Psychiatry* 34:98–111.

· 9 ·

THE BIOLOGICAL CLOCK

LILA J. KALINICH, M.D.

Recently, a middle-aged woman friend shared some reflections with me:

> I remember walking to school one day in the second grade, chatting with my girlfriend's mother as she escorted us. I told her that I had noticed how much more quickly the day seemed to pass than it used to. Seven seemed a very advanced age to me then, so I was sure this phenomenon was related to being finally grown-up. Later that year we moved into a new house in a new community. Moving day was very exciting. The real grown-ups were very busy, so the most entertaining thing I had to do was to sit around and think about my life. Moving seemed to have wrapped up the first part of my life into a discrete little package. And it came to me that there I was, almost *eight* years old, and I didn't have a *feeling* for all that time. I promised myself, as I sat in our old, soft maroon chair, holding some of my accumulated possessions dislocated by their recent journey, that five years later to the day I would sit again in the same spot, in the same position, holding the same objects. Then, I figured, with all the awareness born of old age, I would really know what five years would *feel* like. And five years later I did just that.
>
> I am still trying to comprehend or capture a sense of time passing. Now only the units have changed. Every once in a while I hold very still and try to catch twenty years. Twenty years feel like those five did long ago. Twenty from now, if I'm lucky, I'll be staring my death in the face. It's all so odd. Somewhere inside I *was* all grown-up when I was seven. That "me" hasn't really aged or changed much, and it's still watching as the world wrinkles on the outside. Days are minutes, months are weeks, and years are months. I'll probably be menopausal in the morning!

Women seem to be born with a tide chart somewhere inside which anticipates the lunar rhythm of the biological clock that measures their futures. Each turn of the moon, each wave of menstrual blood, each period punctuates the passage of time in a way that cannot be ignored.

123

This particular woman, as one might predict, given her keen and central sense of time, did not let the years slip away. She seemed to have an internal schedule that paced the major events in her life. She married, embarked on a career, and conceived her first child within one week of obtaining her most advanced degree. Subsequent children came along in a timely way, and her family was complete by the time she was aged thirty-five. The gods granted her good fortune in that no inordinate life obstacles stood in her way. Her children have been well, her marriage and career fulfilling.

But this woman is relatively healthy. The nature of her character or neurosis did not preclude her from taking advantage of the opportunities that knocked at her door. Many other women are not so fortunate. In this chapter, after a glance at cultural factors, I will discuss the problems of a particular group of the less fortunate: single, childless women facing the biological clock. Their difficulties can be especially poignant, and the dilemmas posed in their treatments unique. I will illustrate these with a vignette of a woman patient who, despite a satisfying career, wanted desperately to have a baby.

Culture and the Biological Clock

Until rather recently, women have been freer to allow their biological rhythms to govern their lives. Changes in our culture, however, have complicated and interrupted what seemed to be a simple and innate relationship to the body and its aging. Increasing longevity in both sexes has revised and redefined our notions of youth, the middle years, and old age. Expectations of young people have radically changed, so that adolescence, for a new group of women, starts to fade only at about age twenty-five. Women used to feel like old maids by then. Now they feel too young to marry. This group begins to feel ready to marry at about twenty-eight or twenty-nine. Then, after marriage, as young couples, they look forward to sharing the early years without the responsibilities of a family. Often they feel ready to become parents by age thirty-two or thirty-three. Similar thinking tends to color each subsequent decade in all significant aspects. Until recently, most women past forty were considered "too old" to be hired for ordinary jobs in the work force. In contrast, today, it's entirely possible for women to find rewarding employment and to begin new careers well along in middle age. Few men or women are expected to have achieved full productivity before age fifty.

Feminism has been both an effect of and a catalyst for social changes that have created a disjunction between the contemporary woman and her biological clock. Efforts to guarantee freedom of opportunity for women of this generation have also engendered new imperatives and new standards of achievement which create further problems in the lives of women. Educated women no longer regard a career as optional. Some sort of professional proficiency is today virtually a requirement for a sense of adequacy as an adult woman. Even if a woman stops working, she must feel *capable* of working and commanding an income. After training, additional years are siphoned by the kind of apprenticeship that every serious area of endeavor requires. The woman must establish herself in her occupation of choice, especially if she plans to interrupt it or modify it in order to have children. She cannot allow herself to attend carefully to her internal metronome since it is no longer in synchrony with the demands of her life.

These cultural changes have altered attitudes, aims, and expectations and have opened up new possibilities. Yet the ovarian cycle remains relatively unaltered. It has its own time. For that reason the sense of extended time that today's woman embraces is in a very fundamental way an illusion.

The Clock's Impact on Treatment

Many women seek psychoanalytic treatment when they finally begin to hear the tick of the clock, and for that very reason. The psychodynamic constellations vary from one woman to another. Oedipal and pre-oedipal factors, pathological object relations, feared identifications, gender identity vulnerability, unresolved sibling rivalry, superego and ego-ideal pathology—all make their contributions to the frustration of a woman as she confronts her life and begins to feel that *her* time, especially her time as a childbearing woman, is running out. Further, some women in treatment, precisely because of their deeper understanding of the characterological defenses that have governed their life choices, begin to face the same issues. And other women, who have been dedicated to their careers and frankly antagonistic to marriage and motherhood, may change, but then fear that change has come too late.

Now surely, desire frequently becomes demand during the course of a treatment. The wish to marry and to have a family can function as a powerful resistance to psychoanalytic or psychotherapeutic work. This is very much true of women (and men) who characterologically are depressed, negativistic, demanding, or prone to disappointment reactions. Their failure to find a spouse or to conceive becomes evidence of the failure of the therapy and ultimately of the therapist or analyst. At these times work on the transferential elements of the particular reactions is absolutely central. Yet it is also crucial to help the patient distinguish between life goals and therapeutic goals. For even should the therapeutic outcome be an ideal one, marriage and children simply may not be in the cards. Under these circumstances it is particularly important for patients to comprehend that their treatments may have been successful even in the absence of the life changes for which they have yearned. It is consoling to know that something to which they have devoted time and energy and hope has in fact worked out.

Sometimes, however, the distinction between inner resolution and external goals is not so clear, to analyst or patient, especially during a treatment in progress. Often one points to the other, but not always. For example, a woman who has sought treatment because she wants to marry may find a man and become engaged rather early in the course of an analysis. Occasionally this happens because conflicted areas have become sufficiently unlocked and explored to allow movement and growth. At other times, the identical life change can represent an acting out of a displaced transference. Many a failed marriage has been made on this basis. The analyst's countertransference can complicate the dilemma. It's typically human for the analyst to want for the patient what the patient herself wants. The analyst can be so pleased for the patient that she will at last be married that he or she can neglect the analysis of the selection. At times, even when the analyst sees the displacement, he or she can be tempted to ignore it in the hope that the relationship will somehow work out for the best. Even with all these factors clearly in mind, with analyst and patient working together to sort them out, the two can make a wrong call.

Most unmarried women entering psychoanalysis or psychotherapy in their middle years sense that something in their personal makeup has kept them from marriage. Frequently they have had multiple relationships, some of them long term, with men whom they have understood to be inappropriate life partners for one reason or another. Or they give a history of relative isolation after having had ordinary and satisfying experiences with men during their early and mid-twenties. Women in this group are aware at some level that they have retreated from men when marriage became a serious possibility. So when such women look to the therapist and the therapy to accomplish some sort of internal shift that will help them find a mate and have a family, they are articulating an intuition of the truth. Something inside needs to be understood and altered before life as they desire it can proceed.

A Case Vignette

The following vignette illustrates some of the pertinent issues in the analysis of an unmarried woman in her thirties. Emily, now aged thirty-nine, came for treatment, unmarried, at the age of thirty-four. She sought to enlarge her understanding of her conflicts with Fred, her married lover, thirty years her senior. Although she believed that she wanted Fred to leave his wife for her, she also knew that she was afraid of that possibility. Because Emily's picture of marriage and family life was an oppressive one, the distance and repeated separations built into her liaison suited her. Children were of only remote interest to her; her friends' children irritated her when she was in their company. Emily had been pregnant twice by two different men, and each time had had an abortion with no apparent qualms. Now, at thirty-nine, aware that Fred for various ethical reasons will not leave his wife, Emily is trying desperately to conceive his child, prepared to venture into the uncertain terrain of single parenthood.

A commanding, forceful, beautiful woman, Emily has for years invested the best of her thought, energy, and fantasy in her career. As an executive at a major television studio, she enjoys ongoing relationships with the rich and famous. Emily has regarded ordinary men in ordinary professions as pale and unattractive when compared to the film stars and politicians who people her world. Fred, a publicist, is part of this scene. Although Emily did not find him glamorous, he intrigued her because she felt an unusual sense of comfort with him. "It's almost a bad joke," she said at one point. "He's almost my father's age and looks like my father's brother. I suppose you're going to tell me that this is all my neurosis or oedipal or something. But I can't stand to be around my father. I find him pathetic and infuriating. I can't imagine that I'd want anyone like my father. I've never been with anyone like my father. My old lover, Nick, was married, but he was my age. And Joey was younger than I am. So being with an older man is not a pattern in my life. Don't get that idea. It's just odd that it has worked out this way."

Both of Emily's parents are now retired. They were dedicated to their family and provided a comfortable upper-middle-class life which was rather conventional in the best sense. Her mother stayed at home with the children while they were young, returning to work only after they had completed high school. Despite her devotion to her home and family, the mother saw herself as a longtime feminist. Emily said she never encouraged her two daughters to learn homemaking and cooking skills and instead emphasized education and career training. Recently, when Emily was discussing her decision to stay at home with the family for the holidays rather than travel to Europe on business with a well-known matinee idol, she said, "I'm sure my mother is quite disappointed that I will be at home. She'd much prefer to talk about my being on a glamorous trip with a glamorous guy during a holiday meal than to actually have me at the table."

The oldest of the children, Emily, has had troubled relationships with her siblings, especially with her sister, Faith, one and a half years younger than she. While they were growing up, Emily and Faith hated each other and often fought, sometimes violently. At those times, the parents seemed helpless and unable to intervene in any constructive manner. To Emily Faith seemed the cute, adorable object of her parents' desire, while she herself was the problematic, difficult, mysterious one. Allegedly her father would plaintively ask, "What's wrong with you, Emily?" Emily felt deeply hurt and misunderstood. She managed these feelings, together with the rage that accompanied and concealed them, through a proud self-inflation and isolation. She would disavow her pain and need, embrace the anger that empowered her, and retire to her room, both in fact and metaphorically. There, through the years, she erected an impenetrable fortress to which she retreated whenever narcissistic injury of any sort threatened.

Despite a powerful and intimidating façade, which emerged in the treatment whenever she felt disappointed, criticized, or rejected, Emily was at heart a deeply vulnerable woman who believed that something was wrong with her and that she was unlovable. She was unwilling to put herself in a position where she would actually risk rejection. For example, she knew from the start that her lover was not free to walk away from his wife. His circumstances were even more complicated than the simple reality of his married state would indicate. The impossibility of his choosing Emily precluded true rejection, for that would require Fred's having freedom of choice.

Fred represented a masterful neurotic compromise. He provided Emily with the love, adoration, protection, and sexual response she desired from her father; he guarded her against narcissistic injury by posing no risks; his inability to marry her and to raise a family with her fulfilled her mother's desire by maintaining Emily's focus on her career, thereby ensuring her mother's love and respect; at the same time the painful sibling issues that Emily believed motherhood would arouse could be ignored. (She worried that she would compete with and resent her children as she had her siblings.) Further, in the unmarried state, disparaged identifications with both parents could be held at bay.

I have portrayed the tangle of Emily's psychological life in an over-simplified way, leaving out important areas of complexity, such as her relationship to her own body, which made a crucial contribution to Emily's personality and vision. Her perception of herself as a menstruating female bloodied her view of herself as an adult sexual woman.

Years of work, however, provided Emily with considerable clarity about the intrapsychic issues that seemed to have snagged her life. As she achieved understanding and resolution, she allowed herself to feel more compassion, intimacy, and yearning for virtually everyone in her life. As she comprehended that her angry isolation was a defensive façade, she began to explore how much she feared being alone. She now knew that she wanted marriage, that she wanted a child. As she pondered her desire for a baby, she stumbled upon an even more dreadful set of fears that had existed in comfortable repression, since pregnancy had never been in the realm of possibility.

Within days after she first articulated her desire to have a baby, Emily developed the first of a series of psychosomatic and hysterical symptoms that were to preoccupy her and keep her in something resembling the state of a nightmare for more than a year. Her first complaint was abdominal pain with constipation. She was convinced that "something, cancer, was growing inside" her and would kill her. When she was evaluated medically, she was found to have a spastic colon. This was followed by severe headaches, which she attributed to a brain tumor. Next came so-called panic attacks with a heart rate that exceeded 160, chest pain, and shortness of breath. These frequently occurred on airplanes. And then Emily developed an unexplained low-grade fever in the absence of infection or rheumatoid abnormalities. Finally she was afflicted with menstrual disorders and had a pelvic sonogram, which showed a diffusely enlarged uterus in the face of a negative pregnancy test. No physiological or anatomical basis for the enlargement could be determined.

Symptom after symptom and episode after episode provided opportunities to explore fearful infantile ideas of sex, pregnancy, labor, and delivery. Convinced that the fear that had entrapped her was too great to be overcome through insight, understanding, or education, Emily momentarily gave up the thought of having a baby and turned to her career with increased fervor. She felt enormous relief. Nonetheless, she continued to examine her relationship with Fred. Despite the ups and downs and the intermittent break-ups, they were increasingly close.

Additional work unearthed the castration feelings and claustrophobic fantasies that had organized Emily's reactions to a possible pregnancy. Work within the transference expanded Emily's tolerance for risk and vulnerability and deepened her capacity for love, intimacy, and trust. For example, in response to my occasional vacations and cancelation of sessions, Emily would complain that I was "taking advantage" of her, despite the fact that her own schedule required her to be away a good deal. Through many hours of analytic work, "to take advantage" was transformed into "you will make me know that I miss you and rely on you, and it angers me that you are important enough to be able to hurt me." Five years after the beginning of her treatment, she at last felt ready to be a wife and a mother.

But five years later Emily is biologically an old woman. Even were she to part with Fred, who has loved her so well and guarded her neurosis so vigilantly all this time, making confrontation with change unnecessary, the odds that she will find a suitable mate at her age are small. The likes of *Time* and *Newsweek* have clearly informed every American woman of the statistical realities. So, though she is psychologically ready to be a wife, Emily probably will remain unmarried. It is more likely that she will become a mother. Today's culture treats unwed mothers more kindly than in times past. Although Emily is in all likelihood less fertile at thirty-nine than she was at a younger age, she still has at least three to five years of intermittent ovarian functioning left. Amniocentesis has minimized the risks of bearing a child with certain genetic diseases, making conception during the fifth decade a less hazardous prospect than it was.

Three to five years is not much time, however. The pressures on consolidating a life during this interval in the middle years are enormous. The synchrony of external events must be perfect. Sex has to take place on the right days of the month when ovulation occurs, and neither business trips nor viruses can interfere. Miscarriages must not take place. Fetuses must not be stillborn. The exigencies and misfortunes of ordinary life have no place in the life of a middle-aged woman who wants to bear a child.

If Emily fails to conceive, she can adopt, and she is prepared to do so should her efforts with Fred be unsuccessful. Adoption by a single parent also is better tolerated by society today. But Emily wants very much to experience pregnancy, delivery, and the reality of a child who has grown inside her. Emily today is a woman "obsessed," as she puts it, taking her temperature, using ovulation kits, planning her trips according to her cycle, weeping when she menstruates, and behaving in general like a woman who wants very much to conceive. "I only wish I knew years ago what I know now," said Emily. "I had no sense of the future, and less sense that I could have an impact on the future."

The Longing for a Child

Unmarried childless women are not the only ones who wish to slow the clock. Married women and women with children do so as well. Some of these women desire additional children and feel increasingly frustrated as they grow older. Mrs. N, for example, is a forty-three-year-old woman whose husband left her after twenty years of marriage. Happily she has two adolescent children. For years, however, she badly wanted a third child, which the husband adamantly refused. For most of those years she would cry at the sight of an infant or young child. Her former husband is now remarried, his new wife the lover he took toward the end of his marriage to Mrs. N. The new wife has a child by her previous husband. Ironically, therefore, Mr. N now has three children, which Mrs. N deeply resents: he has the prized child whom he kept from her. Mrs. N is barren while Mr. N's betrayal has borne him fruit. Even should Mrs. N find another man, her capacity to have another child will be seriously diminished by her age.

Mrs. A is thirty-eight and the mother of a four-year-old whom she adores. Her current marriage is her second, a happy one after a disastrous first. Many factors in her life led her to wait a while before attempting to conceive a second child. In some ways these factors were rationalizations for her reluctance to tie herself down again to the responsibilities of an infant. Now, however, she feels eager to have a new baby. She and her husband are attempting to conceive, but Mrs. A seems less fertile than she was five years ago. She dreams recurrently of tiny baby birds whom she is frantically trying to keep alive. In each dream she is working against time. She repeatedly associates to various children with genetic defects and congenital anomalies whom she has seen or heard or read about. She fears that as an older mother she will bear such a child. Mrs. A feels damned by the clock. She believed once that she had enough time to space her children optimally, but this probably will not turn out to be the case. "Time seems to go so fast these days," she said recently. Speaking at a level she did not fully comprehend, she said, "I can't believe it's almost winter."

One could argue that a desperate desire to have a child is simply an expression of a neurotic wish, and this can unquestionably be true. Being pregnant, bearing children, and raising them can serve to gratify neurotic and pathologically narcissistic needs. In working with mid-life women in quest of children, it is extremely important to look for unhealthy motivations that can be clarified and separated from healthier ones. Yet there is something so fundamental, so directly human about wanting children and, for a woman, wanting to experience pregnancy and childbirth that these desires finally defy empty psychoanalytic explanation. At some point in treatment, the desire must be accepted at face value and respected.

Reactions to the frustration of this desire can be understood somewhat better. Take Emily, for example. It is not yet clear whether her efforts to conceive will be successful. But if she fails, it is predictable that her response will be complicated by the narcissistic attitudes that still inform her character. Emily is a woman who believes she ought to be able to get anything she wants. This belief has infantile origins that have been illuminated in her treatment. It is demonstrated by her selection of a married man. Her unwillingness to accept an oedipal defeat, even her refusal to allow her sister entry into the family emotionally will find a parallel in her refusal to accept any failure in childbearing and to mourn its effects.

Most psychoanalysts, being rather ordinary folk, have children. This can create significant countertransference problems in working with a childless person whose chances for conception are slim. Most parents come to have difficulty envisioning life without their children. They are so transformed that their absence or loss, they feel, would be like an endless journey on a sea of unimaginable grief. It is easy, therefore, to project these kinds of feelings onto the childless patient and to feel excessive sorrow on her behalf. The analyst/therapist must keep in mind that life does hold other riches the patient can enjoy; "generativity," as Erikson calls it, can be experienced through a mature and caretaking attitude toward other things in this world as well as through parenthood. Furthermore, it may well be that people without children never really know what they are missing. At best, even when consumed by the desire for a child, they have only a glimmer of the fullness that children can bring to life. An old Slavic proverb addresses this point: "God built a bridge across which men and women without children never pass. To protect them from sadness, God never lets them know exactly what is on the other side."

Nonetheless, when the analyst faces the poignant situation of a woman like Emily, who despite having so much of what life has to offer at age thirty-five, desperately wants a child at thirty-nine, he or she may wonder whether it has been a favor to the patient to stir up the proverbial pot. Yet the patient brings nothing to the analyst if she does not bring her wish to live her own truth. In order to be an analyst, to do analysis, one must commit to truth ahead of well-being. And however painful the frustration of desire, the analyst must keep in mind that the emptiness of desire concealed hurts far worse.

The Experience of Menopause

Like moving day for the seven-year-old at the beginning of this chapter, menopause wraps up a portion of a woman's life into a discrete package: its closure is clear; the ovarian cycle is finished; the womb is quiet once and for all. As a marker in a woman's life, it is so clearly defined that it can bring with it psychological hazards. For most women, however, menopause is basically uneventful. The "change" is experienced quietly and privately, with considerable nostalgia. Even if the menstrual periods were difficult, annoying, or painful, their regular return provided a certain comfort and security. Women can miss this.

And menopause, like retirement, does stand as a concrete reminder of the relative imminence of death. A certain kind of productivity is a thing of the past; most of life has been lived.

Women for whom menopause is problematic have varied reactions. Those who have not had children may become depressed when they experience a resurgence of regret that their children no longer exist, even within the realm of possibility. Women with children whose roles as mothers have been singularly invested may also become depressed because of the loss of capacity. Fears about health and body integrity may reappear at this time of physical and hormonal shifts. Minor physical changes may trigger ancient panics about the mysteries of the body. Narcissistic concerns about aging heighten. Women worry that their sexual appeal and responsiveness will diminish. For some women at menopause, it feels as though life is over when the biological clock has stopped.

Somewhere in the less accessible recesses of my memory is lodged a show from early television bearing the name of a cherished aphorism, "Life Begins at Forty." As a child the thought that life began at forty seemed ludicrous to me, as much a possibility as reindeer that fly and fairies that pay for useless teeth. But now, having myself crossed into the middle years, when the simple facts of passing time are less easily denied, I must say that the message carried by the television show makes more sense to me. The pleasure in feeling a certain consolidation of all the hard-won gains of youth makes me comprehend the point. In certain ways, one really does "arrive" at a destination, or a destiny, which has been prepared by the steps taken in the early years. In that sense, life really does begin.

Menopausal or not, with or without children, the middle years are special ones. And the biological clock, perhaps precisely *because* of its imperatives, because it stops, helps preserve the middle years for living. It preserves them for being in time rather than for passing it through diapering, studying, and all the other seemingly endless tasks that have gone before in a woman's life. It insists that we exist in some way other than the way we did when we were young. In that way it readies us for old age by demanding that we actually live a bit before we are translated from this life. In a culture that privileges youth, this notion of aging is an important one for a therapist or an analyst to grasp. With it he or she will be able to help patients to hear in each tick of the clock the timbre of the music to come rather than the echo of notes already played.

· 10 ·

LESBIANS
A Different Middle Age?

MARTHA KIRKPATRICK, M.D.

I was horrified to learn a few years ago that middle age was the period thirty-five to fifty-five. I have been greatly relieved by my reading of the literature on middle age preparatory to this article to find that some researchers, perhaps having aged a bit themselves, now refer to mid-life as forty to sixty or even sixty-five. Some divide us into early and late mid-lifers. Clearly middle age gets later and longer as life expectancy increases.

At the turn of the century life expectancy was forty-seven years, and only 4 percent of the population passed their sixty-fifth birthday. Women, subject to repeated pregnancies, difficult labors, and a myriad of postpartum complications, had a shorter life expectancy than men. With that fact in mind, we might assume that at the turn of the century the mid-life female population comprised a relatively large percentage of lesbians because they had a better chance of surviving to that age. In fact, Kinsey found a high percentage (16 percent) of lesbians in his middle-aged cohort of women born between 1880 and 1910. Such a notion, however, would be based on the common assumption that lesbians are revolted by men, heterosexual intercourse, and certainly by that quintessential feminine task of bearing and rearing children. This would be a misleading assumption, and not only because women had less control of their marital state and their pregnancies in the past.

Lesbians as Mothers

Lesbians, like heterosexual women, are a diverse group. We might discuss the effect of middle age on lesbians as different from its effect on most heterosexual women because reproduction and child rearing have not structured the phases of their adult lives; but in doing so we must also remember that most studies of a nonclinical population of lesbians reveal that 25 to 35 percent have been married and at least half of these have children (Saghir and Robins, 1973; Bell and Weinberg, 1978). For those women, as for most heterosexual women, the phases of adult life have been organized largely around their children's needs.

135

This came forcibly to my attention when I, along with Dr. Katherine Smith and Dr. Ron Roy, evaluated a group of children being reared by lesbian mothers (half of them alone) and compared them to children being reared by divorced heterosexual mothers (1981). It was an interesting and I think valuable study, but for me the most enduring result was the forced confrontation with my assumptions and prejudices. I thought of myself as sophisticated, liberal, and objective. My assumptions were highlighted when they were disabused by our data. I discovered that I had secretly expected the lesbian mothers to have resisted marriage, thus to have married under some coercion, social or familial; to have shorter and stormier marriages; to have been reluctant, consciously or unconsciously, to bear children and thus to have more difficulties with pregnancy and childbirth; and to demonstrate ambivalence about breast-feeding and the sacrifices involved in maternal care. I expected to hear about dissatisfactions with the roles of wife and mother and especially about sexual frustration. I assumed that these women would be hostile to men, including the children's father, and would deprive their children of male contact. I was wrong on all counts!

The study compared the psychological status, including gender identity and sexual role, of ten boys and ten girls between the ages of five and twelve being reared by mothers self-identified as lesbians with the psychological status of ten boys and ten girls of similar age being reared by divorced single heterosexual mothers. The study's intent was to discover if there were identifiable differences between the two groups in development, especially in the area of gender and sex role. Although we were studying the children, not the mothers, we did collect historical data from each mother about her family, early development, marriage, pregnancy, child-rearing attitudes and practices. Because the children were young, only a few of the mothers were over thirty-five. Much to my surprise, these women had married for love of their husbands and a desire to have a family as often as had their heterosexual counterparts. Evidence of ambivalence toward the process of pregnancy, childbirth, and child rearing was not present, nor was any unconscious conflict revealed by the existence of difficulties during pregnancy or delivery. In fact, the pregnancy and delivery histories of the two groups were remarkably similar. Equal numbers of mothers in both groups breast-fed their infants for similar lengths of time.

Even their responses to questions about their sexual life with their husbands showed little difference from the heterosexual women. Further, they were much less angry and bitter toward men than the divorced heterosexual women and consequently provided more male contact for their children. The one glaring difference we found was the reason for divorce. All but one lesbian had initiated the divorce compared to half of the heterosexual mothers. All the lesbians described the lack or loss of a sense of intimacy as the fundamental cause of the marital failure, whereas the heterosexual mothers pointed to physical abuse, drug and alcohol abuse, infidelity, and neglect.

Middle-aged lesbian mothers with adolescent children suffer the burdens and fears common to all parents at that time. They are also burdened by the fear that their children will turn against them because of their sexual orientation. Adolescents' need to conform to peer attitudes, their fear of embarrassment or ridicule, as well as concern over their own sexuality make their lesbian mothers an easy target for hostility and devaluation, especially by sons. The need of adolescents to devalue parents in the struggle to consolidate a separate self is familiar to all of us. Ethnic origin, foreign accent, age, physical disabilities or features, taste in music or clothes, hair style—all are evidence to our children of our defective natures. Years of society's devaluation and discrimination may have undermined the lesbian mother and made this period especially frightening and painful.

Orientation Changes in Middle Life

A different group of mothers who are lesbians are found in a seemingly new segment of the older lesbian population. These are women who, after twenty to thirty years of marriage and with child rearing completed, leave their husbands and establish enduring lesbian partnerships. Philip Blumstein and Pepper Schwartz engagingly describe one such couple in their large study *The American Couple* (1983). Two women in their mid-fifties, both grandmothers who had had long marriages, met through a personal ad one of the women had placed in a magazine. Both described many years of feeling lonely and empty in their marriages despite the opportunities for feminine fulfillment. They felt they had paid their dues to society and now longed for an intimacy they had not known before. For these women the new experience of being touched lovingly by another woman was deeply gratifying, but a new or better orgasm was neither the motivating force nor the binding experience. In the interview, Grace, one of the women, said, "The thing that is important is the togetherness of our heads and the side-bysideness of our bodies; the sex is just a side issue, . . . an outgrowth of tenderness." Christenson and Johnson (1973) surveyed seventy-one never-married women over fifty, of whom 11 percent were lesbians. All had had sexual experiences with men. Most had had lesbian experiences in their youth, had adopted heterosexual behavior, and had then returned to lesbian relationships. That women might lead long, apparently successful heterosexual lives and then turn to homosexuality in mid-life seems hard to explain. We have some pet concepts to dampen our curiosity: regression in the face of mid-life crises (the empty nest syndrome, intimations of mortality, menopause), loss of impulse control, return of the repressed, superego lacunae, manic defense, and so on. For the couple in the Blumstein and Schwartz book, their action became the courageous fulfillment of a lifelong dream, a different childhood dream than their lives had enacted.

Barbara Ponce (1980), in her study of lesbian identity, found married women with no homosexual experiences identifying themselves as lesbians because of their fantasies and their recognized but inhibited longings. Some of these women may choose to explore the consequences of actualizing these desires as part of the reevaluation process of middle age. They establish lesbian relationships despite the loss of the heterosexual support system and the incredulity and/or disapproval of families and friends. The cost-benefit ratio of such a decision is something the therapist cannot know in advance. Our experience is much too limited. We don't know if or when such behavioral change represents a healthy effort to integrate a valuable but previously abandoned part of the self or represents the loss of ego integration and a retreat to a more limited and more infantile relationship. We thus need to be open, better yet, be acquisitive toward data from all other sources. Bell and Weinberg's (1978) survey of 785 lesbians, for example, showed that the stereotype of the lonely, isolated, bitter homosexual fits only a small group of people whose personality structure impairs their capacity for social and intimate connections. It was these problems that led to isolation and suffering, not homosexuality. In fact, coupled lesbians were very like coupled heterosexual women except that the lesbians had fewer complaints of loneliness.

A Case Vignette: Renewal in Middle Age

I was recently consulted by a woman dentist in her mid-fifties. She had always been shy, slow to make friends, and slow to complain or demand anything of those friends she had. She had married shortly after college in the hope of establishing a family and had had three children in seven years. Finding herself inexplicably depressed when her youngest child was two, she entered a five-year analysis with an experienced woman analyst. She reported being terrified throughout the analysis of revealing something that would be used to point out how bad she really was. The source of this expectation was never uncovered, although she found great comfort in what she perceived to be the analyst's genuine interest in her and patience with her inhibitions. She felt deeply grateful and experienced a sense of great love for the analyst which she carefully concealed. The analysis terminated. Life went on in its shy and lonely way. During the children's late adolescence a mass was found in one breast and she underwent a mastectomy. Faced with morbidity and mortality and the realization that her husband's presence did not comfort her, she separated from him. She cared for her children until they left for college, feeling relief and pride in the discovery of her competence to manage her own life for the first time.

Now, eight years after the mastectomy and separation, she was planning breast reconstruction. Why now? She found herself in love with a woman bridge instructor, a revival of her analyst and the analytic secret. She believed for a while that her sexual longing was reciprocated, and this supported a new sense of worth and lovability that had begun to grow in her. She got corrective lens surgery and a permanent and began dressing in a more stylish and more feminine way. Her new concept of herself as a lovable and feminine woman led to the breast reconstruction. She has since realized that her interest was not returned in kind, but despite the sadness this caused, she has maintained her new pride in herself, her reconstructed self. This discovery and acceptance of a capacity for intimate feelings toward women have strengthened her self-esteem and loosened the constrictive forces in her emotional life. She is much less shy and has enlarged her circle of friends with a new hope that she may yet experience an intimate loving relationship.

New Options

Middle age for some heterosexual women opens the possibility of finding a new level of intimacy with a woman, an important option considering the diminished outlook for finding male partners at later ages. For some lesbians it may be the time to try to find or return to heterosexual relationships. One such story is reported by Blumstein and Schwartz. In my clinical experience this wish to become comfortably heterosexual is experienced more typically by young lesbian women, frightened about their future as lesbians, unsure of the cost of social stigma, and faced with the loss of potential motherhood. This provides a motivation not commonly found in middle-aged lesbians. In actuality, the mid-age lesbian may have little reason to envy her heterosexual sister's life.

For example, like their heterosexual counterparts most lesbians at middle age have a partner with whom they expect to grow old (Saghir and Robins, 1973, pp. 311–312). Heterosexual women are often younger than their husbands and, with a longer life expectancy than their mates, may be widows for a considerable period of their lives. Remember, there are 245 widows for every 100 widowers. Heterosexual remarriage or sexual partners are hard to find for older women. After age forty-four only 56 women remarry for every 100 men who remarry (Blumstein and Schwartz, 1983). On the other hand, lesbian couples share the same life-expectancy curve. Furthermore, should a partner die or leave, the pool of peers remains. Since women often believe, and men often confirm, that the physical appearance of the woman is the greatest motivator for a man to begin a relationship, middle-aged women face the future fearful of losing their ability to attract (or maintain) a partnership. Lesbians, like other women, place less emphasis on youth and/or beauty and are generally less threatened by the changes in appearance age brings. A curious study of personal ads undertaken by Mary Riege Laner (1978) found that 98 percent of lesbian advertisers stated their age compared to 76 percent of heterosexual women. Also, far fewer lesbians restricted the age of the respondent. And Raphael and Robinson (1984) found that lesbians over fifty preferred partners of the same age.

A number of features of lifelong lesbian orientation may contribute to the more sanguine approach to aging of many lesbians. Although women in general have lower incomes than men and lifelong lesbians have not shared in a husband's income, surveys usually find that lesbians are better educated and hold higher paying jobs than heterosexual women (Bell and Weinberg, 1978).[1] They have been free to direct their time and energy toward building careers, and the money they have made has been used to enhance their lives. It is expected in lesbian relationships that both partners will work. Supporting oneself and managing one's own affairs if one is left alone in later middle age is not new

1. Bell and Weinberg's (1978) large-scale survey in San Francisco included educational and occupational histories of 229 lesbians.

or something to be feared. Moreover, the stigma of middle age has less sting for those who have coped with stigma throughout their life. They know, through experience, that a satisfying life is possible without society's positive evaluation. Saghir and Robins's (1973) study found lesbians to be more involved in leisure-time activities, artistic pursuits, and individual sports than heterosexual women and thus connected to more sources of satisfaction.[2] Lesbians tend to have a close network of friends which may substitute for estranged family and kin, and these networks do not depend on couple status. Raphael and Robinson's (1984) survey of twenty lesbians over fifty found no evidence of the lonely, isolated lives older lesbians are thought to lead. Strong friendship ties provided support and correlated positively with high self-esteem.

Intimacy and Sexuality

The search for intimacy is a major theme in many if not most women's lives. In fact, I think of intimacy as the major organizer of femininity. The girl's psychological and physiological environment both encourage her to find stimulation and comfort in the social rather than the physical world. This search for intimacy seems to be an even greater imperative in the lives of lesbians. Perhaps this represents an unconscious effort to reinforce or complete their feminine development. The high value of intimacy is shared by both partners in a lesbian relationship and by others in the lesbian community. This fuels and helps maintain the supportive network of friendships characteristic of many older lesbians (Wolf, 1978).

Lillian Rubin's sensitive book *Women of a Certain Age* (1979) tells us that many a married woman's sexual life becomes freer, more flexible, and more satisfying at middle age. The children have left, she is less tired, there is no fear of unwanted pregnancy, and the capacity to respond increases. Mid-life releases possibilities for new forms of creativity as well as making old forms more pleasurable as fears and superego rigidities give way to increased desires for personal gratification. At the same time in life, the male partner is apt to be less interested sexually and may experience occasional erectile failures. This imbalance in sexual response need not weigh heavily on lesbian couples. Raphael

2. Saghir and Robins's interviews with fifty-seven lesbians included questions about use of leisure time, hobbies, and interests.

and Robinson (1984) discovered that many of their sample of lesbians over fifty had a continuing interest in a sexual life and, unlike heterosexual older women, looked forward to having sexual partners in their later years. Although many lesbian couples remain sexually active into old age, Blumstein and Schwartz (1983) and others found, however, that the frequency of sexual relations is less among lesbian couples than among other couples, even at young ages and early in a relationship, when excitement and desire are intense. But in later years nonsexual contact remains high and is greatly valued. The womanly valued qualities of mutual understanding, expression of feelings, sensitivity toward others, and mutual nurturing are rated as more important to a relationship than sexual excitement. Despite the lower frequency, lesbians report greater satisfaction with the sexual aspect of their relationship than do other couples.

Nevertheless, lesbian couples, like heterosexual couples, may break up in middle age under the impact of a closer view of life's ending and the fear of having missed something exciting. They may feel they have a last chance for the fulfillment of earlier expectations. Separations, however, are often followed by deep depression and the need for therapy.

Relationship to Community

The lesbian couple's relationship to the group or community is a complicated one. The relationship to the larger community provides none of the supportive rituals or rules that surround and sustain heterosexual marriages. A couple may keep their relationship a secret for fear of job loss or censure by coworkers. Colleagues do not acknowledge the couple as a unit or provide support if the relationship is severed. Thus retirement may remove the strain of leading a double life. Middle age may provide some relief from social pressures to date men, but the larger community still opposes the couple's integrity.

The lesbian community, on the other hand, although acknowledging the couple, poses a threat as well. Susan Krieger, in an excellent review article (1982), states that the lesbian community, like many stigmatized minority groups, offers the individual lesbian a sense of self, especially in that the community commands recognition of a distinctly lesbian sensibility and places an unusual value on intimacy between women. But it also conflicts with efforts to enhance individuality and to recognize and benefit from internal deviance: it demands loyalty and conformity to group standards. For women who are enmeshed in this community the tension between its demands and the demands of the couple relationship result in what Elizabeth Barnhart (1975) describes as the "lesbian shuffle"—a continual changing or exchanging of pair relationships within the community. Unlike many heterosexuals who have separated, lesbian ex-lovers tend to remain friends; thus the community stays intact.

Blumstein and Schwartz (1983) reported that lesbian couples who were actively involved with the lesbian community were more likely to break up than those who were not. In some sense this is similar to the tension Otto Kernberg (1980) has described between the heterosexual couple and the group. He says, "The couple in a love relationship is in opposition to the group and yet needs it for survival" (p. 82). In the heterosexual woman's world the breakup of a marriage, especially in middle age, means not only a 68 percent lowering of her standard of living, frequently the loss of her home, the loss of credit (social and financial), the loss of membership in "the club," and the loss of a sexual partner, but also often the loss of a supportive network of married women friends. This comes as a shock and deep disappointment to many women who find themselves isolated and ignored when they most need comfort and support. The married couples' world is elitist and chauvinistic, and it has no room for dropouts. The profound sense of one's betrayal by old and trusted friends is often the most painful loss for divorced women. The lesbian community responds very differently to the breakup of a couple. Although some choosing of sides may result in strained friendships, the community as a whole tends to rush to the aid of the separated member and provides comfort and participation in the search for a new relationship. I believe that the greater hostility and bitterness our study revealed among divorced heterosexual women compared to lesbian women was related to the difference in community response.

Partnership Difficulties

Lesbian couples and heterosexual couples present some distinct differences in their dissatisfactions with their relationships. Rather than the complaints of loneliness, distance, and lack of communication and understanding that are common among heterosexual women, lesbian couples suffer from excessive intensity, lack of privacy, and an overly strong tendency for fusion with a concomitant loss of the sense of one's separate feelings and an inability to express or tolerate differences. The requirement of a sensitive mutual understanding may inhibit healthy aggression and tend toward a suffocating exclusivity. Interestingly, these same features are often described in admiring rather than pejorative terms for heterosexual couples: "they are so close"; "they've never been apart in thirty years of marriage"; "the perfect helpmate"; "my better half." I can't resist giving the closing lines of a Victorian poem quoted by Ehrenreich and English in *For Her Own Good: 150 Years of the Experts' Advice to Women* (1978). Extolling the ideal woman's development, the poem ends with:

> There's nothing left of what she was;
> Back to the babe the woman dies,
> And all the wisdom that she has
> Is to love him for being wise.

This idealization of merger, vicarious union, or loss of boundaries between self and partner (not loss of boundaries between ego, id, and superego) continues to be a millstone around women's necks, lesbian or heterosexual, interfering with individualization.

Despite the feminist movement's occasional admiration of lesbians as women who have survived without men and who have valued women, lesbians are less protected from merger in their relationships. Identification with the father or with male values of independence, competence, and courage may have arisen partly to protect against a pull toward merger with the mother. In many lesbian relationships similarities are valued; differences are diminished and often feared as divisive. Also, the lack of differentiation in socialization for sex roles as well as the actual role expectations of compliance and nurturance make the struggle toward individuation conflicted and guilt-ridden. Two women urgently moving toward each other for intimacy, with their nesting "instincts" intensified, can create a mutual prison. Occasionally such merger is patently obvious, as when the women dress alike, have the same hair style, finish each other's sentences, do everything together. Space or difference is feared and experienced as abandonment or hostility. To want space is a source of guilt, for it suggests a lack of love.

Although these features may exist long before middle age, it is nonetheless common that the prison bars begin to show in middle age, and symptoms of depression, apathy, loss of libido, and phobic states make it clear that something is wrong. Although we can speculate on the unresolved symbiotic tie to mother, reenactment of a flawed separation-individuation process, fear of abandonment and eroticization as a defense against it, and various other pre-oedipal and oedipal calamities, our purpose here is to focus on the experience of middle age as such. In the case report that follows these issues were dominant and extreme.

A Case Vignette: Merger in a Relationship

A forty-four-year-old woman attorney came for treatment of depression and an increasing sense of emptiness and futility. During therapy she recalled occasional episodes of claustrophobia and has recently complained of a sense of suffocation. She is an extremely attractive, stylishly dressed woman, highly motivated, introspective, and articulate.

Her mother was described as a beautiful, vivacious, highly social woman with a myriad of lifelong hypochondriacal fears, mostly related to anxiety and intermittent panic attacks. The mother abhorred physical contact and was never known to touch her children. When she was present, however, her interactions were intense, and she dominated the household. There were frequent changes of child caretakers during the patient's early years, and she remembers the intense despair that followed these losses. Her relationship with her parents was also intense, and she suffered greatly during their frequent periods of travel. The patient was responsible for keeping her mother calm, taking her to the doctor, providing companionship at the mother's behest, and responding to her unpredictable moods.

During a summer vacation from college she became swept up in a chaotic love affair with another woman. Her family became alarmed and demanded that she enter analysis. The analyst supported her through the traumatic breakup of the affair and her college career. After four years, she married a young man with whom she was best friends. She was glad that she could please her analyst in this way and did not reveal any dissatisfaction with the marriage, although she felt empty and in pain. The analysis terminated one year after she had married. After three years of marriage she became deeply depressed. She eventually made a suicide attempt and was briefly hospitalized. She divorced despite her parents' threats to disinherit her.

Some supportive psychotherapy helped her establish herself in her own apartment and enter professional training. She had a few brief affairs with both men and women and then became infatuated with a woman of her age whom she met at a tennis club. They became engulfed in a passionate affair which led after two years to their moving in together. The partner is almost ludicrously similar to her mother— she is beautiful, unpredictable, extremely possessive, full of anxiety, and unable to tolerate the patient's attention not being focused on her. In recent years my patient has become increasingly unable to protect herself from being used by her partner as narcissistic balm, as she was used by her mother. Until this therapy she was completely blind to the striking similarities with her early relationship with her mother. She felt she had totally detached herself from her mother and cited her inability to mourn her mother's death in a car accident two years ago as proof.

Although the demand on a partner to supply repairs for narcissistic wounds and to supply all narcissistic needs is not limited to homosexuals, lesbians seem especially prone to confuse these demands with love. This patient's sense of worth depends on being enslaved and used. When she first came for consultation, she answered every question about herself by telling me about her friend. She seemed to have lost track of her own feelings and ideas. She no longer knew what she liked or didn't like or what she wanted. Their sexual life has continued to be very active and orgasmic for both, but for my patient it is meaningless, as are most other experiences of daily life. Her partner has carried all the feelings and meanings for both. She has given up all friends, interests, and activities that do not place her partner in center stage. Her partner's demands, however, continue, and my patient feels inadequate and depressed that she has nothing more to give. She has become a necessary but insufficient appendage of her partner. In her experience, the partner's insatiable demands represent love. There was no precedent for mutuality or any kind of nonfused partnership.

The discovery or rediscovery of herself has been fraught with fear —both fear of losing her partner and fear that her feelings, so alien and overwhelming, will close in on her or suffocate her. She is now aware of her imprisonment and the ambivalence of the attachment, but freedom to assert herself and make use of the consequences is not yet available. Apparently it will depend on her capacity to discover and integrate both the loving and the hostile attachment to her mother and to experience mourning. This may allow her new freedom in participating in relationships of all kinds.

Comments on a Few Other Mid-Life Issues

Homosexual women once were thought to be disinterested in motherhood. We know now that the desire for children has many roots and does not originate only in resolution of the oedipal configuration. It is not the desire for a baby but the discovery and wish for the father's participation that originates during the process of resolution. The longing of lesbians for children has been made manifest in recent years now that single motherhood is more acceptable and available through artificial insemination and adoption.

Older lesbians for whom motherhood was not a possibility, like other women who are infertile or have elected to be childless, have usually come to terms with that loss earlier than middle age. Curiously enough, postsurgical depression following hysterectomy or the onset of menopause is less likely to occur in childless women than in mothers. Having invested all one's energy in motherhood seems to make a woman more vulnerable to a pathological experience of loss at this time. Medical problems, particularly gynecological problems, however, may be ignored by middle-age lesbians because of apprehension about revealing their sexual preference or being embarrassed by questions about birth control or intercourse. Lesbians in this age group are also at a disadvantage in tending to the health needs of their partners. "Family only" visiting rules prevent them and their partners from caring for each other and taking responsibility for necessary decisions. Estate planning is fraught with uncertainty about whether a lover can receive what a partner wishes to give without legal barriers (Adelman, 1986, pp. 219–256). The support of a nonjudgmental therapist may assist them in reaching creative solutions to these problems of middle age.

The middle years occupy the largest portion of our lifetime and of our investigative energy. Being there, I'm glad it does. For lesbian women as for others, it can be a time of discovery of new creative potential, especially if a sense of having weathered slings and arrows over the years gives support to one's adult confidence, and the integration of adult experience enhances the use of the future. Neither homosexuality nor heterosexuality can guarantee this capacity.

REFERENCES

Adelman, M. 1986. *Long time passing: Lives of older lesbians.* Boston: Alyson Publications.

Barnhart, E. 1975. Friends and lovers in a lesbian counterculture community. In *Old family/new family.* Ed. Nona Glazer-Malbin. New York: Van Nostrand.

Bell, A., and Weinberg, M. 1978. *Homosexualities: A study of diversity among men and women.* New York: Simon and Schuster.

Blumstein, P., and Schwartz, P. 1983. *American couples.* New York: William Morrow.

Christenson, V., and Johnson, A. 1973. Sexual patterns in a group of older never married women. *Journal of Geriatric Psychiatry* 6:80–89.

Ehrenreich, B., and English, D. 1978. *For her own good: 150 years of the experts' advice to women.* Garden City, N.Y.: Anchor Press.

Kernberg, O. 1980. Love, the couple, and the group: A psychoanalytic frame. *Psychoanalytic Quarterly* 49:78–108.

Kinsey, A.; Pomeroy, W.; Martin, C.; and Gebhard, P. 1953. *Sexual behavior in the human female.* Philadelphia: W. B. Saunders.

Kirkpatrick, M.; Smith, C.; and Ron, R. 1981. Lesbian mothers and their children. *American Journal of Orthopsychiatry* 51:545–551.

Krieger, S. 1982. Lesbian identity and community. *Signs: Journal of Women in Culture & Society* 8:91–108.

Laner, M. 1978. Media mating II: "Personals" advertisements of lesbian women. *Journal of Homosexuality* 4:41–61.

Ponce, B. 1980. Lesbians and their worlds. In *Homosexual behavior: A modern reappraisal.* Ed. Judd Marmor, 157–175. New York: Basic Books.

Raphael, S., and Robinson, M. 1984. The older lesbian: Love relationships and friendship patterns. In *Women-identified women.* Ed. Trudy Darty and Sandee Potter, 67–82. Palo Alto, Calif.: Mayfield Publishing.

Rubin, L. 1979. *Women of a certain age: The midlife search for self.* New York: Harper and Row.

Saghir, M., and Robins, E. 1973. *Male and female homosexuality: A comprehensive investigation.* Baltimore: Wilkins and Wilkins.

Wolf, D. 1978. Close friendship patterns of older lesbians. Paper presented at the meeting of the Gerontological Society. Dallas, November. Quoted in Raphael and Robinson (1984).

· 11 ·

MIDDLE-AGED HOMOSEXUAL MEN
Issues in Treatment

ROBERT S. LIEBERT, M.D.

A man in his mid-forties,[1] several years into analysis, mused in one session:

> Why is being gay so confusing? I was thinking, when I first came out in Boston it was wonderful. But underneath there was a sadness and always, always guilt. I think of one traumatic experience I had when I was going through Hell Week at the fraternity in college. I had been up without sleep for three nights. One of the brothers came into my room and propositioned me. He said, "Do it and you're in." I knew that he really wanted to have sex with me, but I wouldn't dare under these circumstances. There has always been something about the nature of being gay, not just sleeping with men—a whole other part of feeling vulnerable.

This reflection was spoken a week after his lover of the past decade had precipitously announced that he was infatuated with someone else and was going to move out for an indefinite period.

The patient, a successful, well-liked, and respected person, was profoundly frightened, fearful that in his remaining years no one whom he found desirable would seriously consider him. His view of the years ahead contrasted starkly with his recollections of his desirability and the excitement and pleasure of the gay aspects of his life when he was in his twenties. His fantasies now were of a progressively deteriorating body, humiliating encounters, apprehension over AIDS, and loneliness, with nobody to leave his earthly possessions to except distant siblings in remote cities.

His morbid expectations were the product of fears attending middle age and beyond and a scenario determined by guilt and self-punitive need. The guilt pertained not so much to his overt life of homosexu-

---

1. Each of the patient vignettes in this chapter is a composite of clinical material spliced together from several patients who have been either in treatment with me or in a treatment supervised by me.

ality as to his reservoir of unconscious aggressive and defiant impulses, which were the subject of much of the analytic work.

To explore what is specific to the treatment of the male homosexual in his middle years requires that we first consider some of the meanings this period of life potentially holds regardless of sexual orientation.

As far back as the riddle of the Sphinx in the myth of Oedipus, we humans have been concerned with drawing chronological divisions in our lives, in order, as Frank Kermode (1966) puts it, to bear the weight of our anxieties and hopes. These divisions are an attempt to give our lives order and coherence. Beyond this, they provide a framework within which we measure the meaningfulness of our lives.

The subjective sense of meaningfulness reflects a complex interaction between, on the one hand, the achievement of what the culture prescribes as both expected and rewarded and, on the other, the achievements of the imagination—that is, whether the organizing fantasies of one's mental life, of one's representation of his or her self, are being reasonably actualized.

Let me illustrate this issue with a clinical vignette. A man in his late twenties, who was rising in a creative field, entered analysis. His reasons for seeking treatment were quite general and poorly defined. Yet he seemed intent on continuing. Movement was very slow however, in terms of both changes in his life and progress in the analysis. This was, in part, because there was little manifest pain in his life to serve as a catalyst to his participation in the analysis of his pervasive resistance. The form of the resistance was primarily his being a "good patient." He followed the rules and produced a continuous flow of "analytic" material for the analyst alone to chew on.

For several years he had been the secret lover of a glamorous public figure his father's age. But now over the course of the next few years, the relationship came to an end because of growing disenchantment on the part of both men, and because of the patient's unconscious expectation that the analyst would henceforth fulfill these same needs. As he moved along into his thirties, appropriate artistic advancement continued, and he formed a bond with a seemingly more suitable same-aged lover. Nevertheless, he sank into an ongoing low-grade depression with a growing sense of purposelessness and ennui. I will not go into the complexities of his object choices or the vicissitudes of the emerging transference neurosis. Rather, I want to make the point that in his earlier years a central and organizing fantasy was that of being the adored boy lover and giver of pleasure to an idealized parental figure —a male transformation of the frustrating imago of his mother of early childhood—who, in turn, would protect and lovingly guide him. As long as this fantasy system could be actualized, he experienced life as full, exciting, and relatively meaningful. Without its actualization outside or sufficient gratification of the fantasy by the analyst in treatment, an increasing sense of emptiness predominated, which could not be compensated for by either external accomplishments or a new kind of symmetrical relationship with a man.

In retrospect, one of the primary forces inducing this man to begin what appeared to be a poorly motivated analysis in his late twenties was his emerging, but denied, awareness that as he moved into middle age he could no longer sustain this particular fantasy system as an active way of life.

This patient exemplifies a not uncommon pattern in the life cycle of homosexuals. In their twenties they are the lovers of men a generation older than themselves. Then, in their late middle years and beyond, they are the lovers of men a generation younger than themselves. What is directly gratified in this erotic parentified reliving in their twenties is gratified in their later years in the projective identification with the young lover. Thus, the inexorable forward motion of time is slowed down—indeed, magically turned back—by such unions.

This was the theme of Aschenbach's obsession with Tadzio in Thomas Mann's *Death in Venice* (1930). Aschenbach, exhausted and increasingly preoccupied with his spiritual barrenness and forebodings of death, first seeks the suspension of time in the otherworldly beauty of the isle of Venice. Destiny, however, cannot be forestalled, and signs of a plague progressively engulf Venice. We then witness the disintegration of Aschenbach's defensive structure and ego functioning with the breakthrough of his desperate obsession with a beautiful Polish boy. Tadzio, with whom he never exchanges a word, is never out of his thoughts for a moment. In his eroticized, obsessional union with the boy, Aschenbach attempts to infuse a passionate purpose into the subjective meaninglessness of his life.

Like Mann's fictional character or my patient mentioned above, men whose fantasies involve a union between generations confront the problem of how to negotiate the years between the role of young lover and older lover—that is, the middle years. Success in negotiating these years depends more on the organization of the character structure than on the content of the fantasy system. That is, if the hierarchical organization of the person's fantasies, which are the controlling force behind both behavior and the potential for satisfaction, is flexible and adaptive, then the present can be meaningful and the future can be anticipated with optimism. Even with psychoanalytic therapy, earlier controlling fantasies, which are no longer adaptive, do not disappear or change substantially. Rather, they lose their insistent power and become subordinated to other, more adaptive fantasies that then exert primary influence on thought and behavior. We may, incidentally, rarely see as patients individuals with these characteristics. If, on the other hand, the organization of fantasies is relatively rigid and fixed, despair and lack of a sense of meaning or joy will inevitably prevail. And this is the group from which we do see patients.

The degree of flexibility and the capacity to rewrite central fantasies and dampen their imperative call to action depend largely on the nature of the defense mechanisms the individual characteristically employs and the relative integrity of the personality organization. Clinically, we generally observe significant correlation between the conscious and unconscious fantasies that represent a higher level of psychological development (that is, oedipal) and more flexible and adaptive mechanisms of defense. In contrast, conscious and unconscious fantasies rooted in more primitive, pre-oedipal conflicts are accompanied by more rigid and less adaptive defenses. Kernberg (1986) has recently elaborated on this issue. He has observed that in patients with a more borderline personality organization, homosexual behavior was commonly a resolution of the unconscious wish to submit to the father in order to obtain the oral gratifications that they had never received from the dangerous and frustrating mother. The defensive operations surrounding the oral conflicts of frustration and sadistic impulses in these individuals are weighted in the direction of *splitting* and *projection*. Reliance on these more primitive mechanisms renders the individual relatively inaccessible to change in psychic organization without imposing a serious threat to the entire fabric of personality integration.

In contrast, patients with a neurotic personality organization reveal the predominance of oedipal conflicts. In this group the homosexual activity often represents unconscious submission to the father related to guilt over longings for mother and fears of retaliative castration. Here the defensive resolution of the negative oedipal complex primarily involves *repression*. As a consequence, there is less rigid structuralization of psychic organization than we find in the borderline patient inasmuch as the threat of disorganization if the defensive system is confronted is less immediate.[2]

Having just related some forms of homosexual behavior to particular pre-oedipal and oedipal experiences and conflicts, I want to emphasize that I am not suggesting that these conflicts are the *cause* of an individual's homosexual orientation, for we observe the same family constellations and conflicts in our heterosexual patients. Nor am I suggesting a monolithic motivational pathway to the homosexual outcome. I do not think that at this time we understand why the majority of homosexuals become homosexual. This, however, is not to say that, like most complex behavior, homosexuality serves as a resolution of multiple intrapsychic conflicts, rooted in different periods of development.

The reorganization of a patient's major constellations of fantasy in a new hierarchical order and the resulting shift in the insistent quality of these fantasies are issues I shall return to shortly. Here I shall address the essential element in the construction of the chronological divisions that compose the life cycle—that is, the always present but continuously changing manner in which our thought and adaptation are informed and organized by the concept of *time*. I would postulate that the psychology of time is different for homosexuals in their middle years as a group than for individuals who participate as the adults in nuclear family arrangements.

The awareness and meaning of time and one's relation to its passage shift with each epoch of the life cycle and with one's particular life circumstances during that epoch. Time as a symbol and principle has always represented a dialectic between, on the one hand, time as a unidirectional, inexorably destructive force—concretized by Freud in his concept of Thanatos—and, on the other, time as the revealer of truth and wisdom.[3] For all of us, the point on which we fall on the continuum from graceful acceptance to protest, from contentment to

2. Also see McDougall (1986) and Person and Ovesey (1983) for discussions of the relationship between homosexual behavior and the developmental level of conflict and psychic organization.

3. The icon that Father Time traditionally carries is the sickle—the instrument of both castration and agricultural fertility. Father Time derives from the Greek god Kronos (who provides the etymological root for time [chronos]), who castrates his father, Uranus, with the sickle, becomes the patron of agriculture, and then is overthrown by his own son Zeus.

despair, which characterizes our state of mind during the middle years, is determined in significant measure by the balance of our own distinctively personal psychology of time.

Among the very limited writings on middle age in the psychoanalytic literature, an important contribution was made by Elliott Jaques (1965), who focused on a crucial psychological feature of this epoch: realization of the inevitability of one's own eventual personal death. In contrast with the period before, when we tend to concentrate on what we want and how to obtain it, most of us arrive at mid-middle age having laid the foundations for all the principal structures that will fulfill our lives. At the same time, with somewhat grim irony, these achievements and fulfillments are now foreseeably limited by the end of our lives, however near or far away that will be. Thus, the middle years demand an acceptance that we cannot achieve all we had hoped and planned and cannot hold on to all we have achieved.[4]

One of the tasks of the middle years, therefore, is to adapt to this new awareness. Prominent among the less adaptive means resorted to are various depressive positions, which necessarily involve the regressive reactivation of earlier intrapsychic organization, with the compelling object attachment being that of the "good" and "bad" parents of childhood. In the depressive state the revivified internal relation to earlier objects ascends to precedence over here-and-now relationships in one's life. How, then, do we ward off what appears to be a powerful draw toward depression in the middle years, as denial weakens and one is caught more urgently in the dilemma posed by Freud (1915): "We were of course prepared to maintain that death was the necessary outcome of life. . . . however, . . . in the unconscious every one of us is convinced of his own immortality" (p. 289)?

The capacity to withstand the regressive draw to depression depends largely on two factors: the relative success of having mourned and relinquished the early childhood objects along with having come to terms with one's capacity for ambivalence and unconscious sadistic fantasies; and the nature of the primary relationships in the middle years.[5]

It is with respect to this latter point—the nature of the present-day object relationships—that we see a significant difference between

4. Jaques writes: "The issue of resignation is of such importance. It is resignation in the sense of conscious and unconscious acceptance of the inevitable frustration on the grand scale of life as a whole" (1965, p. 513).

5. I am disregarding in this discussion the relative genetic and/or physiological factors that create a diathesis toward depression.

homosexual men and their married heterosexual and even married homosexual counterparts. It is a difference that holds profound clinical significance. Just above, I referred to Freud's statement, "In the unconscious every one of us is convinced of his own immortality." The existential dilemma of the contradiction between accepting the insistent idea of death and comforting oneself with the unconscious notion of immortal existence is best resolved by knowing that one will be preserved as a presence by someone who primarily loves one and further, by one's children and grandchildren as extensions of oneself into the future. For a few, artistic or intellectual creations can, to some extent, serve this purpose.

In my experience, the most frequent presenting problem in consultation with the middle-aged male homosexual is mounting depression in connection with the awareness that to this point in his life he has had a long list of relationships each of which ended in disenchantment, if not bitterness, and now he increasingly dreads a future of fading attractiveness and loneliness. His situation and clinical response parallel those of the single, childless middle-aged woman. For both there is the powerful social reality that middle-aged physical appearance is a handicap in finding desirable partners. This reality must be borne in mind while also exploring the particular individual neurotic contribution to the unhappy situation.

The central therapeutic task with many of the patients who fit this description is to enable them to mourn and relinquish the too active inner representation of parental figures of the past in order to be free to love without the unconscious fear of destroying the object of love in the present. My observation has been that the degree of the heretofore contained resentment and sadistic feelings that would be unleashed in the process of mourning and relinquishing these objects from the past has militated against that mourning and individuation ever having taken place.

I will illustrate this issue with a clinical vignette of a patient whose analysis I supervised over many years.

Francis, an attorney in his late thirties, entered analysis with considerable apprehension because of increasing depression and an unrelentingly high level of anxiety regarding his work. In addition, intimate relationships had been an endless chain of lovers of no more than a few weeks' duration. Interspersed with these relationships was much compulsive cruising in which, contrary to his usual presentation of himself, he sought to be the sexual servant of an idealized, anonymous young man. Although highly successful and well liked in his profession, Francis was never for a moment free from the anxiety that any older man who had some authority or influence over him would capriciously turn on him. With his reputation destroyed, he would then, he feared, suddenly be without income or future prospects.

Francis's father, a minister, had always been remote with his wife and children. He looked the other way as Francis's mother cultivated in the boy certain aspects of sissyhood. Then, his father died after a progressive illness when Francis was a senior in high school, just about to go off to college. His recollection was that he felt nothing other than relief when father died—no tears, loss, or guilt. Although he had been continuously, actively homosexual since his early teens and exclusively interested in males in fantasy, Francis had never defined himself to himself as homosexual or contemplated homosexuality as his future orientation. But, upon his father's death, he immediately experienced enormous liberation and acknowledged to himself that of course he was and always would be homosexual.

In the course of analysis, Francis developed the beginnings of his first stable relationship, in part to buffer the intensity of his transference to the analyst. He and his lover soon bought a little dog. The puppy, however, proved resistant to training, and after he had bitten a second person, it was clear that he had to be put away. Francis was overwhelmed with grief, uncontrolled sobbing, and the guilty conviction that he had caused the dog's untoward fate because he had allowed it, on the night before the second biting episode, to watch him in one of his anonymous sexual encounters. Although he recognized its irrationality, the causal connection was obsessively compelling.

This loss, a minor one in the ordinary human scheme, allowed Francis to face for the first time in an affectively connected way his fantasy that his adolescent homosexuality had killed his father. The thought ran something along these lines: "If my father knew that I sucked cock, it would kill him." In his father's untimely death, it seemed to Francis that his unconscious murderous thoughts were magically actualized. Thus freed of father as a projected superego presence, but without the work of mourning having taken place, Francis produced an idealization of his father and the clear belief that, had his father lived, he would have been fully accepting of Francis's sexuality and unambivalently pleased with his professional accomplishments. The analysis of his reaction to the dog's death and his dread of the analyst's condemnation of his sexual behavior, which he regarded as having caused the dog's death, enabled him to come in touch for the first time with his boyhood and adolescent yearnings, frustration, and sadistic retaliative feelings and fantasies toward his father.

With this turn in the analysis, he began to mourn the loss of the occasional good moments he had enjoyed with his father along with the loss of the idealized fantasy he maintained of the father he never did and never would have. Once sufficient mourning had taken place to enable him to relinquish the powerful internal hold his father had on his psychic life, Francis experienced appreciable relief from his self-tormenting necessity to expect at every turn some older authority to destroy the fabric of his life. Also, his need for humiliating and self-punishing sexual rituals diminished. He was then able for the first time to develop a long-lasting, mutually devoted relationship. Interestingly, lustful sexuality between Francis and his lover was virtually absent because of its consolidated foundation in sadomasochistic fantasy. This body of thought and activity had to be isolated lest its sadistic component injure and alienate his partner.

Francis revealed only after this period of mourning that he was convinced he would die by age forty-six, the age his father was when he died. He had been living a life with only a fragmented sense of future. All his daily fears of having his work life destroyed by authorities were still more tolerable than the dread of what he regarded as a deserved death by the age his father was when Francis was unconsciously convinced that he had destroyed him.

In this vignette I have attempted to highlight elements of unconscious aggression that suffused Francis's sexual fantasies and activities. They interfered with his capacity to sustain an intimate and affectionate relationship, thereby leaving him bereft of the primary and necessary means of adapting to the middle years.

History is quixotic, and the male homosexual is suddenly confronted by existential conditions that were unimaginable only five years ago. I am referring to the AIDS epidemic, in which unconscious fantasy merges with a significant degree of reality. Now, every prospective lover or sexual mate is potentially dangerous. No less significant, one may, in the act of lovemaking, be an infectious agent oneself. With the enormous level of anxiety attending this problem it is often extremely difficult in treatment to maintain a necessary figure-ground contrast between the patient's fantasized fears of aggression, with their long antecedent history, and what is actual danger. The observing ego is at times overwhelmed by the situation—by the fact that one's worst fantasies could indeed become manifestly realized. The psychoanalytic process, which involves weakening the oppressive hold that self-punitive attitudes exert on the potential for pleasurable fulfilling of self ideals, is greatly complicated now by this new reality and its ramifications for both patient and analyst.

Since the early 1970s there has been a dramatic increase in social tolerance of homosexuality, accompanied by equally changing attitudes on the part of most clinicians. With this we have seen male homosexuals whose goal is not to effect change in orientation or to "accept" their condition but to resolve the neurotic and characterological conflicts that have prevented them from achieving deeper and lasting homosexual relationships. They need also to dissolve some of the psychic scar tissue that has invariably resulted from growing up in a family with traditional values, knowing that their fantasies are homosexual and that they are expected to take their place in a culture whose structure is decidedly heterosexual. Now, in response to the terror of AIDS, we are increasingly seeing both young adult and early middle-aged homosexuals who, either at the beginning of treatment or in the course of it, wish to work toward the goal of achieving a heterosexual adaptation. In their view, what is most preferable in terms of sexual pleasure is subordinated to other values—stable family life and children, and physical safety.

In tandem, there has been a shift in attitude and outlook among therapists. In terms of survival, it is advantageous to be heterosexual at this time, and this stark fact cannot but influence the conscious and unconscious approach of a therapist—whether heterosexual or homosexual. We are now at a historical moment when directions of lives are being decided in a frightening and radically changing social climate, without knowledge of whether a cure or vaccine for AIDS is upon the immediate horizon or off in the indefinite future.

Because of space constraints I can only allude to the many countertransference entanglements that can intrude into the therapeutic situation. To maintain a neutral position with respect to the patient's libidinal disposition as well as superego prohibitions remains as essential as ever. Only then can the homosexual patient reach goals, whatever they may turn out to be, that he experiences as self-determined and authentic.

REFERENCES

Freud, S. 1915. Thoughts for the times on war and death. In *Standard edition*, 14:275–302.

Jaques, E. 1965. Death and the mid-life crisis. *International Journal of Psycho-analysis* 46:502–514.

Kermode, F. 1966. *The sense of an ending.* Oxford: Oxford University Press.

Kernberg, O. 1986. A conceptual model of male perversion. In *The psychology of men: New psychoanalytic perspectives.* Ed. G. I. Fogel, F. M. Lane, and R. S. Liebert. New York: Basic Books.

Mann, T. 1930. *Death in Venice.* New York: Alfred A. Knopf.

McDougall, J. 1986. Identifications, neoneeds and neosexualities. *International Journal of Psychoanalysis* 67:19–32.

Person, E. S., and Ovesey, L. 1983. Psychoanalytic theories of gender identity. *Journal of the American Academy of Psychoanalysis* 11:203–226.

· 12 ·
MARITAL CONFLICT AND PSYCHOANALYTIC THERAPY IN THE MIDDLE YEARS

FRED M. SANDER, M. D.

Psychoanalytic writings pertaining to marriage are virtually non-existent, an omission apparent from the beginning. The index to the *Standard Edition* of Freud's writings lists eleven references under "marriage," in contrast to two thousand under "dreams and dreaming." The neglect continues: the indexes of the *Journal of the American Psychoanalytic Association*, the *Psychoanalytic Quarterly*, and the *International Journal of Psychoanalysis* for the last ten years give no references at all under "marriage."

Although Freud neglected marriage as a subject of study, he certainly recognized it as the arena for the enactment of neurotic conflicts. In 1919, seeing the potential for patients' acting out unconscious conflicts in their marriages, Freud recommended that such vital life decisions be postponed when psychoanalytic therapy was undertaken. In those days, when psychoanalyses lasted months and marriages, whether happy or not, were long, this was an understandable recommendation. In the past fifty years, however, psychoanalyses have significantly lengthened while marriages have become briefer. This fact serves as a stimulus in this chapter first to note briefly the rapidly changing externals of marriage and family life in the modern era before turning attention to the perennial presence of marital conflicts, their internal dynamics, and their treatment.

Broadly speaking, the way we view the middle years is affected by both sociological and historical conditions. For example, in the pre-modern era, when the life span was relatively short, those elders who survived the middle years were venerated for their accumulated wisdom. In the past century, owing largely to advances in science and medicine, life expectancy has increased dramatically. We are facing an era in which the increasingly infirm elderly are about to outnumber the young, who in turn are the object of heightened attention and admiration; this culture worships its youth. People in their middle years are thus, culturally speaking, en route from revered youth to the losses and despair of the later years.

Also in the past century, a period of time roughly corresponding with the formulation and evolution of psychoanalysis, our view of the life cycle has undergone changes reflecting its insights. As Aries (1962) noted, the concept of "childhood" was discovered and delineated in the modern era. Although some attention has been paid of late to adult development (Vaillant, 1977; Gould, 1972), the most recent version of the life cycle emphasizes the importance of childhood. Erikson's (1950) often cited schema, for example, allots five of eight stages to childhood and adolescence, underscoring the predominant analytic view that childhood is when character is formed. His stages of development contrast sharply with Shakespeare's "all the world's a stage" version in *As You Like It* (act 2, scene 7). Man progresses in seven stages from the "mewling and puking" infant, through the "whining school-boy," the lover, the soldier, the justice, to declining age and finally his childlike dotage. Interestingly, this schema, like others of the premodern era (and like the psychoanalytic literature), neglects marriage.

In this chapter, after noting some of the structural changes in marriage in the modern era, I will review the few observations that Freud and more recent psychoanalytic writers have made about marriage and the treatment of marital conflicts. I will then introduce the concept of shared unconscious wishes, fantasies, and conflicts as they impinge on marital life. From the perspective of treatment, such interlocking pathology with its associated reciprocal or complementary identifications may require, at least at the start, modalities other than individual treatment (Sander, 1979). I shall then address the related question of a couple's individual or marital treatment and conclude with two case illustrations.

External Changes in the Family

While the psychoanalytic literature has been silent on the subject of marriage, the other social sciences have documented the dramatic changes in the family's structure and functions wrought by industrialization and other modern developments. Talcott Parsons (1955) was particularly acute in discerning the profound changes in the family produced by the increasing structural differentiation of the social order. Whereas the family once subsumed many social, political, and economic functions, in the modern era it has retained only two, the socialization of children and the stabilization of the adult personality. With this development came the emergence of the primacy and privacy of the nuclear family. Parsons concluded that this shift was a source of significant strain upon both the individual and the family:

> In particular, [the nuclear family's] spouses are thrown upon each other, and their ties with members of their own families of orientation, notably parents and adult siblings, are correspondingly weakened. . . . The consequence of this may be stated as the fact that the family of procreation, and in particular the marriage pair, are in a "structurally unsupported" situation. Neither party has any other adult kin on whom they have a right to "lean for support" in a sense closely comparable to the position of the spouse. (pp. 19–20)

Since Parsons's cogent sociological observations we have witnessed and experienced yet another revolutionary development. The advent of feminism and an unprecedented number of women entering the work force have shaken the traditional roles of spouses in the nuclear family. In addition the 40–50 percent divorce rate and its sequelae have further destabilized the family. Consequently, the intact nuclear family, so recently described by Parsons as typical, has become a minority variant. It is no accident that the mental health professions generally, and the field of family therapy specifically, have arisen in this context of family dysfunction and instability (Sander, 1979).

The complaints of our patients in their middle years reflect the new realities: they are unable to find a suitable marriage partner; their marriages increasingly are childless; they are between marriages; they are coping with the problems of stepparenthood; or they are having children only now in their later middle years. It is increasingly rare to see a patient in his or her first marriage. Nonetheless, despite these sociological changes, the ubiquitous oedipal and pre-oedipal conflicts we are familiar with still contribute to individual distress and marital disharmony. As analysts we are always aware of the unique intrapsychic determinants of each person's experience of either marriage or the midlife years. Thus, we turn now to the sparse psychoanalytic writings on marriage.

Psychoanalytic Writings on Marriage

I began this chapter with Freud's 1919 interdiction against the patient's marrying during the course of psychoanalysis. He had earlier observed in a letter to Abraham that psychoanalytic treatment inevitably seemed to bring about the dissolution of marriages. In 1908 he wrote a critique in which he blamed the cultural repression of women for the inevitable failures of most marriages:

> The harmful results which the strict demand for abstinence before marriage produces in women's natures are quite especially apparent. It is clear that education is far from underestimating the task of suppressing a girl's sensuality till her marriage, for it makes use of the most drastic measures. Not only does it forbid sexual intercourse and set a high premium on the preservation of female chastity, but it also protects the young woman from temptation as she grows up, by keeping her ignorant of all the facts of the part she has to play and by not tolerating any impulse of love in her which cannot lead to marriage. The result is that when the girl's parental authorities suddenly allow her to fall in love, she is unequal to this psychical achievement and enters marriage uncertain of her own feelings. In consequence of this artificial retardation in her function of love, she has nothing but disappointments to offer the man who has saved up all his desire for her. In her mental feelings she is still attached to her parents, whose authority has brought about the suppression of her sexuality; and in her physical behavior she shows herself frigid, which deprives the man of any high degree of sexual enjoyment. (1908, pp. 197–198)

A decade later Freud noted the tendency of many patients to act out their neuroses by prematurely forming an inappropriate attachment. He concluded with the observation that "unhappy marriage and physical infirmity are the two things that most often supercede a neurosis. They satisfy, in particular, the sense of guilt (need for punishment) which makes many patients cling so fast to their neuroses. By a foolish choice in marriage, they punish themselves" (1919, p. 163).

It is still the case that patients' neurotic conflicts are superseded and acted out in the arena of family life. Their intrapsychic conflicts are externalized and "lived out" (acted out) with those who are significant to them. Although this is not a new idea, we do not always fully appreciate how our patients defend against anxiety, depression, or symptoms through complex enactments with others.

In the mid-twenties Karen Horney contributed to a volume edited by Keyserling in which she addressed the question of "why people marry given the likelihood of marital unhappiness." Her reply that "we shall find in [marriage] the fulfillment of all the old desires arising out of the oedipus situation in childhood" (1926, p. 319) today sounds like a glib recounting of the Prince Charming fairy tales of childhood. She went on to note the pre-oedipal contributions to the desire for monogamy out of which further difficulties can arise. The derivative of the oral phase, she wrote, "takes the form of the desire to incorporate the object in order to have sole possession of it." To this she added the anal-sadistic demand for possession. She concluded that the opposing polygamous and monogamous instincts arising out of childhood are essentially not resolvable by any general principle. But, she thought, psychoanalytic insight could help moderate the intensity of marital conflicts.

Not until the mid-fifties was the marital bond directly addressed as possibly representing an unconscious fantasy. Stein (1956) noted a frequent unconscious male fantasy that sees the wife as an intrapsychic representation of the man's phallus. It is perhaps a counterpart of a female fantasy of a husband or son representing a replacement of her own lost phallus. Such fantasies, of varying intensities, are layered and undoubtedly latent in most marriages. I would add that they are consciously or unconsciously shared. To the degree that they are *not* shared, but are rather disparate, they can become in themselves a source of conflict.

Why and how do these shared fantasies occur? From earliest childhood aggressive and libidinal impulses are projected onto objects in the outside world. This proclivity continues in varying degrees into adult life as the catastrophic anxieties of childhood are projected onto a spouse or child and thus experienced in an interpersonal context through what Wangh (1962) called the "evocation of a proxy." In this elaboration of a defense first described by Anna Freud, which she called "altruistic surrender," another person is used by the ego for defensive purposes. In keeping with Waelder's (1930) principle of multiple function, id, superego, reality, and repetition-compulsion factors are all held in a delicate equilibrium.

What is minimized in this perspective, as well as in Freud's observation of an unhappy marriage superseding a neurosis, is the requirement of a willing other, a colluding reality. The other shares, for his or her own psychic economy, the fantasies, conflicts, or needs evoked by another self. For this to occur there must be internalized reciprocal or complementary identifications and fantasies (Blum, 1987). Some authors have described this as mutual projective identifications (Zinner, 1976; Dicks, 1967). In its most pathological form such collusive sharing is evident in the clinical picture of a *folie à famille*, where a delusion is shared because of the profound dependency of one or more participants (Wikler, 1980). In its sublimated form the defense subsumes our participation, as artists and audience, in cultural activities such as movies, theater, and dance. We "willingly suspend our disbelief" in order to enjoy and share in the representations of universal unconscious fantasies (Arlow, 1986). In families the sharing of such unconscious conflicts, wishes, and needs is ubiquitous. It determines the choice of the marital partner (Ottenheimer, 1968) and the unfolding of the marriage relationship as well as the quality of parents' interaction with their children (Johnson and Szurek, 1952).

The complementary nature of neuroses in marriages became much more evident when some practitioners, confronted with frequent impasses in analyses, experimented with the treatment of both spouses concurrently or sequentially (although not conjointly) (Oberndorf, 1938; Mittelmann, 1944, 1948). Although the unfolding of the analytic process would be disrupted by the analyst's seeing the patient's spouse, these clinicians were the first to begin to spell out the nature of "unhappy marriages that supersede neuroses" and that at times interfere with individual treatment. Giovacchini (1958, 1961) emphasized that such "external object relations" contributing to treatment resistances could be interpreted and that, when appropriate, the spouse could be referred to another analyst.

More recently some analytically oriented family therapists have variably described the shared externalization of internal conflicts: "neurotic complementarity" (Ackerman, 1967), "marital collusion" (Dicks, 1967; Willi, 1982), "mutual adaptation" (Giovacchini, 1958, 1961), "conscious and unconscious contracts" (Sager, 1976), "the marital quid pro quo" (Jackson, 1965), "equal levels of undifferentiation" (Bowen, 1978), and these concepts characterize the fixed interpersonal patterns of closely related individuals. Object relations theorists (for example, Fairbairn, Guntrip, Winnicott), while still working in the one-to-one psychoanalytic modality, have all along provided conceptual building blocks for the development of an object relations approach to marital and family therapy (Slipp, 1985; Scharff and Scharff, 1987).

Thus, we are noting explicitly what earlier authors from Freud on implicitly noted: the shared participation in neurotic conflicts. The threats of object loss, loss of love, castration, and superego disapproval—the calamities of childhood in all ages and cultures—continue to affect our relations to others, especially those with whom we live and work. The repression of such universal childhood experiences and conflicts leads to their repetition with important others who reciprocally enact similar or complementary unconscious conflicts.

Utilizing Mahler's separation-individuation schema, Blum (1987) has spelled out the ubiquity and structure of reciprocal identifications and shared unconscious fantasies. In an elegant application of this concept he reexamined the marital bond in Shakespeare's *Macbeth* (1986), going beyond the play's more obvious parricidal theme with its punishment of childlessness and death for oedipal crimes. Beginning with Freud's observation that Macbeth and Lady Macbeth are split aspects of one character, Blum points out that they share a phallic narcissistic fantasy with its corollary idealization of masculine power and aggression. Indeed, the very magnitude of the pre-oedipal wishes makes *Macbeth* Shakespeare's bloodiest play.

The two having failed to achieve separate identities, separation-individuation and narcissistic issues are intertwined with oedipal ones. Blum observes that the drama is "replete with reversals, splits, bisexuality, and paired opposite identifications." He continues:

> Macbeth is initially the proxy agent and passive partner to Lady Macbeth's ruthless, phallic narcissism. He tries to cling to the passive position of the child without responsibility, directed by others and external forces. . . . As he disengages from his initially dominant and controlling wife/mother, he emerges as the ruthless, omnipotent tyrant. . . . He wishes for and fears merger and femininity and defends to the death his masculine autonomy. . . . [Lady Macbeth] idealizes only her own possessed, illusory omnipotent penis, her husband/son. Macbeth recognizes her masculine drive, identifies with it. . . . there is a hidden shared fantasy that this son is his mother's phallus and omnipotent object. (p. 592)

Blum then suggests that Macbeth and Lady Macbeth demonstrate reciprocal identifications, a phenomenon commonly seen in marital partners with mutual projection and introjection of primitive aggression and incomplete separation-individuation. The Oedipus complex is here distorted as pre-oedipal issues fuse with oedipal ones.

Narcissistic frustration and its oral greed, envy and rage, ultimately threaten the viability of many marriages. Aggression has reached levels that threaten the stability of the relationship. In the midst of threats of separation, patients turn to individual or couples therapy for assistance. These unhappy marriages, as Freud understood, mask intrapsychic neurotic conflicts. Each party blames the other for the impasse, and depression, anxiety, or symptoms are repressed. The intrapsychic problems have become externalized (Coen, 1989; Lansky, 1980). What is the appropriate treatment for such a couple?

Individual or Marital Treatment

In an earlier review of determinants of therapeutic modality (Sander, 1986), I noted that a patient's choice of modality may defensively reflect one of the conflicts with which he is struggling. Thus a parent unable to separate from an adolescent may insist on family treatment in the hope that the therapist may keep the dreaded separation from occurring. So also a couple fearful of separation may lean toward marital treatment and use the therapist as a kind of "accessory object" (Winnicott, 1951) to minimize or prevent the pain of separation. On the other hand, a patient may choose individual therapy when contemplating divorce. The therapist is here also used as an accessory object to ease the transition to being single again (Whitaker and Miller, 1969). In such instances, the splitting of positive and negative transferences between therapist and spouse can lead to a further deterioration of the marriage. The therapist is often increasingly idealized as the spouse is devalued. I recall one couple, each in analysis, who realized that the times they got along best were during their analysts' vacations. Graller (1981) described in this regard the conjoint treatment of narcissistic couples whose individual analyses have developed this kind of split transference between spouse and analyst.

The more fixed these interpersonal systems, the less self-object differentiation, and the more primitive the defenses, the more one is likely to find shared, often archaic fantasy structures contributing to blaming, impulsivity, and acting out. These systems often require quite active management by other than interpretive interventions. Many of the more active prescriptive family therapy approaches have been developed to deal with families having such disorders as psychoses, addictions, eating disorders, and delinquency.

Toward the other end of the continuum, individuals with healthier levels of functioning and object relations are more differentiated. They utilize higher-level defenses and are usually more accessible to insight-oriented treatment or analysis. Here there are also shared fantasies and reciprocal identifications of a less archaic or intense nature.

Inevitably the interweaving of intrapsyychic and interpersonal conflicts is evident in the ubiquitous distorting attitudes that accompany the transference of early object relationships, usually via projective mechanisms, to current interpersonal pathology. There are usually varying degrees of incomplete separation-individuation, a process Mahler was quick to emphasize unfolds throughout the life cycle. Loewald (1984), in reviewing Mahler's contributions, also pointed to the importance of our turning to "transindividual psychic fields" as a primary datum in clinical theory, research, and practice.

Both as a psychoanalyst and as a family therapist I have come to view conjoint marital treatment as the logical place to begin when the presenting and primary complaints deal with interpersonal conflict. After a period of conjoint treatment, during which such conflicts and ready-made transferences can be interpreted, the partners often become symptomatic and more aware of their internal conflicts. They can then go on to further individual treatment or analysis. In the case examples that follow, the role of such shared unconscious conflicts is illustrated. In one case the marital treatment culminated in a referral for analysis of one of the partners. In the second case an incomplete analysis preceded the marital treatment.

Case Illustrations

RICHARD AND KATHRYN

Richard, a thirty-three-year-old research economist, and Kathryn, a twenty-eight-year-old editor who was pregnant, came for consultation as their marriage of eight years was deteriorating. Their initial crisis concerned the pregnancy, which Kathryn wanted but Richard, feeling unready for fatherhood, did not. When Richard was seven years old his own father had left him with his three-year-old brother, his mother, and his maternal grandmother. He described his family as a powerful matriarchy. He did not see his father again until his adult years. At that time he learned that his mother and grandmother had thrown his father out because of his extramarital affairs.

Kathryn also had a younger brother and had grown up in a female-dominated household with a remote father who was also an economist. It is relevant that the couple had met nine years previously when Kathryn, still in college, had just had an abortion soon after a girl-friend of Richard's also had an abortion. When they met he helped her through, and unconsciously shared, some of "her" guilt feelings about the abortion. During the course of their marital therapy their mutual guilt-ridden infanticidal impulses toward their younger siblings was acknowledged and seen as uniting them. In sharing these impulses they tried to minimize their own guilt feelings. Their guilt, however, over sibling rivalry, as well as their marked oedipal guilt, contributed to a sterile and distant marriage punctuated by Richard's extramarital affairs. It is also relevant that three years prior to their beginning ther-apy Kathryn's younger brother fell to his death down an elevator shaft, and she felt her pregnancy was partly precipitated by a wish to replace him.

She finally decided upon an abortion because, as she put it, she was the stronger of the two, a decision reflecting an unconsciously shared view of men as damaged and of women as strong and powerful. Her view of women as stronger than men repeated the manifest constella-tions of their families of origin while simultaneously serving the intra-psychic balance of their positive and negative oedipal conflicts. Kathryn had alternately identified and competed with her dominant mother as well as her father. She had given up her wish to become an economist when she married and was living out that wish by proxy through her husband.

Richard, on the other hand, warded off a feminine identification by compulsive womanizing, which he curtailed during most of the mari-tal therapy. He also worked in a low-paying academic job despite the availability of more lucrative opportunities in the private sector.

In the fifth month of marital therapy Kathryn suggested that Richard relate a dream he had had that morning. The night of the dream Kathryn had angrily moved out of their bedroom, after realizing that she was not pregnant. (There had almost been another "unplanned" pregnancy.) He dreamed that he was on the terrace of a tall city build-ing where people were playing baseball. There was no railing. When the younger brother of a sister who was present fell off the terrace, Richard tried to get the mother to do something, but she was not inter-ested. Kathryn then spontaneously reported an episode in Richard's childhood. At age six he had been in an auto accident with his father and brother after playing baseball. Richard, sitting between his father and his brother, was protected, but his brother was thrown through the window of the car and was hospitalized for a leg injury. A related later memory of playing baseball with his brother emerged. As the pitcher, Richard had accidentally hit his catcher brother in the head, resulting in the brother's undergoing an operation for a deviated septum.

In the middle of this session I asked Kathryn if she knew of a sister whose brother had fallen. She was stunned that she had not recognized the connection to her own history. I again noted their tendency to repress their own past histories by displacing their conflicts onto each other. I pointed out their shared ambivalence and guilt over their relationships to their younger brothers and asked, why have children when so much can go wrong? She recalled in this context that when her brother died she had said to herself that she would never have children, although within a few months she had begun talking of her wish to become pregnant.

Of interest in this dream report was Kathryn's generally dominant stance in bringing up Richard's dream for examination in the first place. Further, both had used it to repress their own conflicts and displace them onto the other. Such displacements are made more readily when the partners share a similar conflict or past history. The manifest content of Richard's dream picked up on Kathryn's brother's death, while her associations to his dream shifted the focus to *his* brother's childhood accidents from her own brother's death—this all in the context of another lost pregnancy the day before and her rejection of him by moving into another room. She was thus the mother he couldn't get to be interested in the brother (and himself).

After a year of treatment the neurotic basis of the marriage was increasingly clarified without a corresponding strengthening of their marriage. When the neurotic tie is the only significant bond its analysis in either individual or marital treatment will often precede the ending of the marriage. Richard's resumption of extramarital affairs brought the marriage and the therapy to a swift conclusion. He, however, saw his compulsive promiscuity as a problem he wanted to resolve, and I referred him to a psychoanalytic clinic where he is presently in his eighth year of analysis. Kathryn felt less need for intensive treatment and continued with me once weekly for about six months during which time she began a new relationship that included a similar pattern of tolerating the friend's infidelity. Her repeated need to lose to other women, reflecting a deeper unconscious homosexual tie to them, again illustrates Freud's view that unhappy relationships can supersede a neurotic conflict.

This couple's shared unconscious conflicts interfered, in their middle years, with tasks generally begun in the preceding years—the formation of a stabilizing marriage and of a family. As so often happens in our time, the culturally supported delay of such life-cycle events was reinforced by underlying neurotic conflicts requiring, in this instance, couple therapy that evolved into individual treatment.

VIRGINIA AND REYNOLDS

Virginia, a thirty-nine-year-old middle management bank employee, had had two years of a control analysis in her late twenties for her depression and inability to find a suitable mate. Her continued masochistic relationship with a married lawyer while she was a paralegal in his firm, however, had ultimately raised questions as to her analyzability. The analysis was terminated around the time that Reynolds, her married friend, also now thirty-nine, left his wife and six-year-old son to live with her.

When they came to consult me they had lived together for nine years and been married for one. A pattern of interaction, repeatedly enacted by the two, was the only presenting complaint; it had led to Virginia's wish to separate, a phone call to her former analyst, and the referral for marital therapy.

Once to three times per week Reynolds would come home anywhere from two to seven hours after a prearranged agreed-upon time. He always went to the same neighborhood bar with a masculine-sounding name that catered to sports fans and writers. This was in keeping with his general character and past. He had fished and hunted as a youth in the South before going to college and law school and becoming a New York lawyer. His first marriage to a law student had deteriorated rapidly after the birth of a son, Amos, while both actively pursued their respective careers. At the time of the consultation Amos, now fifteen, was living with his mother and having school difficulties which culminated in his going to boarding school. Aside from the presenting complaint, Reynolds and Virginia got along quite well, sharing friends and a pleasure in cooking—especially so on weekends, which tended to be romantic reconciliations after the more conflicted weeks.

As I regularly do in initial consultations with couples, I elicited a biographical sketch from each of them. She had also been raised in the South, where her parents separated when she was six. Her father, a lawyer, then moved to another city, and she had seen him only on holidays and during the summer. She lived with her mother and a brother, who was a year younger, until she went to college. She felt bitterly deprived of fathering and had been disappointed that her first analyst was a female; she continues to long for a perfect father to care for her. Her longing for and anger at her father is reenacted each time Reynolds comes home late.

Reynold's father died of a heart attack at the age of fifty-two, when Reynolds was ten. He and his sister, two years younger than he, lived with their schoolteacher mother until he went to college. Neither his mother nor Virginia's mother ever remarried.

During the first three consultations, despite relatively active questioning on my part, Reynolds and Virginia asked whether I would be providing more structure and input. Although transference (to the therapist) interpretations are not always initially as central in marital as they are in individual therapy, in this instance the history and initial presentation and quickly emerging shared transference were so manifestly congruent that I made the observation that their shared loss of a father in childhood was underlining their problems with each other and showed itself in their wish for more participation from me. Shared or complementary conflicts are regularly the determinants of marital interaction and tensions, although not always as transparently as was the case with this couple. There were many overdetermined aspects and multiple functions of their repetitious and monosymptomatic marital disorder.

Their intense confrontations over his repeated lateness served a number of functions for each of them. The pattern itself served each of their needs to *repeat* the loss of the father, followed each time by his return. He projected feelings of "squirrelly hormonal" feminine vulnerability and father hunger onto her and identified with his "outdoorsman" abandoning father. At the same time he was punished each week for displacing his father. Each week their marriage was consummated on the weekend and guiltily undone the following week. Well into the treatment Virginia dreamed of having affairs, including one with me. This was interpreted as Reynolds's facilitating the return of the oedipal father by repeatedly abandoning her to me. This pattern was especially pronounced on the nights before their morning sessions with me at which he would arrive bleary-eyed, sleepy, and inaudible. Thus mother/wife was reunited with father/analyst and Reynolds reassumed the role of the son.

The oscillating quality of their relationship also recapitulated some aspect of their relationships to their respective opposite-sex siblings. She was particularly close to and protective of her younger brother, whereas he was quite distanced from his younger sister. Their need to repeat their respective sibling constellations further added to their weekly confrontations. She wanted closeness and he, distance, in relation to the spouse as sibling.

Shared fantasies and complementary conflicts are not always present at all levels, however. In the case of this couple Reynolds also had claustrophobic anxieties. He feared being swallowed up by what he experienced as Virginia's voracious needs. As Reynolds's defenses were worked with he began to acknowledge some of his own needs, and he became less removed and more accessible. In the middle of the second year of treatment he reported a first treatment dream, in which he killed a deer while hunting with a male friend. In the second part of the dream he was escaping punishment by making a public offering before some Orwellian dictator. Before I could suggest the theme of punishment for an oedipal crime, they reported that on the night of the dream Virginia had joined him for a special occasion sponsored by the bar—the first time she had done so during the entire course of the therapy. At the bar there was mention of an acquaintance who died of a heart attack at age fifty-two (the age his father was at his death). Reynolds thought my interpretation of the dream as suggesting guilt over his oedipal success (represented by his going to the bar with his wife) was ingenious, but with characteristic skepticism and rebelliousness, he thought perhaps it was "not correct." As the session unfolded further he connected his fishing practice of catching and releasing trout as similar to his catching and releasing his wife each week. In effect he was ambivalent that his wife was with him at the bar. There was a not quite conscious acknowledgment that the deer he shot in the dream might have represented his "dear" wife, thus expressing a more repressed homosexual wish to be united with his father and hunting partner at the expense of his wife/mother.

A few sessions later some reconstruction of his childhood need to distance himself from his grief-stricken, but otherwise stoical, schoolteacher mother was possible. It had been his eight-year-old sister who had stayed with the mother when she banged her head in despair. Meanwhile the ten-year-old new "man of the house" would take off on his bicycle to avoid all that "feminine emotionality." This was a pattern that had continued to the present, as Reynolds was compelled to escape from the anticipated engulfment of his mother's grief. Virginia found in the abandoning husband a situation in which she could repeat her experience of loss of her father. Thus the unconscious fit perpetuated the cycle.

Interpretation and working through, however, modified the mutual pattern so that the marriage could continue in ways more gratifying and less threatening to intrapsychic vulnerabilities. Termination of analysis was warranted after two years and shortly after their purchase of a country house which was to be the only "child" they were actually to share. It remains to be seen whether their decision to remain childless contains the seeds of later strains as menopause approaches in the later middle years.

Conclusion and Implications

In a rather casual aside, Freud observed in 1919 that unhappy marriages can supersede neuroses while satisfying an individual's need for unconscious punishment. Today we can be more precise in noting the almost universal presence in unhappy marriages of shared conscious and unconscious fantasies and conflicts. Also, we might see interpersonal conflict not as superseding a neurosis but rather as the inevitable resonance of neurotic processes with an external reality that fits the neurotic structure. Individual treatment in many such cases is often not possible at the start. Conjoint treatment can at times resolve the presenting conflict; at other times it can be preparatory for analysis or individual treatment, as patients become aware of their externalizing defenses as well as experience more directly their underlying internal conflicts.

Unfortunately, one of the many complex reasons that fewer patients are seeking analysis these days is that their neuroses are imbedded in marital disorders that are increasingly being treated by nonanalytically trained therapists. As a result, these masked neuroses are being neither diagnosed nor adequately treated.

Aside from the technical consideration of beginning exploration via conjoint treatment, there are theoretical implications of this contribution. For some time now there has been controversy over the relative weight of intrapsychic versus environmental factors in the etiology of neuroses. Although this controversy generally is more polemical than illuminating, I have noted in this chapter the frequency with which "external reality" is, in part, informed by a significant "other's" psychic reality and that often these lead to shared internal *and* external "realities." With such reciprocal internalizations the distinction between external reality and internal "psychic" reality is not as well defined as we usually assume. In psychoses the distinction is so blurred that such shared conflicts and wishes parallel the loss of self and ego boundaries. In higher level clinical states they can contribute to sadomasochistic struggles for power as well as Freud's early observation—that is, the shared need for punishment for oedipal and pre-oedipal wishes.

REFERENCES

Ackerman, N. 1967. *Treating the troubled family.* New York: Basic Books.

Aries, P. 1962. *Centuries of childhood: A social history of family life.* New York: Vintage Books.

Arlow, J. 1986. The poet as prophet: A psychoanalytic perspective. *Psychoanalytic Quarterly* 55:53–68.

Blum, H. P. 1986. Psychoanalytic studies and "Macbeth": Shared fantasy and reciprocal identification. In *The psychoanalytic study of the child,* 41:585–599. New Haven: Yale University Press.

———. 1987. Shared fantasy and reciprocal identification: General considerations and gender disorder. In *Unconscious fantasy: Myth and reality.* Ed. H. P. Blum et al. New York: International Universities Press.

Bowen, M. 1978. *Family therapy in clinical practice.* New York: Jason Aronson.

Coen, S. J. 1989. Intolerance of responsibility for internal conflict. *Journal of the American Psychoanalytic Association* (in press).

Dicks, H. V. 1967. *Marital tensions.* New York: Basic Books.

Erikson, E. 1950. *Childhood and society.* New York: W. W. Norton.

Freud, S. 1908. Civilized sexual morality and modern nervous illness. In *Standard edition,* 9:179–204.

———. 1919. Lines of advance in psychoanalytic therapy. In *Standard edition,* 17:159–168.

Giovacchini, P. 1958. Mutual adaptation in various object relations. *International Journal of Psychoanalysis* 39:547–554.

———. 1961. Resistance and external object relations. *International Journal of Psychoanalysis* 42:246–254.

Gould, R. 1972. The phases of adult life: A study in developmental psychology. *American Journal of Psychiatry* 129:521–531.

Graller, J. 1981. Adjunctive marital therapy. In *The annual of psychoanalysis,* 9: 175–187. New York: International Universities Press.

Horney, K. 1926. The problem of the monogamous ideal. In *The book of marriage.* Ed. H. Keyserling. New York: Harcourt, Brace.

Jackson, D. D. 1965. Family rules: The marital quid pro quo. *Archives of General Psychiatry* 12:589–594.

Johnson, A., and Szurek, S. A. 1952. The genesis of antisocial acting out in children and adults. *Psychoanalytic Quarterly* 21.

Keyserling, H., ed. 1926. *The book of marriage*. New York: Harcourt, Brace.

Lansky, M. 1980. On blame. *International Journal of Psychoanalysis and Psychotherapy* 8:429–456.

Loewald, H. 1984. Review of the selected papers of Margaret S. Mahler. *Journal of the American Psychoanalytic Association* 32:165–175.

Mittelmann, B. 1944. Complementary neurotic reactions in intimate relationships. *Psychoanalytic Quarterly* 13:479–491.

———. 1948. The concurrent analysis of married couples. *Psychoanalytic Quarterly* 17:182–197.

Oberndorf, C. 1938. Psychoanalysis of married couples. *Psychoanalytic Review* 25:453–475.

Ottenheimer, L. 1968. Psychodynamics of the choice of a mate. In *The marriage relationship*. Ed. I. Alger and S. Rosenbaum. New York: Basic Books.

Parsons, T. 1955. The American family: Its relations to personality and to the social structure. In *Family socialization and interaction process*. Ed. T. Parsons, R. F. Bales, et al. Glencoe, Ill.: Free Press.

Sager, C. 1976. *Marriage contracts and couple therapy*. New York: Brunner-Mazel.

Sander, F. M. 1979. *Individual and family therapy: Toward an integration*. New York: Jason Aronson.

———. 1986. Family or individual therapy: The determinants of modality choice. *Hillside Hospital Journal of Psychiatry* 7(1):37–41.

Scharff, D. E., and Scharff, J. S. 1987. *Object relations family therapy*. New York: Jason Aronson.

Slipp, S. 1985. *Object relations: A dynamic bridge between individual and family treatment*. New York: Jason Aronson.

Stein, M. 1956. The marriage bond. *Psychoanalytic Quarterly* 25:238–259.

Vaillant, G. 1977. *Adaptation to life*. Boston: Little, Brown.

Waelder, R. 1930. The principle of multiple function. *Psychoanalytic Quarterly* 5:45–62.

Wangh, M. 1962. The evocation of a proxy. In *The psychoanalytic study of the child*, 17:451–477. New York: International Universities Press.

Whitaker, C., and Miller, M. 1969. A re-evaluation of "psychiatric help" when divorce impends. *American Journal of Psychiatry* 126:611–616.

Wikler, L. 1980. Folie à famille. *Family Process* 19:257.

Willi, J. 1982. *Couples in collusion*. New York: Jason Aronson.

Winnicott, D. W. 1951. Transitional objects and transitional phenomena. *International Journal of Psychoanalysis* 34:229–242.

Zinner, J. 1976. The implications of projective identification for marital interaction. In *Contemporary marriage: Structure, dynamics, and therapy*. Ed. H. Grunebaum and J. Christ, 293–308. Boston: Little, Brown.

Part III

The Biological-Psychoanalytic Interface

· 13 ·

BIOLOGICAL CONSIDERATIONS
IN THE MIDDLE YEARS

STEVEN P. ROOSE, M.D.

HERBERT PARDES, M.D.

As the middle years begin, one becomes aware of subtle, often disquieting changes in the body: our reflexes are a little slower, our muscle tone seems harder to maintain and weight distressingly easier to accumulate, our hair takes leave, our eyes focus with less acuity. In sum, it is as if one feels a chill from a fall wind, inexplicably blowing on an August day. Discussions of the biological considerations in middle years often focus on these subtle decrements in body function and how they are translated into psychological terms as losses, narcissistic hurts, or new realities, with a consequent impact on self-esteem, ego ideal, and so on. But, considering the question in this way once again creates a kind of mind/body split: the deterioration of the body and the mind's reaction to it. Rather, if one considers the problem from the perspective of the mind *in* the body—that is, the brain—a major question would be, what (if anything) of significance is happening to the structure of the brain during the middle years?

It may be well to state explicitly some of the assumptions on which this chapter is based. It is not known how the brain operates so as to produce all of what are considered to be functions of the mind, whether they be thought, creativity, affect, or memory. Nonetheless, there is consensus that the brain is the organ of the mind or, as Eric Kandel (1979) has said, that "what we conceive of as our mind is an expression of the functioning of our brain". This is not a new concept, for it was long ago that Hippocrates said, "From the brain, and from the brain only, arise our pleasure, joys, laughter and jests, as well as our sorrows, pain, grief and tears". Thus, if there are significant changes in the structure of the brain, one would expect that they would have significant impact on the mind. Actually, this is an equation that is well demonstrated when the brain has suffered a gross trauma such as a stroke or a tumor. It has long been recognized that such disruption of brain function can produce and, indeed, first present as subtle or gross changes in personality, cognition, or mood. More specifically, one can consider whether there are significant changes in the brain that occur as a normal process of aging during the middle years and, if so, whether this might have implications for both our understanding of psychological development in this part of the life cycle and the treatment of patients.

This chapter will concentrate on two points. The first is that there is a structural deterioration that occurs during the middle years in specific areas in the brain stem whose normal function involves the experience of anxiety, arousal, and fear. Juxtaposed to this loss of brain function, the second point is that other areas of the brain are continuously changing, not deteriorating, in structure. This would imply that, contrary to the popular conception that advancing age is equivalent to rigidity, the brain and presumably the mind remain open to change and learning in rather significant ways throughout the middle years.

The Effects of Aging on the Locus Coeruleus

Anatomically, the brain is separated into three major components, the brain stem, the cortex, and the cerebellum. In terms of evolution, the cortex is the most recently developed structure and the one generally associated with cognition, learning, and other complex functions. The brain stem has been seen as providing sophisticated "housekeeping" functions—for example, regulating sleep/wake cycles and integrating complex motor functions. Also contained within the brain stem, however, are areas that play a major role in such complex mental functions as anxiety and dreaming.

Specifically, there is an area in the brain stem called the locus coeruleus which has drawn the attention of neurobiologists because of its apparent importance as a center involved in arousal, anxiety, and fear and its accessibility to study in humans through pharmacological probes. Located at the base of the fourth ventricle, it is a small area containing fewer than twenty thousand cells (Van Dongen, 1981). The locus coeruleus, however, appears to be the most extensively projecting neuronal system in the central nervous system. Its function in monkeys and in man has been elegantly elucidated by groups at Yale, notably Gene Redmond (Redmond, 1977, 1981; Redmond et al., 1976) and Dennis Charney (Charney et al., 1982a, 1982b) and, in California by Floyd Bloom and his coworkers, Foote and Aston-Jones (Foote et al., 1983). Redmond et al. (1976) demonstrated that electrical stimulation of the locus coeruleus in monkeys elicited behavioral responses and physiological measures that are characteristic of fear or anxiety. Interestingly, moderate levels of activation of the locus coeruleus are correlated with attentiveness and vigilance to relevant stimuli (Redmond, 1977). Conversely, abnormally low levels of function of the locus coeruleus induced by electrolytic lesions are characterized by inattentiveness, impulsiveness, carelessness, recklessness, and the failure of external threats to elicit the expected fear response (Redmond et al., 1976).

In humans it is possible to study the effect of stimulating or inhibiting the activity of the locus coeruleus by the use of certain drugs that are specific alpha-2 agonists (clonidine) or antagonists (yohimbine). Through either stimulation (by agonists) or inhibition (by antagonists) of the alpha-2 receptor system, the locus coeruleus can be either "turned on" or "turned off." When given drugs that stimulate the locus coeruleus, normal human volunteers reliably report feeling anxious (Charney et al., 1982a). This effect can be reversed by drugs that are known to inhibit the locus coeruleus (Redmond, 1981). Thus, there is strong evidence that in humans as well as in monkeys, the locus coeruleus plays a significant role in the experience of anxiety. However, although there are compelling data that the locus coeruleus is a necessary, even pivotal, component of the behavioral and physiological expression of anxiety, it is not the only brain system critically associated with anxiety, nor is the expression of anxiety its only function. Thus, it is somewhat misleading, although partly correct, to call the locus coeruleus the "anxiety system," since expression of anxiety requires other brain systems and the locus coeruleus is involved in functions other than anxiety (Foote et al., 1983). As Gene Redmond (1977) has said, "Perhaps alarm system is a better name for the locus coeruleus' apparent function, since alarm function conveys an adaptive nature, the deficit which would be present if the system were missing, and the unpleasantness of its ringing loudly or too long."

Besides its normal function as an anxiety or alarm system, the locus coeruleus—actually, the dysfunction of the locus coeruleus—has been implicated in a number of discrete pathological entities, namely, panic attack syndrome (Charney et al., 1982a), drug addiction (Charney et al., 1982b), and, more speculatively, bulimia (Roose et al., 1987). The data are most compelling for panic attack syndrome because agents that cause intense firing of the locus coeruleus can produce panic attack in patients with the syndrome (Charney et al., 1982a). Conversely, all the drugs that have been found to be effective in treating panic attack syndrome are known to quiet the locus coeruleus (Liebowitz et al., 1984).

There is speculation that there is a cluster of psychiatric disorders in which dysfunctional hyperactivity of the locus coeruleus leads to either symptoms of anxiety itself or a behavior such as drug addiction, in an attempt to attenuate that anxiety.

Thus, in summary, the locus coeruleus is a small area in the brain stem which, because of its extensive network of connections to other areas in the brain, exerts a significant influence on a number of complex mental functions both cognitive and affective. Its normal functioning is associated with anxiety, and its pathological hyperactivity is strongly associated with panic attack disorder and speculatively with drug addiction and bulimia as well.

An awareness of the critical importance of the locus coeruleus is an essential backdrop against which to consider what happens to this specific area during the middle years. The aging process in the locus coeruleus can be understood from two interrelated but distinct perspectives: functional capacity and structural integrity. In the brain the predominant mode of communication between two cells is through substances called neurotransmitters which chemically communicate a message of excitement or inhibition from one cell to its neighbor. Norepinephrine is such a neurotransmitter, but it is notable that only 1 percent of the cells in the brain use norepinephrine as a neurotransmitter. Furthermore, the vast majority (70 percent) of the cells that use norepinephrine as the primary neurotransmitter are concentrated in the locus coeruleus.

There are critical steps in both the synthesis and the metabolism of norepinephrine that are regulated by the availability of enzymes. Specifically, in the process of synthesis the rate-limiting enzyme—that is, the enzyme that determines the rate of production—is tyrosine hydroxylase. In the central nervous system, norepinephrine is metabolized predominantly by the enzyme monoamine oxidase B. Thus, if there were significant changes in either of these enzymes, tyrosine hydroxylase or MAO B, it would significantly affect either the rate of synthesis or the rate of metabolism of norepinephrine and consequently would significantly affect the availability of this neurotransmitter. This, in turn, would have a significant impact on cells that depend on norepinephrine as a neurotransmitter—the cells in the locus coeruleus. Through the remarkable dedication of certain investigators such as Lucien Cote, data have become available on what happens to these critical enzymes as people age (Cote and Kremzner, 1983; McGeer, 1978; Pradhan, 1980). Gathering such data is exceedingly difficult because these enzymes decay rapidly after death, thereby necessitating immediate access to autopsy material. Despite these logistical difficulties, Cote and others have been able to demonstrate that the critical enzyme tyrosine hydroxylase, in the synthesis of norepinephrine, undergoes significant reduction in activity specifically between the ages of forty and sixty years. This reduction in enzyme activity would imply that there is less capacity to synthesize the neurotransmitter. In contrast, the enzyme monoamine oxidase, which is responsible for the metabolism of norepinephrine, actually has a significant increase in its activity during the years forty to sixty (Robinson, 1975). Thus, there is a pincer movement in which the availability of neurotransmitter is compromised by both a decrease in synthesis and an acceleration of metabolism. Such a decrease in neurotransmitter availability raises the possibility that the activity of the locus coeruleus itself may be significantly attenuated starting in the middle years.

Besides a decrease in functional capacity, other striking changes happen to the cells that make up the locus coeruleus beginning at the age of forty. In cells that predominantly use norepinephrine as a neurotransmitter there is a progressive, age-related increase in neuromelanin, a substance that accumulates within the cells (Graham, 1979; Mann and Yates, 1974, 1979). The general view is that neuromelanin is an inert waste product of norepinephrine metabolism (Graham, 1979). Therefore, it would be expected that as the years increase, the amount of this "garbage" within the cells would also increase. By the fourth decade of life, there is a striking increase in the area of the individual cell that is occupied by this inert neuromelanin pigment (Graham, 1979). A consequence is that the cell loses its internal structural integrity, its capacity to function, and eventually dies (Mann et al., 1980; Wree et al., 1980). Thus, the accumulation of neuromelanin would imply a decrease in locus coeruleus activity (Mann et al., 1980).

Furthermore, the progressive accumulation of neuromelanin pigment within cells is compatible with data on the number of viable cells still present within the locus coeruleus as age increases. The actual number of intact cells in the locus coeruleus decreases dramatically in direct proportion to the increase in neuromelanin (Wree et al., 1980; Vijayashankar and Brody, 1979; Tomlinson et al., 1981).

Thus, three obviously interrelated but independently collected sets of data, (1) the changes in enzyme capacity, (2) the increase in neuromelanin, and (3) the decrease in the number of cells, support the hypothesis that as we are entering our middle years, the locus coeruleus is beginning its senescence.

If, in fact, this is the case what could the clinical implications of such an event be? Before proceeding with clinical speculations, it is prudent to emphasize some cautions. In general, neurobiological data, such as those just discussed, and psychological phenomena are, for the most part, best considered as trains running on parallel tracks. It is safer to be satisfied to look over to the other train rather than to reach out and make direct contact, except at rare moments when both trains are stopped at a station. Furthermore, whatever happens to the locus coeruleus happens concurrently with many other biological, psychological, and social events. Therefore, it would be reductionistic to try to understand any psychological or behavioral phenomenon as the product of only one biological event. Specifically, one should be very cautious about equating the "anxiety" generated in the locus coeruleus to any one of the multiple meanings that the word *anxiety* has in analytic metapsychology, including the concept of signal anxiety.

Nonetheless, it is intriguing to consider certain clinical observations that have been made repeatedly about character and age while keeping a biological perspective in mind. Many authors have commented that people observe a change in themselves or, more accurately, that it is often first observed by others around that person. This has variously been described as a decrease in intensity, a softening of tone, and a reduction in anger, anxiety, and impulsivity. All these subtle shifts are incorporated into the ultimate description of the phenomenon— "mellowing."

This mellowing phenomenon may be reflected in the data from George Vaillant's study (1976) of the natural history of male psychological health, in which he tried to document and define this clinical observation more precisely. He proposed that there was an orderly shift during the adult life cycle from immature defenses (passive aggression, hypochondriasis, acting out) to more mature defenses (suppression, altruism, sublimation). Not surprisingly, the predominant use of mature defenses correlated well with career achievement, stable object relations, psychological health, and life satisfaction in general. Of course, not all men develop in this way; it is important to emphasize that the perpetuation of immature defenses is not unusual and perhaps is as common as development in the other direction. But it was the shift to mature defenses that led Vaillant (1976) to conclude that "over the course of the adult life cycle, character is dynamic."

Obviously, many internal and external factors must contribute to such a change in character. One of those factors must certainly be a biological shift, and it would be hard to conceive how the deterioration of the locus coeruleus would not be a significant part of such a shift.

Furthermore, it is compelling to consider what effect the deterioration of the locus coeruleus might have on the course of more specific diagnoses, such as addictive disorders, panic attacks, generalized anxiety disorder, and, more speculatively, bulimia. All these disorders are illnesses of younger people; the age of onset is usually in the twenties. It has been clinically observed, although not well documented, that as patients get older, in many cases the illness "burns out." This has been noted even for such entities as pathological narcissism, and, as Otto Kernberg has observed, "Some middle-aged narcissistic personalities may 'settle down' in a relatively routine, strangely flat, and nondescript social life. A 'burning out' seems to have occurred" (1980, p. 149). As these disorders lessen in intensity, patients may become more accessible to analytically oriented treatment.

A further association between changes in the locus coeruleus and psychological state can be drawn within the concept of the well-documented observation that depression increases with age (Weissman et al., 1982). Deficient norepinephrine and dysfunction of the locus coeruleus have long been implicated in depressive disorders (Van Dongen, 1981). Thus, if the deterioration of the locus coeruleus does play a part in the psychological changes seen in middle years, its effect may not be restricted to anxiety alone.

Brain Plasticity and the Capacity for Change

In contrast to the deterioration of certain brain areas, the second point of this chapter is to highlight that the brain remains a vital, structurally plastic, and adaptable organ throughout the middle years. Psychoanalysts were not the only group to believe that critical development occurred predominantly in the early years of life. Neuropathologists and neurobiologists also held to the concept that most of what was important in brain development was essentially complete in early childhood. The brain was then essentially fixed in structure, with the only significant change being the deterioration associated with aging. Thus, the brain was condemned to a life of development, rigidity, and decay. However, new data on the plasticity of cell structure and the conditioning of cell response stand in opposition to this conclusion.

The structure of the brain cell itself contains (1) dendrites, short, branching fibers that receive nerve impulses from other cells and conduct them toward the cell body, and (2) axons, which conduct impulses away from the cell body. At the end of the axon is the presynaptic terminal, at which are concentrated the synaptic vesicles containing the cell-specific neurotransmitter. It is by release of the neurotransmitter from the synaptic vesicles into the synaptic cleft (the space between cells) that one cell communicates a message of stimulation or inhibition to another cell. It has long been recognized that in response to peripheral nerve damage, the neurons in the central nervous system can acquire new response properties so as to restore orderly communication between the periphery and the central nervous system (Brenowitz and Pubols, 1981). There have been two types of explanation for this phenomenon: one is that previously formed but as yet dormant connections now become activated (Kass et al., 1983); second is that entirely new connections are formed by virtue of cell growth, particularly at the parts of the cell that are critical for communication with other cells (Kass et al., 1983).

More recently, a series of remarkably complex and elegant experiments have highlighted that alteration in cell structure occurs not only in response to major trauma; in fact, significant changes occur as part of normal function on a literally day-to-day basis. The investigators, Dale Purves and colleagues (1986), were able to isolate individual nerve cells in superior cervical ganglia (a collection of nerve cells in the neck) in mice. They identified individual cells and injected them with dye in order to be able to take a photograph of their structures. Then, from three to ninety days later, they were able to identify the same individual cell and rephotograph it. The results of this procedure dramatically illustrated that extensive morphological changes occurred in these cells between study days. Some dendrite structures disappeared and new ones were formed, thus indicating that structural plasticity is perhaps the norm rather than the exception for nerve cells.

Besides this dramatic morphological plasticity, the functional response of an individual cell can be made more or less intense. Eric Kandel and his colleagues (1983), in work of inestimable importance, have illustrated the biochemical mechanism by which a cell can modify its response during classical aversive conditioning. Using the snail aplysia, Kandel constructed experimental paradigms to produce states of chronic and anticipatory anxiety. Both forms of anxiety are expressed through enhanced cellular connections that rely on modifications of synaptic transmission. Augmented neurotransmitter release is accomplished through depressing a potassium channel, thus increasing the influx of calcium, which helps prolong cell excitation.

Kandel's work implies that there is a basic "molecular grammar" the composites of which can be combined in different ways, thereby expressing different phenology. The modification of neurotransmitter release is a process that occurs over time and explicitly illustrates the power of experience in modifying brain function. This process is a further example that the brain cell maintains a functional capacity to adapt to changing realities.

What possible relevance does cell plasticity have to psychoanalytic treatment? To consider this question it must be appreciated that at some point learning, whether it takes place in psychotherapy or another setting, must ultimately involve the alteration of currently existing neuronal pathways to allow for the expression of new patterns of behavior. As Kandel (1979) wrote, "In so far as psychotherapy works, it works by acting on brain function, not on single synapses, but on synapses nevertheless. Indeed, I would argue that it is only so far as our words produce changes in each other's brains that psychotherapeutic intervention produces changes in patients' minds."

Freud's view on the potential for change during middle years was somewhat more pessimistic. In his paper on psychotherapy written in 1904, he said, "The age of patients has this much importance in determining their fitness for psychoanalytic treatment, that, on the one hand, near or above the age of 50 the elasticity of the mental processes, on which the treatment depends, is as a rule lacking." Nevertheless, the evidence that there is significant plasticity in the cell must encourage the view that at least a psychotherapeutic, if not a psychoanalytic, treatment is a possible endeavor well into the middle years.[1]

In summary, this chapter has focused on two biological considerations that may have special relevance for the understanding and treatment of patients in their middle years. First is the concept that certain parts of the brain are encoded to begin significant deterioration during

---

1. Since 1975, the analytic literature on treatment of older patients has supported this contention. Several authors, notably P. King (1980), A. M. Sandler (1978), and W. A. Myers (1984), have published extensive case material on psychoanalytically oriented psychotherapy and psychoanalysis of patients in their sixties and seventies. The psychotherapeutic process itself—for example, transference, countertransference, dream interpretation—and the range of outcomes from significant character change to interrupted and unsuccessful treatments are similar to those noted for younger patients.

the middle years. This may have an impact on character and defenses and, by lessening the intensity of certain psychiatric disorders, may make a whole new group of patients more amenable to a psychoanalytic treatment. Second, the central nervous system maintains plasticity and flexibility well into the middle years, perhaps a biological precondition for a successful psychotherapeutic experience. Thus in the middle years, whether the deterioration of the locus coeruleus produces new problems or new possibilities, we maintain the capacity to adapt to new realities.

REFERENCES

Brenowitz, G. L., and Pubols, L. M. 1981. Increased receptive field sizes of dorsal horn neurons following chronic spinal cord hemisections in cats. *Brain Research* 216:45–49.

Charney, D. S.; Heninger, G. R.; and Sternberg, D. E. 1982a. Assessment of alpha-2 adrenergic autoreceptor function in humans: Effects of oral yohimbine. *Life Sciences* 30:2033–2041.

Charney, D. S.; Riordan, C. E.; Kleber, H. D. et al. 1982b. Clonidine and naltrexone: A safe, effective and rapid treatment of abrupt withdrawal from methadone therapy. *Archives of General Psychiatry* 39:1327–1332.

Cote, L. J., and Kremzner, L. T. 1983. Biochemical changes in normal aging in human brain. In *The Dementias*. Ed. R. Mayeux and W. G. Rosen. New York: Raven Press.

Foote, S. L.; Bloom, F. E.; and Aston-Jones, G. 1983. Nucleus locus ceruleus: New evidence of anatomical and physiological specificity. *Physiological Reviews* 63:844–914.

Freud, S. 1904. On psychotherapy. In *Standard edition*, 7:264.

Graham, D. G. 1979. On the origin and significance of neuromelanin. *Archives of Pathology and Laboratory Medicine* 103:359–362.

Kandel, E. R. 1979. Psychotherapy and the single synapse: The impact of psychiatric thought on neurobiologic research. *New England Journal of Medicine* 301:1028–1037.

———. 1983. From metapsychology to molecular biology: Explorations into the nature of anxiety. *American Journal of Psychiatry* 140:1277–1293.

Kass, J. H., Merzenich, M. M., and Killackey, H. P. 1983. The reorganization of somatosensory cortex following peripheral nerve damage in adult and developing mammals. *Annual Review of Neuroscience* 6:325–356.

Kernberg, O. F. 1980. *Internal world and external reality: Object relations theory applied*. New York: Jason Aronson.

King, P. 1980. The life cycle as indicated by the nature of the transference in the psychoanalysis of the middle-aged and elderly. *International Journal of Psychoanalysis* 61:153–160.

Liebowitz, M. R.; Quitkin, F. M.; Stewart, J. W.; McGrath, P. J.; et al. 1984. Phenelzine v imipramine in atypical depression: A preliminary report. *Archives of General Psychiatry* 41:669–677.

Mann, D. M. A.; Lincoln, J.; Yates, P. O.; Stamp, J. E.; and Toper, S. 1980. Changes in the monamine containing neurones of the human CNS in senile dementia. *British Journal of Psychiatry* 136:533–541.

Mann, D. M. A., and Yates, P. O. 1974. Lipoprotein pigments: Their relationship to aging in the human nervous system. II. The melanin content of pigmented nerve cells. *Brain* 97:489–498.

————. 1979. The effects of aging on the pigmented nerve cells of the human locus coeruleus and substantia nigra. *Acta Neuropathologica* 47:93–97.

McGeer, E. C. 1978. Aging and neurotransmitter metabolism in the human brain. In *Alzheimer's disease: Senile dementia and related disorders*. Vol. 7, *Aging*. Ed. R. Katzman, R. D. Terry, and K. L. Bick. New York: Raven Press.

Myers, W. A. 1984. *Dynamic therapy of the older patient*. New York: Jason Aronson.

Pradhan, S. N. 1980. Central neurotransmitters and aging. *Life Sciences* 26:1643–1656.

Purves, D.; Hadley, R. D.; and Voyvodic, J. T. 1986. Dynamic changes in the dendritic geometry of individual neurons visualized over periods of up to three months in the superior cervical ganglion of living mice. *Journal of Neuroscience* 6:1051–1060.

Redmond, D. E., Jr. 1977. Alterations in the function of the nucleus locus coeruleus: A possible model for studies of anxiety. In *Animal models in psychiatry and neurology*. Ed. I. Hanin and E. Usdin. New York: Pergamon Press.

————. 1981. Clonidine and the primate locus coeruleus: Evidence suggesting anxiolytic and anti-withdrawal effects. In *Psychopharmacology of clonidine*. Ed. H. Lal and S. Fielding. New York: Alan R. Liss.

Redmond, D. E., Jr.; Huang, Y. H.; Snyder, D. R. et al. 1976. Behavioral effects of stimulation of the nucleus locus coeruleus in the stump-tailed monkey Macaca arctoides. *Brain Research* 116:502–510.

Robinson, D. S. 1975. Changes in monoamine oxidase and monoamines with human development and aging. *Federation Proceedings* 34:103–107.

Roose, S. P.; Walsh, B. T.; Lindy, D. C.; Gladis, M.; and Glassman, A. H. 1987. Biological probes of anxiety in bulimia. In *Psychobiology of bulimia*. Ed. J. I. Hudson and H. G. Pope, 177–184. Washington, D.C.: American Psychiatric Association Press.

Sandler, A. M. 1978. Psychoanalysis in later life: Problems in the psychoanalysis of an aging narcissistic patient. *Journal of Geriatric Psychiatry* 11:5–36.

Tomlinson, B. E., Irving, D., and Blessed, G. 1981. Cell loss in the locus coeruleus in senile dementia of Alzheimer type. *Journal of the Neurological Sciences* 49:419–428.

Vaillant, G. E. 1976. Natural history of male psychological health. V. The relation of choice of ego mechanisms of defense to adult adjustment. *Archives of General Psychiatry* 33:535–545.

Van Dongen, P. A. M. 1981. The human locus coeruleus in neurology and psychiatry. *Progress in Neurobiology* 17:97–139.

Vijayashankar, N., and Brody, H. 1979. A quantitative study of the pigmented neurons in the nuclei locus coeruleus and subcoeruleus in man as related to aging. *Journal of Neuropathology and Experimental Neurology* 38:490–497.

Weissman, M. M.; Tischler, G. L.; Holzer, C. E., III; Orvaschel, H. et al. 1982. Psychiatric disorders (DSM-III) in the elderly: 1980–1981. Paper read at the Annual Meeting of the American Psychiatric Association. Toronto, May 20.

Wree, A.; Braak, H.; Schleicher, A.; and Zilles, K. 1980. Biomathematical analysis of the neuronal loss in the aging human brain of both sexes, demonstrated in pigment preparations of the pars cerebellaris loci coerulei. *Anatomy and Embryology* 160:105–119.

· 14 ·

THE PHANTOM SELF OF MIDDLE AGE

SAMUEL W. PERRY, M. D.

To introduce the aspect of middle age I discuss in this chapter, let me begin with an anecdote. It may not be true—but there is truth in it.

The story goes that a woman in her late fifties returned after many years to visit her hometown and, upon learning that a former high school classmate was a dentist in the area, called to make an appointment, using her married name in hopes of surprising him. The scheduled day arrived, and when the dentist came out into the waiting room and greeted his new patient with a pleasant but blank expression, she exclaimed, "Don't you remember me? You were in my class!" "Oh, really," he responded politely. "And what class did you *teach*?"

Although the dentist was no doubt embarrassed to discover his error, we have no problem understanding how it could happen: curiously, no matter what our age, we all maintain a view of ourselves as being somewhat younger than we actually are. At the inner core, the sense of ourselves does not quite match with our years, nor with how old our peers appear to be.

This phenomenon is so common that we do not think of it as pathological. On the contrary, if a patient feels *older* than his stated age, we are likely to suspect that a depressive process is operating. Although having a younger sense of oneself is not seen as abnormal, it is generally seen as an attempt to defend against the harsh reality of time. Various dynamics have been offered to explain this defensive distortion, including the narcissistic reluctance to accept one's limitations, or the existential avoidance of one's mortality, or oedipal inhibitions in identifying with the sexualized parental role, or the dependent need to remain young and cared for rather than to be a grown-up responsible for oneself and others.

As many chapters in this book attest, these and other psychodynamic formulations can be useful in helping us understand why some individuals are especially vulnerable to the impact of middle age—why the descending narcissist may vainly turn to face lifts or weight lifting, why buying a new sports car may be a futile attempt to race away from death's approaching shadow, why decreasing sexual desire in marriage

191

may stem from the unconscious guilt associated with an oedipal victory, and why physical illness in one's self or parents can jar the view that one is still an invincible and nurtured child. In this chapter, however, I propose that the tendency to think of ourselves as younger than our years may not only be based on a reluctance to accept growing old; it may also be related to psychological processes that ironically have little to do with the passing of time.

The Body Ego and Self-Definition

When Freud was laying the groundwork on which to build his structural model of the mind, he stated "the ego is first and foremost a bodily ego" (1923), by which he meant that the sense of self is gradually acquired as the young child experiences, through pain and other sensations, what is "me" and "not me." Since Freud's initial formulation, others have elaborated on how bodily sensations help consolidate our separateness from the external world. Anna Freud, for example, suggested that "the pain produced by head-knocking may serve the purpose of establishing an otherwise missing body reality for the child" (1954); and Mahler's systematic studies have documented the link between separation-individuation and the child's quest for bodily sensations (Mahler and McDevitt, 1982). Similarly, clinicians have noted that autistic children often resort to head banging for self-definition (Greenacre, 1954), that those born with a congenital indifference to pain suffer from poorly established ego boundaries (Frances and Gale, 1975), that medical staff and patients themselves may undermedicate for pain to preserve self-other differentiation (Perry, 1985a), and, conversely, that borderline personalities during severe bouts of depersonalization will attempt to regain their identities by inflicting pain upon themselves, such as cutting or burning their skin (Bychowski, 1954).

In addition to these more dramatic examples, there are also subtle indications of how we use bodily perceptions to define ourselves and clarify our relationship with the external world. For example, during the course of a day we frequently touch our nose, rub our ears, brush back our hair, or scratch the back of the head—sometimes because these places itch or are irritating, but more often automatically for no apparent reason. Moreover, these gestures have three other notable features: they most often involve bodily areas we can neither see nor move voluntarily; they produce a "double-touch" (Hoffer, 1949), a tactile sensation in both the touching hand and touched area that is different from the sensation of touching someone or something else; and the gestures tend to occur more frequently when we feel anxious or self-conscious (indeed, it is the rare person who walks through a restaurant to be seated without scratching the back of the head, brushing back hair, or double-touching another area that is not felt or seen or in volitional control).

These gestures are not so puzzling if we agree that just as bodily stimuli define a body ego for the child, our double-touching throughout the day consolidates our bodily boundaries and sense of self. This explanation also helps us understand the inherent reassurance and pleasure that comes from those external stimuli that make us more aware of unseen or unfelt bodily surfaces—such as the hot sun on our naked back or a gentle breeze on our face; furthermore, this explanation helps us understand why the reduction of external stimuli can be so disquieting or even psychotomimetic, such as may occur with sensory deprivation, scuba diving, or water tank isolation (Lilly, 1977), and drugs like ketamine or pancuronium (Perry, 1985a, 1985b). Furthermore, when people speak of pinching themselves "to make sure it is not a dream," they are implying how bodily sensations can help demarcate our relationship with the real external world. Possibly certain nervous habits— biting a pencil, tapping fingers on a desk, fondling silver or glassware at the table, and so on—serve in part to define our boundaries by discriminating the animate from the inanimate, a faculty Monakow termed *protodiakrisis* (Stirnimann, 1947).

The Mind's Response to a Changing Body

Although we may concur with Freud that the perception of our body helps establish our identity and our relationship to the external world, the question still before us is why the sense of ourselves does not match with our years—why, as it were, our body percept fails to keep up with the subtle and insidious changes that occur during middle age. In search of an answer, we can first briefly turn to what we know about the psychological responses to more overt and circumscribed somatic changes, such as those associated with adolescence, pregnancy, plastic surgery, mastectomy, facial disfigurement and limb amputation. As we will see, although these situations are quite different, a common theme does emerge.

Erikson (1968) emphasized the psychosocial events that induce an "identity crisis" in the adolescent, but rapid and profound somatic changes clearly also play a leading role. To assimilate these changes, the adolescent typically spends hours viewing and touching this strange new surface and, partly to impose mastery over this alien shell, experiments with haircuts, clothes, makeup, movement, and mannerisms until, if successful, early adulthood is approached with an alignment between who one is and how one appears, that is, between identity and body image. As Pines (1982) has noted, this new alignment can later be jarred by pregnancy, the enlarging breasts and other rapid and pronounced bodily changes being reminiscent of puberty. The complex psychological responses to pregnancy are of course partly psychodynamic and hormonal, but of interest to us here is the observation by Bibring (1959) that the altered body image in the *normal* pregnant woman can have a temporary but pronounced effect on her identity and ego boundaries until she assimilates her new self.

In addition to the physiological somatic changes induced by adolescence and pregnancy, changes that are pathological or iatrogenic indicate not only the close link between the sense of ourselves and how we perceive our bodies but also how permanent change is assimilated only over time. For example, Meyer et al. (1960) have described the gradual process that occurs after plastic surgery in which the bodily change, even if highly desired, can nevertheless be disquieting and require time before the new external image is internalized. Similarly, Druss (1973) provides poignant and detailed accounts of how women in the weeks following mastectomy enclose themselves in a dark quiet room and, at first quickly, then for more prolonged periods, touch, massage, and fondle the surgical area until gradually the altered bodily surface is incorporated into the self-representational world. Burn victims, especially those with facial disfigurement, can go through a similar process; but the data regarding amputees supply the most compelling support for the thesis that our body image is normally refractory to change.

The phenomenon of the phantom limb following amputation has been so well documented and described (Kolb, 1959; Straus, 1963; Lofgren, 1968) that for our purposes only four relevant points need to be itemized here: first and foremost, imagining that one's arm or leg is still present during the first few weeks after amputation is entirely normal and, as best as can be discerned, is primarily based on an inherent difficulty in modifying one's body percept; second, the phantom limb does not fade away like an entire dream into the morning light, but rather the illusion may persist for some missing bodily surfaces and not for others (for example, months after a below-the-knee amputation a patient may imagine that his big toe is still protruding from beneath the kneecap while the rest of his leg has "telescoped" into his thigh); third, before the phantom limb phenomenon gradually resolves and the patient assimilates a new body image, he may experience intermittent cognitive dissonance (for example, when thinking the leg is still there, the patient starts to get out of bed in the morning, then is suddenly reminded of what another part of his mind already knows); and fourth, although a normal phenomenon, the phantom limb can be influenced by psychodynamic factors (for example, phantom limb pain has been related to a sympathetic identification with another amputee who was ambivalently regarded during one's youth, and it has also been related to what the patient believed happened to the amputated limb—"burning" pain is associated with its being placed in an incinerator; "crushing" pain with its being buried; and "stabbing" pain with its being dissected by a pathologist).

The Phantom Self

If I have been successful in presenting my argument so far, a central point of this chapter has already been implied: although maintaining a younger sense of ourselves may be partly based on a reluctance to accept growing old, it may also be based on a psychological factor that is unrelated to fears associated with the passage of time. Because our body percept is so tightly linked with our sense of self, bodily changes threaten our very identity. Awareness of these changes therefore not only evokes the three signal anxieties originally described by Freud (1926)—fears of losing love, power, or self-regard—but also evokes fears of losing one's primal sense of self. Just as adolescence, pregnancy, plastic surgery, disfigurement, or amputation will commonly elicit the feeling "I'm just not myself," in a similar way a sudden reminder of how one's body has changed with age—such as the initial glance at a recently taken picture—will often elicit as a first response not concern about growing old but rather the disquieting sense of appearing different than one's internalized image of self. I propose that the anxiety evoked by this discrepancy is fundamentally unrelated to time and that the maintenance of our core identity is one reason our body percept does not keep up with the bodily changes induced by the aging process.

For purposes of conceptualization, I have chosen to call this illusionary misperception of the body a *phantom self*. The term is intended to convey a phenomenon analogous to a phantom limb in that this younger sense of self is preconscious and is fundamentally based on an inherent difficulty in modifying one's body percept rather than on conscious or unconscious fears about growing old. Like the telescoping phenomenon in the amputee, some bodily changes of age are integrated before others: one may more readily assimilate those changes of which one is constantly reminded, such as decreased vision or increased waistline, whereas changes less accessible to more constant perception may still "protrude," such as incomplete appreciation of one's gray hair, wrinkles, or diminished flexibility.

The younger phantom self is also like a phantom limb in that both can induce a cognitive dissonance when the illusion is confronted by reality. At times this confrontation between how old one is and how old one feels can be triggered directly by somatic events, such as not recovering as fast from jet lag, from the flu, from walking up an extra flight of stairs, or from a night of heavy drinking. At other times the younger phantom self may be confronted indirectly by the perception of others, such as meeting a former classmate after many years or, as one of my patients put it, realizing that "the cop on the corner has acne and you no longer do." These direct and indirect confrontations cause a momentary collision between one's sense of self and one's actual age; but as with the phantom limb phenomenon, the illusionary phantom self may persist despite these corrective experiences.

Finally, the phantom self and phantom limb are analogous in one other important respect: although both can be explained in part by a basic resistance to changing our body percept, they can nonetheless be additionally influenced by psychodynamic factors. In no way do I mean to suggest that intrapsychic conflicts about growing old cannot maladaptively sustain an exaggerated discrepancy between one's body percept and one's actual age.

Normal Grief and the Phantom Self

I am aware that the concept of the phantom self is a hard sell. The idea that we maintain a younger sense of ourselves for reasons that are unrelated to fears of growing old seems contrary both to common sense and to the psychoanalytic tenets of unconscious struggle. Although skeptics would probably agree with Freud (1923) that the infant's sense of self develops in part through pain and other sensations and they may even agree that these bodily sensations can continue throughout life to reinforce ego boundaries, they would contend that I am on shaky ground in setting up a parallel between the difficulty of assimilating acute bodily changes and that of assimilating the insidious bodily changes of middle age. Whereas the delayed assimilation of acute changes after trauma or surgery is easily viewed as unrelated to time, the gradual physical changes of aging are so inherently associated with loss, vulnerability, and mortality that it is much harder to accept the proposition that the delayed integration of these changes into the body percept is not primarily due to conscious and unconscious fears about growing old.

The argument against my proposition is given additional weight by the wealth of clinical data, such as that reported throughout this book, that indicates the defensive need to avoid accepting the disheartening fact that one is not as young as one would like to be. The skeptical reader rightfully asks for countering data that support my contention that the presence of a younger phantom self does not derive from these defensive constructs—but admittedly the evidence I can offer is far from compelling. I realize that it is insufficient to repeat the observation, shared by so many, that having a younger sense of self is extraordinarily common; for the phenomenon could be ubiquitous, even among those who profess no real concerns about growing old, and still stem from unconscious fears. I also realize that it is insufficient to note that the distorted body image in children (Klein, 1946; Spitz, 1957) and in psychotic adults (Rosenfeld, 1950; Elkisch, 1957; Searles, 1963) derives from problems about self-identity and not primarily from concerns about growing old; for one could counter that mental processes in these populations are not generalizable to normal adults. And finally, to support my contention that the younger phantom self is fundamentally linked to core identity, I could recount those occasions when a nonpsychotic analysand experiences a diffusion of ego boundaries during a transient period of depersonalization; but these episodes would support only half of my proposition, namely, that body percept and sense of self are tightly related. The depersonalized experiences would not in themselves indicate that the younger view of ourselves derives from this relationship.

The skeptic might further argue that just as individuals with acute body change eventually modify their body percept and reach a more accurate alignment, the discrepancy between the younger sense of self and one's chronological age should also fade over time unless it is being maintained for defensive reasons; but I contend that this discrepancy is not necessarily an indication of a continuing struggle against growing old, but rather is the expected consequence of normal grief and the nature of the physical changes that occur with aging.

The process of normal grief has been well elucidated by Freud (1917), Lindemann (1944), Parkes (1972, 1985), Clayton et al. (1974), Horowitz et al. (1980), and Solsberry and Krupnick (1984), so that for our purposes here I need only point out two features of the grieving process that help explain why there is a persistent gap between the younger phantom self and one's actual age. First, the physical losses of aging are not circumscribed; rather, they are continuous and require a grieving process throughout the life cycle. This requirement is similar to that associated with prolonged physical illnesses; for example, individuals with diabetes, arthritis, or systemic lupus erythematosus must intermittently continue to grieve over increasing physical losses after they occur (Jacobs and Douglas, 1979; Perry, 1986). Although this mourning can be somewhat buffered by anticipatory grief, it generally *follows* recognition of the loss and accordingly lags behind the actual event. By analogy, because the physical losses of aging are more or less constant, they too require this intermittent grieving *after* appreciation of the loss. It is therefore understandable why our body percept never quite "catches up" to our declining physical state.

A second feature of normal grief that helps explain why the younger phantom self never completely resolves in middle age is that the mourning process is catalyzed by reminders of the loss; for example, the work of mourning after the death of a loved one is facilitated by eulogies, anniversaries, sorting through belongings, visiting the grave site, or returning to places where experiences were shared. These memories encourage the begrieved to work through the loss in tolerable fragments over an extended period of time; and in between these reminders, disavowal and dissociation from the loss may normally occur in varying degrees. Because the physical losses of aging occur so insidiously, however, and because many remain outside of awareness in our day-to-day lives, reminders of the loss are not always accessible to catalyze the grieving process. For example, the gradual enlargement of ears, nose, hands, and feet; the shortened stature secondary to osteoporosis; the less specific immunological response to antigens; the decrease in cardiac, pulmonary, and renal reserve; and the diminished adrenocortical and hypothalamic response to stress—all may go unnoticed until an event brings them into sharp focus; and if the event is circumscribed— a bout with the flu, an all-nighter, an extra set of tennis—the reminder may again fade from view after the event passes and before sufficient grieving over the loss has occurred. Even though some reminders may be more constantly accessible to awareness, such as decreased elasticity in the skin, altered sexual function, and modified sleep cycle with more frequent nocturnal awakenings, these only partially represent the losses that are due to aging; they therefore do not allow for a complete working through and accurate alignment between the younger sense of self and all the insidious somatic changes.

But of all the gradual changes accompanying the aging process, those that involve the central nervous system (CNS) can best explain why the younger phantom self normally persists throughout adulthood and well into our later years. The biological changes within the CNS have already been reviewed in this book by Roose and Pardes (chapter 13) and elsewhere by Cote and Kremzner (1983); and the effects of these changes on mental processes have been summarized by Pitt (1982) and Weinberg (1980). For our purposes, what needs to be noted here is that although certain mental functions begin to decline in early adulthood, such as memory and reaction time, the normal aging brain retains remarkable plasticity and flexibility well into later life. As a result, although individuals may become increasingly aware of their benign senescent forgetfulness, they generally do not feel that their brain is growing old to any marked degree. Furthermore, the decrease in "fluid intelligence" (for example, the capacity to memorize) is offset by an increase in "crystallized intelligence" (for example, the capacity to conceptualize issues and place them in perspective). In short, over the years we become less smart but more wise.

Given the capacity of the brain to retain most of its functions well into our later years, given the subtlety of the insidious changes that do occur and the compensatory capacity to offset these losses, and given that the sense of ourselves is heavily dependent on our mental processes, it is not surprising that at the core we do not view ourselves as old as we are. It therefore makes sense that our younger phantom self is maintained even long after other somatic changes can no longer be ignored. Indeed, a recent sociological study of geriatric populations (Kaufman, 1987) documented that retirees typically feel that they are young people trapped in an old body, a perception not discernibly linked to fears of aging or death but rather linked to an acknowledgment that their mental processes—how they think and feel and act—have not aged as rapidly as other functions.

The Phantom Self in Psychoanalysis

So far I have proposed that the younger phantom self is due in part to the tight relationship between our body image and core identity, and I have argued that the persistence of this illusion throughout middle age is consistent with the normal grieving process and with the continuous, insidious somatic changes of aging. My intention in developing this concept is that I believe it may be an error to assume that a younger sense of self derives only from fears of growing old. Does this assumption occur frequently in psychoanalysis? I doubt it. In fact, judging from my own clinical experience and conversations with colleagues, I do not believe that the discrepancy between how old one is and how old one feels is often addressed during the course of an analysis. I do not mean that analysands do not discuss their concerns about growing old and grieve over the limitations posed by time; I mean only that an analysis can be viewed as successful without a totally accurate alignment between sense of self and chronological age. I suspect there are at least three reasons for this.

First, the discrepancy is generally experienced as being egosyntonic, and although perhaps mentioned from time to time, it is not identified by the analysand as a problem to be resolved. Similarly, unless the discrepancy is marked and dynamically related to other material, the analyst is not inclined to view its reduction as a specific task of the analysis and may even judge the illusionary phantom self to be adaptive —feeling younger than one's years is after all not such a bad thing.

Second, in both theory and method, adult psychoanalysis tends to emphasize the impact of the past on the present rather than the influence of the present on the future. In terms of understanding intrapsychic conflict, the profound psychosocial and biological events of childhood are given more weight; and in terms of technique, the importance of transference interpretations is based on this theoretical perspective. As a result, the less dramatic and more gradual physical changes of aging are not targeted as especially germane. It is true that since the contributions of Erikson, this view has been increasingly challenged; this book and many others (for example, Levinson et al., 1978; Neugarten, 1975; Vaillant, 1977; Offer and Sabshin, 1984) attest to the recognition that events throughout the life cycle affect intrapsychic structure. As Michels (1980) has stated, "It would be as great an error to 'infantomorphize' adult psychological processes as it was to 'adultomorphize' childhood in the last century." Nonetheless, psychoanalysis has persuasively shown that adults are far more like grown children than children are like small adults; and as analysands come to appreciate this fact, they too are generally less concerned about current aging processes outside of awareness. Even those older patients seeking psychoanalysis (King, 1980) have more a sense of "becoming" than of "being"; they reflect Kierkegaard's observation that "life can only be understood backwards" and, like the rest of us, rarely portray themselves in dreams as being as old as they are. Given that both analysts and their patients are focused more on the past than on the present and given the iatrogenic regression of psychoanalysis, it follows that the younger sense of self would be not only accepted but even encouraged by the analytic process.

A third reason that psychoanalytic treatment may not totally align the sense of self with one's chronological age regards the emphasis of analysis on psychological rather than somatic data. The following case vignette illustrates what I have in mind.

A successful businessman in his mid-forties entered analysis because of obsessive thoughts that his fiancée was having secret affairs. He acknowledged that this suspiciousness might be his problem because there was no supporting evidence and because his childless first marriage had ended in divorce because of his endlessly accusing his wife of infidelity with no basis. Within weeks, distressing homoerotic fantasies evolved in the transference and ignited fears of latent homosexuality until the yearning was traced to the death of the father from chronic tuberculosis during the patient's early adolescence. By analyzing concomitant fantasies about having an affair with the analyst's wife, the patient eventually came to understand that his pathological jealousy derived in part from an unconscious wish to have the woman serve as a conduit to make contact with the lost idealized father.

The ensuing months during the first year of the analysis were characterized by a poignant delayed grieving; as childhood memories resurfaced about the sickly father, both the father and the analyst were increasingly seen as more human and less magically powerful. By the end of the first year of analysis, the patient had married his fiancée and had no concerns about his new wife's fidelity except during periods of separation from the analyst when doubts, but no accusations, about her behavior would recur—one indication that the analytic work was not complete.

The sessions at issue occurred in this context during the start of the second year when the patient reported the "shock" of seeing himself in an angled mirror when being fitted for a new suit. He was struck in particular by the extent of his baldness but more generally how he did not appear as he imagined himself to look. I was not impressed by this material and silently speculated that this man's younger phantom self was consistent with the dynamics so far uncovered in the analysis: by maintaining a more youthful sense of self, he could perpetuate the illusion of being protected by an older man, a wish reflected not only in the analysis but also in his overly deferential manner with bosses at work. I was therefore surprised when during the next several sessions this now familiar defensive constellation did not unfold as I had anticipated.

The experience at the tailor's had catalyzed a process the patient later labeled "an internal audit." Whereas until then the analytic material could best be described as interpersonal—that is, interactions with wife, boss, father, analyst—the sessions were now far more involuted without apparent transferential implications. In fact, at times I was not even sure the patient was aware that I was in the room as he took stock in the most intimate detail of his bodily appearance: the hair around his ear canal, a crooked front tooth, a toenail too curled to clip easily, a small café au lait patch on his shoulder, the slight uneven slant to his circumcision, the ridge of skin between his anus and scrotum, and so on. Although I felt somewhat embarrassed by such disclosures, my strongest reaction was bewilderment, not only about why the patient was presenting this material at this time, but also about his complete lack of self-consciousness; it were as though he were standing alone naked in front of a bathroom mirror.

I remained at a loss until the following week when he reported a dream in which an older woman unexpectedly comes into my office with the patient and together they lie down on the couch. He believed the woman in the dream was a patient of my colleague with whom I share an office suite and who frequently arrives at the same time for her appointment. Since the patient had previously remarked that this older woman reminded him of his mother, this connection was not obscure. The novel element, however, was that the dream produced a flood of repressed childhood memories involving his mother's intrusiveness, including sleeping with the patient when his father was in a sanitorium, bathing him nightly until fifth grade, and closely monitoring his every bruise, blemish, and bite of food. The analysis had already revealed the mother's anguish over her husband's chronic illness and death, but the extent of her clinging to her only child for solace was new material.

I need not recount here all the dynamic themes that emerged as the patient recalled through the transference the wish for the father to return and intercept the mother's clinging bond and, conversely, the resentment when the father did return and the subsequent resentment toward bosses, peer competitors, and the analyst when they were perceived as interrupting the "blissful union" with his current wife. A discussion of these dynamics, although interesting in themselves, might distract from the main point I wish to make—namely, that the patient's shock over his appearance at the tailor's had relatively little to do with fears of growing old. For him, the experience was more associated with how his intrusive mother was "always under my skin" and interfered with the normal development of a consolidated identity and body percept. ("If I fell and scraped my knee, I didn't even know I should hurt unless she said so.")

In retrospect, I realize that the preliminary work in the analysis had led to sufficient trust, self-definition, and intrapsychic presence of a "real" father to enable the patient to deal with this more primitive material. I also now suspect that had I interpreted the experience at the tailor's as being related to the wish to be young, I might have short-circuited or at least delayed the recovery of memories related to how the mother had impeded the development of solid ego boundaries. Unwittingly, when I remained silent both about the tailor incident and during the subsequent sessions in which the patient took his remarkable internal audit, I was assuming the role of one who could unobtrusively permit the very private process of aligning one's body percept and sense of self. Of course, I was also placed in the position of *being* obtrusive, a situation that reflected the other side of the patient's conflict—the wish to have the mother illicitly barge through the bedroom door (which she insisted must never be locked).

Intermittently throughout his analysis, the patient referred to his internal audit as a benchmark, that time in his life when he finally took stock of his body and in the most intimate way came to terms with who he was and who he was not. And while those extraordinary sessions remain memorable to me as well, a more general response has been to note how rarely in my experience this most intimate and detailed discussion of one's bodily appearance occurs during an analysis, even in patients who otherwise are quite forthcoming. It is for this reason I have presented this vignette—to point out that the emphasis in psychoanalysis on psychological rather than somatic events may be an additional factor to explain why the younger phantom self eludes analytic exploration.

This chapter has examined the common experience of feeling younger than one's chronological age. While recognizing that this phenomenon can relate to conscious and unconscious fears of growing old, I contend that the younger phantom self can also be explained by the fundamental link between body percept and identity and how the physical changes of middle age can threaten one's very sense of self, a threat not directly related to the passage of time. I further argue that the discrepancy between how old one is and how old one feels is consistent with normal grief and with the nature of the aging process. I conclude by pointing out why this discrepancy may elude the analytic process.

REFERENCES

Bibring, G. L. 1959. Psychological process during pregnancy. *Psychoanalytic Study of the Child* 42:1390–91.

Bychowski, G. 1954. Discussant: Problems of infantile neurosis. *Psychoanalytic Study of the Child* 19:16.

Clayton, P. J.; Herjanic, M.; Murphy, E. E.; and Woodrugg, R. 1974. Mourning and depression: Their similarities and differences. *Canadian Psychological Association Journal* 19:309–312.

Cote, L. J., and Kremzner, L. T. 1983. Biochemical changes in normal aging in the human brain. In *The dementias.* Ed. R. Mayeux and W. G. Rosen, 19–30. New York: Raven Press.

Druss, R. 1973. Changes in body image following breast augmentations. *International Journal of Psychoanalysis and Psychotherapy* 2:248–256.

Elkisch, P. 1957. The psychological significance of the mirror. *Journal of the American Psychoanalytic Association* 5:235–44.

Erikson, E. H. 1968. *Identity: Youth and crisis.* New York: W. W. Norton.

Frances, A., and Gale, L. 1975. The proprioceptive body image in self-object differentiation: A case of congenital indifference to pain and head-banging. *Psychoanalytic Quarterly* 44:107.

Freud, A. 1954. Discussant: Problems of infantile neurosis. *Psychoanalytic Study of the Child* 19:16.

Freud, S. 1926. Inhibitions, symptoms and anxiety. In *Standard edition*, 20.

———. 1923. The ego and the id. In *Standard edition*, 19.

———. 1917. Mourning and melancholia. In *Standard edition*, 14.

———. 1900. The interpretation of dreams. In *Standard edition*, 5.

Greenacre, P. 1954. Discussant: Problems of infantile neurosis. *Psychoanalytic Study of the Child* 19:16.

Hoffer, W. 1949. Development of the body ego. *Psychoanalytic Study of the Child* 5:18.

Horowitz, M. J.; Wilner, N.; Marmar, C.; and Krupnick, J. 1980. Pathological grief and the activation of latent self-images. *American Journal of Psychiatry* 137:1157–1162.

Jacobs, S., and Douglas, L. 1979. Grief: A mediating process between a loss and illness. *Comprehensive Psychiatry* 10:165–176, 1979.

Kaufman, S. 1986. *The ageless self: Sources of meaning in late life.* Madison: University of Wisconsin Press.

King, P. 1980. The life cycle as indicated by the nature of the transference in the psychoanalysis of the middle-aged and elderly. *International Journal of Psychoanalysis* 61:153–160.

Klein, M. 1946. *The psycho-analysis of children.* London: Hogarth.

Kolb, L. C. 1959. Disturbances of the body image. In *American handbook of psychiatry.* Ed. S. Arieti. New York: Basic Books.

Levinson, D.; Darrow, C.; Klein, E.; Levinson, M.; and McKee, B. 1978. *The seasons of a man's life.* New York: Alfred A. Knopf.

Lilly, J. C. 1977. *The deep self.* New York: Simon & Schuster.

Lindemann, E. 1944. Symptomatology and management of acute grief. *American Journal of Psychiatry* 100:141–145.

Lofgren, B. L. 1968. Castration anxiety and the body ego. *International Journal of Psychoanalysis* 49:408.

Mahler, M. S., and McDevitt, J. B. 1982. Thoughts on the emergence of the sense of self, with particular emphasis on the body self. *Journal of the American Psychoanalytic Association* 30:827.

Meyer, E.; Jacobson, W. E.; Edgerton, M. T.; and Cater, A. 1960. Motivational patterns in patients seeking elective plastic surgery. *Psychosomatic Medicine* 22:193–203.

Michels, R. 1980. Adulthood. In *The course of life: Psychoanalytic contributions toward understanding personality development.* Vol. 3, *Adulthood and the aging process.* Ed. S. I. Greenspan and G. H. Pollock, 25–34. Washington, D.C.: National Institute of Mental Health.

Neugarten, B. L. 1975. Adult personality: Toward a psychology of the life cycle. In *Human life cycle*. Ed. W. C. Sze, 379–394. New York: Jason Aronson.

Offer, D., and Sabshin, M., eds. 1984. *Normality and the life cycle*. New York: Basic Books.

Parkes, C. M. 1985. Bereavement. *British Journal of Psychiatry* 146:11–17.

———. 1972. *Bereavement*. New York: International Universities Press.

Perry, S. 1986. Psychiatric aspects of SLE. In *Systemic lupus erythematosus*. Ed. R. Lahita. New York: John Wiley.

———. 1985a. Irrational attitudes towards narcotics and addicts. *Bulletin of the New York Academy of Medicine* 61:706–729.

———. 1985b. Psychological reactions to pancuronium. *American Journal of Psychiatry* 142:1390–91.

Pines, D. 1982. The relevance of early psychic development to pregnancy and abortion. *International Journal of Psychoanalysis* 63:311–320.

Pitt, B. 1982. *Psychogeriatrics*. London: Churchill Livingston.

Rosenfeld, H. 1950. Notes on the psychopathology of confusional states in chronic schizophrenias. *International Journal of Psychoanalysis* 31:132–137.

Searles, H. F. 1963. The place of neutral therapist responses in psychotherapy with the schizophrenic patient. *International Journal of Psychoanalysis* 44:42–56.

Solsberry, V., and Krupnick, J. 1984. Adults' reactions to bereavement. In *Bereavement: Reactions, consequences and care*. Ed. M. Osterweis, F. Solomon, and M. Green, 47–68. Washington, D.C.: National Academy Press.

Spitz, R. A. 1957. The primal cavity. *Psychoanalytic Study of the Child* 10:215–240.

Stirnimann, F. 1947. Das kind und seine fruheste unwelt. Psychol Praxis 6:1.

Straus, E. W. 1963. *The primary world of the senses*. New York: Macmillan.

Vaillant, G. 1977. *Adaptation to life*. Boston: Little, Brown.

Weinberg, J. 1980. Geriatric psychiatry. In *Comprehensive textbook of psychiatry/III*. Vol. 3. Ed. H. I. Kaplan, A. M. Freedman, and B. J. Sadock, 3024–3042. Baltimore: Williams & Wilkins.

Part IV

Clinical Papers

· 15 ·

THE INTERACTION OF MIDDLE AGE AND CHARACTER PATHOLOGY
Treatment Implications

OTTO F. KERNBERG, M. D.

I shall explore here the middle years, which I define, in agreement with Levinson et al. (1978), as ranging from forty to sixty. This range appropriately signals the dramatic changes in psychoanalytic perspectives since the time of Fenichel's (1945) proposal that the optimal years for psychoanalytic treatment started at about age fifteen and stopped at age forty.

I shall spell out my evaluation of patients in this age group who consult me because of neurotic and characterological problems. The particular questions and concerns I focus on reflect my understanding of the developmental frame of the middle years.

Physical Appearance

I always observe, as the patient enters my office, what the individual has done with his or her body. During these years, neglect of the body as evidenced by muscular atrophy, obesity, or unattended medical problems begins to show. These may be telltale indications of unacknowledged self-destructiveness. At this age, the patient's natural attractiveness or lack of attractiveness, expressive movements, and manner of speaking may provide immediate information regarding emotional maturity and whether he or she enjoys sexual freedom and pleasure or is bitter because of overwhelming envy and unsatisfied greed. A patient's physical appearance must be viewed in the context of his socioeconomic background, but it also can indicate the deteriorating effects of severe narcissistic pathology, the growing emotional stagnation of the infantile personality, and the effects of drug abuse and alcohol. I am alert to both the exaggerated youthfulness of appearance characteristic of narcissistic personalities and the self-demeaning implications of a manner that might indicate, for example, a man's sense that it is useless to compete with other men for a desirable woman or a woman's conviction that her body is distasteful and certainly no source of sexual enjoyment. Above all, I wonder whether the patient is comfortable with or cannot accept the changes occurring in his body. As always, it is crucial to register such first impressions before developments in the transference and countertransference reduce the analyst's ability to see how others would perceive this patient and what this may indicate in terms of the patient's psychopathology.

Case Vignette 1. A forty-eight-year-old woman with an infantile or histrionic personality, borderline personality organization, and severe psychogenic obesity sought psychoanalytic psychotherapy to help her overcome her obesity and to establish a satisfactory relationship with a man. In the past, she had unsuccessfully undergone several psychotherapeutic treatments intended to overcome her eating disturbance. Her position as a schoolteacher provided her with some social contacts, but her almost grotesque appearance had interfered, she said, with her interactions with men. In the course of her evaluation, it became clear that psychotherapeutic treatment had a magic quality for her; in her fantasy, it would resolve her obesity without her having to go through the discomfort of dieting. Her assessment of the possibility of establishing a satisfactory relation with a man under such conditions seemed highly unrealistic.

She was referred to a program for eating disturbances, with the recommendation that she undergo a supervised course in weight reduction simultaneously with supportive psychotherapy and the understanding that psychotherapeutic treatment would be made contingent upon a commitment on her part to effective weight loss. The patient rejected this treatment recommendation and interrupted the consultation.

Work and Profession

I would expect that by the middle years the individual will have found an area of gratifying and successful work within the boundaries of available opportunities, given the socioeconomic, cultural, and familial background. Hence, the "eternal student," the social drifter, and the patient presenting parasitic dependency upon others have prognostically graver implications in mid-life than would be true if these trends were manifest at an earlier age. This personality trait may reflect severe masochistic features which may already have ruined important opportunities. Character problems may have caused failure in important professional functions, or severe work inhibition may have interfered with expectable promotions. In the course of the evaluation, I raise questions about the relation between achievements and aspirations and the extent to which previous aspirations have been suppressed by a sense of impotence or hopelessness.

This is a difficult area to investigate. The analyst must be careful not to convey a critical attitude regarding the patient's achievements, yet not to succumb to the patient's denial of areas of failure. Particularly if patient and analyst are of the same sex, cultural background, and age, there exists the danger that the analyst's guilt over having higher achievements than the patient's or fear of arousing the patient's envy or concern over the patient's narcissistic lesion when the denial of failure is explored may induce countertransference reactions. These reactions could inhibit exploration of important areas of failure and contribute to setting up "silent areas" or "bastions" (Baranger and Baranger, 1966) where mutual collusion between patient and analyst permits psychopathology to go into hiding.

The counterpart of these observations is the patient whose phenomenal success at work, in a profession, in politics, or in unusually creative endeavors of any kind raises the analyst's admiration and envy, which may lead to an underestimation of the patient's psychopathology and risk of self-destructive behavior. Even if the patient seems to have been successful in work or profession in terms of external, social criteria, the next and crucial question is the extent to which success has been gratifying. Perhaps unbridled ambition reflecting narcissistic psychopathology or unconscious guilt feelings may be ruining the patient's capacity for enjoyment of what he has achieved. Pathological, driven ambitiousness may create relentless pressures at work, neglect of other areas of life, and the illusion that the next success will put to rest a chronic internal dissatisfaction that has unconscious origins. Again, the danger is that the patient may experience the analyst as questioning what seems to the patient to be natural ambition, and he may project his own dissociated or repressed envy onto the analyst. And indeed, when the analyst is faced with a prominent, famous, or unusual patient, narcissistic gratification at treating such a person may interfere with the capacity to assess the patient's narcissistic pathology.

I carefully explore the patient's interests in areas other than his primary work or profession. In the middle years, such additional private interests indicate sublimatory capacities, are an important expression of ego strength, and have prognostically favorable implications.

Above all, the question is, how much has already been ruined or destroyed, how much can still be salvaged, what is the patient's potential for turning a new leaf and making his work effective, satisfactory, and creative? Creativity at work is reflected in the enjoyment of work, in pleasure in new contributions, or in discovery, while collaborating with others, of the pleasure of learning and contributing through this learning.

The female psychoanalyst confronting a female patient who is a housewife has the delicate task of evaluating whether the patient finds this role creative and a source of gratification or whether she is masochistically submitting to a culturally or psychopathologically imposed norm. In a time of rapid changes in cultural values, such a probing and technically neutral inquiry should become easier; but again, fear of and submission to the patient's envy and resentment and the analyst's unconscious guilt over her own achievements may interfere with a full exploration of this issue. In any event, for many middle-aged married women, this is a time when children leave for college, when the mourning process over the end of a stage of life and the relief over the renewed increase in personal freedom lead to expectable conflicts, the realistic or neurotic working through of which need exploration.

Love and Sex

Two related developments should have been achieved by this stage of life: first, the capacity to experience fully sexual pleasure in the context of an intimate relation with another person, and second, a growing awareness of repetitive cycles or patterns within one's intimate relations. Although this statement may seem obvious, I cannot underline sufficiently how inadequately these areas are often explored, with far-reaching consequences regarding prognosis, treatment indication, and psychoanalytic treatment itself.

First, patients who have never been able to enjoy a full sexual experience, the activation of an internal world of fantasy in the context of mutual sexual exploration, and gratification with another human being reveal, by this, severe character pathology and, if they present borderline personality organization, have an unfavorable prognosis regarding the treatment of their sexual difficulties. Second, sexual inhibitions that may have improved or disappeared in early adulthood may by now have reasserted themselves. They reflect deep conflicts that undermine stable love relations, whether homosexual or heterosexual, inside marriage or in multiple relationships. For example, sexual boredom is a frequent symptom reflecting unconscious conflicts that gradually infiltrate a couple's relationship and character pathology in one or both sexual partners. Sexual boredom may stem from unconscious oedipal guilt, narcissistic conflicts over unconscious envy of the sexual partner, or the widening repression of sexual urges as part of a defensive warding off of polymorphous perverse fantasies and urges. Patients in the middle years should be expected to be able to talk openly with the analyst about their sexual experiences and difficulties when asked about these matters; difficulty in doing so in itself is a sign of a severe developmental lag.

Many patients tend to dismiss or underemphasize their sexual difficulties for narcissistic reasons, as part of severe superego pathology, or as a manifestation of denial. The capacity for sexual enjoyment, the availability of an erotic dimension in life, is a basic cement for object relations, a counterpart to the equally important capacity for expressing aggression in nondestructive ways. Dr. Henriette Klein (personal communication) has alerted us to the fact that, whereas after analytic treatment many former patients experience further improvement in significant areas, sexual life tends not to improve further after treatment. To bring the erotic and aggressive fantasy life of early object relations into the excitement of adult sexuality is a major task of psychoanalytic treatment. I inquire carefully about the nature of a patient's sexual experiences, his or her fantasies and dreams, the relation between sexual and emotional involvements, with particular focus on the patient's ability to integrate polymorphous perverse sexual trends, love and hatred, in a love relation, and, of course, the extent to which the patient has an integrated view of his or her sexual partner.

The exploration of patterns of intimate love relations represents my effort to evaluate the development of direct and reverse triangulation in fantasy and reality. By direct triangulation I mean the conflicts reflecting oedipal rivalries with "excluded third parties," expressed in feelings of inferiority, sexual inhibition, and jealousy. Reverse triangulation refers to the revengeful aspects of the search for "forbidden" relations and the construction in reality or fantasy of a triangular situation in which two persons compete for the individual's sexual interest. I explore in detail sexual fantasies, affairs and their impact on a marriage, and the degree to which the patient's evaluation of his own and the partner's contribution to conflict is realistic or naive. The capacity for emotional commitment, the availability of normal superego functions as opposed to overwhelming projective mechanisms in dealing with a marital partner, the capacity for a sense of guilt over one's own aggressions, the capacity for romantic love and longing and for jealousy—all contribute to clarify whether oedipal or pre-oedipal conflicts predominate in the marital relationship and the extent and severity of narcissistic conflicts. At the same time it is possible to detect the presence or absence of identity diffusion (the capacity, or lack of capacity, for an integrated view of self and significant others). The analyst's freedom from the conventional, the moralistic, his or her ability to avoid an inhibited approach to these issues with the middle-aged patient, are absolutely central to the diagnostic evaluation.

Case Vignette 2. A forty-three-year-old mid-level executive in a large corporation consulted because of sexual inhibition with his wife (he was having intercourse once or twice a month), chronic depressive reactions, and inhibition in the social life connected with his work. He presented an obsessive-compulsive personality. His wife also suffered from severe sexual inhibition—an incapacity to achieve any excitement in intercourse. After several brief attempts at psychiatric treatment, she refused further consultation.

This man had a typical neurotic personality organization and a capacity for relations with others in depth; he had been able to achieve full sexual pleasure in premarital relations with several women, but not as part of a stable relation with any of them. He was effective and satisfied in his work and highly regarded; in spite of his social awkwardness and shy demeanor, he had a small group of close friends. In the course of psychoanalytic treatment, he first was adamant in asserting that, given his profound Catholic convictions, he would never divorce his wife and leave their five children, ranging from preschool age to early adolescence.

The psychoanalytic resolution of his profound submission to his father and his guilt-determined unconscious selection of a wife who was very different from the unconscious image of his mother resulted in his rebelling against his wife's sexual rejection of him. Later on, he was able to have extramarital relations for the first time during his marriage. Finally, he met a sexually mature, fully satisfactory woman who shared his interests and whom he eventually married in the course of his treatment. His sexual inhibitions were fully resolved, he obtained significant changes in his social life, and he established a rich and satisfactory relation with his new wife, which persisted after a ten-year follow-up.

The single man and the single woman in this age group may have serious problems, but the analyst may erroneously attribute to character pathology what may be in part a consequence of social, cultural, economic, and/or ideological factors. In homosexual patients, the stability and depth of a relationship over an extended period of time may reflect neurotic, in contrast to borderline, personality organization, a predominance of oedipal over pre-oedipal issues, and the capacity to integrate a full sexual engagement with tenderness and an object relation in depth. In contrast, homosexuality based in a narcissistic personality may be reflected in persistent instability of object relations and be manifest as a gradual emptying out of sexual pleasure, sexual boredom, and a significant decrease of all intimate engagements. Narcissistic types of homosexuality have a much more reserved prognosis for psychoanalytic treatment, so that, paradoxically, the fading out of homosexual engagements may signal a poorer prognosis.

In heterosexual patients, where social and cultural pressures usually facilitate the establishment of stability at this stage of life, marital failure or difficulty may reflect a mild neurosis or the entire spectrum of character pathology. When heterosexual patients consult because of marital difficulty in middle age, the analyst must be alert to the danger of colluding with sociocultural values in evaluating the patient's capacity for benefiting from treatment. Demographics suggest that it is harder for women to find a new partner at this stage of life, and the biological clock limits a woman's capacity to have children. But this reality should not be confused with the psychopathology of masochistic and hysterical characters who feel that life is meaningless without a man and who, for neurotic reasons, cannot perceive themselves as autonomous. Paradoxically, a real capacity to commit oneself in depth to a mature love relationship goes hand in hand with a firm sense of autonomy. Independence and a capacity to depend on another person are mutually complementary capabilities. As Ernst Ticho (1972) has pointed out, in this area the differentiation of life goals from treatment goals needs to be explored early and fully. Psychoanalysis may help resolve neurotic psychopathology, but it cannot guarantee the patient's finding an appropriate spouse.

Case Vignette 3. A forty-seven-year-old woman entered psychoanalytic treatment because of frequent disappointments in her involvements with men, involvements that turned out to be with highly sadistic and unsatisfactory partners. She was the buyer of art objects for a major department store and had a few close woman friends and good interpersonal relations on her job. She also had a moderate degree of sexual inhibition—she could reach orgasm only by masturbating, not as part of her sexual relations with men. She was diagnosed as a depressive-masochistic personality structure.

In the course of a six-year psychoanalytic treatment she was able to resolve the masochistic personality traits that had prompted her selection of men and to mourn successfully the fact that she was not going to have children. She established a stable and satisfactory relation with a married man who, because of a severe, chronic illness of his wife, was not willing to obtain a divorce. At the completion of her analysis, her sexual inhibition was completely resolved, and she obtained profound gratification from her fulfillment as a woman and as an art expert.

Case Vignette 4. A fifty-three-year-old woman with an infantile or histrionic personality disorder sought psychoanalysis to help her with her chronic marital conflict. Although she accepted on principle that she might be contributing to her difficulties with her husband, in practice she blamed him and showed a predominance of projective mechanisms, passive aggressive exploitation of her husband, and a manipulative and guilt-raising pattern of relations with her children that had in effect alienated them from her. A few months after the beginning of the treatment she separated from her husband, developed an intense sexualized transference to the analyst, and from then on successfully defeated his efforts to point to her many problems in relating to herself and others, problems clearly implicated in her inability to find another husband. She was adamant in expecting the analyst to be her man. Consistent efforts to interpret this transference resistance proved unsuccessful. After three years of psychoanalysis, the analyst decided to terminate the treatment and referred her for psychotherapy to a colleague.

In retrospect it was evident that the differentiation between life goals and treatment goals had not been explored sufficiently at the initiation of the treatment. This patient's parasitic dependency upon her husband and her children, the chronic acting out of severe sadomasochistic behavior patterns, the lack of any achievement of personal interests, work, or a profession, the lack of any distance or introspection toward her ambivalent and pathological relations with her family—all militated against an expressive modality of treatment.

Early middle age is the time of maximum marital infidelity, usually rationalized in terms of intolerable personality features of or interactions with the marital partner. The psychoanalyst has to be prepared to look beyond these rationalizations. Sexual intercourse provides an ideal means of living out sadomasochistic impulses and primitive aggression from all possible sources. The intensity of the unconscious envy of the other sex, a dominant narcissistic pathology in the sexual realm, may combine with the effects of unconscious prohibitions against satisfactory sexual relations stemming from the oedipal superego. During middle age, the sexual partner comes close in age to the age of the actual parent of the opposite sex when the patient was in early adolescence, which may reactivate oedipal guilt and inhibitions. The search for younger sexual partners does not stem only from sexual boredom but may reflect, at a deeper level, the oedipal taboo.

Case Vignette 5. A fifty-three-year-old marketing consultant entered psychoanalytic treatment because of occasional impotence in relations with his wife and compulsive masturbation with sadomasochistic pornographic material for several hours daily, which interfered significantly with his work. This patient presented a childlike, dependent attitude toward his wife and a seductive, pseudohypermasculine approach to other women. His diagnosis was that of a hysterical personality with infantile features and secondary, moderate impotence. In the course of five years of psychoanalytic treatment, his masturbatory behavior shifted into an overt pattern of sexually sadistic behavior toward women, which was expressed in the form of typical perverse scenarios involving women friends and prostitutes, within which actual aggression was playfully contained. In the analysis, his defensive reaction formation against homosexual submission to a powerful oedipal father and the perverse solution to this conflict by a dissociated identification with a sadistic father were gradually explored. He began to experience his wife consciously as so similar to his dominant, guilt-raising, and sexually teasing mother that, after awakening from a dream with manifest contents of sexual involvement with his mother, he would experience a frightening uncertainty of who was in reality lying next to him.

The analysis of his rivalry with father and of his corresponding intense castration anxiety led to a gradual resolution of the perversion and a corresponding resolution of his sexual inhibition with his wife as well. He finally dared to become more affirmative and independent in his interaction with her and more aggressive in his sexual behavior toward her, resolving in this context the dissociation in his sexual life. An unexpected consequence of his treatment was a significant change in his relation to colleagues and superiors at work and also a significant increase in his satisfaction and effectiveness in his work.

Intergenerational Relations, Intimacy, Loneliness, and Autonomy

The capacity to enjoy relations in depth with their own children as well as to tolerate jealousy and envy of them without love being threatened by such emotions is another life task that the middle-aged should have achieved. The counterparts of this achievement are improved relations with one's own parents and the ability to be free of irrational submission to and idealization of parents as well as of irrational hostility, rebelliousness, and devaluation of them. The capacity to accept and work through the identification with their parents is a precondition of middle-aged patients' capacity to identify with their own image over an extended life span. In other words, we must explore the extent to which our patients have been able to reevaluate internal relations with their parents, project themselves into the parents' role in the future, and acquire a new distance regarding their role toward their own children. Intimately related to these issues is a patient's capacity to experience himself as part of an "older" generation, to accept, for example, that there is a younger generation at work as well as socially and a still older generation to which he can in turn relate. A lack of this normal broadening of the time span of ego identity is one of the most frequent symptoms of severe character pathology in this age group. A middle-aged patient who gives the impression of standing alone in the world rather than actually experiencing a sense of loneliness as he projects his life span into the past and the future is another manifestation of this same problem.

Case Vignette 6. A forty-year-old heir to an important fortune consulted because of growing dissatisfaction with his incapacity to establish a stable relation with a woman and his sense of social isolation in spite of a busy social life. He had been married briefly twice and had had numerous affairs, but as he experienced a repeating pattern of idealization and rapid loss of interest in the women he became involved with, he finally became concerned over the loss of excitement and enjoyment in his sexual life. In recent years, he had become aware that some of the women with whom he had been involved in the past and whom he had left were actually very attractive, but he could not overcome sexual boredom and intense suspiciousness of their intentions toward him. Were they interested in him or in his money? And if they were not interested in his money, were they too stupid or naive to appreciate his power and the impact of his wealth? He had a strikingly youthful appearance and, in spite of an extended family network, conveyed the impression of being a man without a past and without any stable roots in life.

While he was being evaluated, he expressed enormous satisfaction in the power and influence his wealth gave him, hinted at his unusual capacity for assessing other people, particularly their negative features, and manifested subtle grandiosity and arrogance together with fearfulness of being found out as an emotional failure. He created overall a chaotic impression. He was also afraid of not being able to function adequately sexually and wondered whether any stable relation with a woman would condemn him to sexual impotence. The diagnosis was of a narcissistic personality without prognostically unfavorable complications (antisocial features, paranoid tendencies, lack of impulse control and anxiety tolerance). Psychoanalytic treatment was recommended as the treatment of choice.

Conventionality, Creativity, Triviality

A normal task in the middle years is to free oneself gradually from conventional social pressures. There is a connection between freedom from conventionality and group pressures and a sense of gratification and achievement of personal ambitions and an acceptable place in life. Relentless ambitions are usually the counterpart of overdependency on other people's views and reactions, reflecting, at best, overcompensation for feelings of inferiority and unconscious guilt from many sources and, at worst, severe narcissistic character pathology.

Creativity in any area of life, gratification that stems from what a person does rather than from how he is perceived by others, is the healthy, compensating counterpart to conventionality. The interplay of creativity and conventionality, together with the quality of object relations, will codetermine the extent to which a person's life is meaningful or trivial. Triviality is another nonspecific manifestation of character pathology at this stage of life. It can result from general repression of sexual longings as well as aggression or may be a product of a deterioration of object relations and consequent overdependency on external sources of applause, gratification, and reassurance.

The Management of Aggression

In the middle years, the individual should have achieved an appropriate degree of self-assertion, the capacity to rely on others but not to be submissive toward idealized parental figures and their derivatives. Handling one's aggression means recognizing one's capacity to react with hatred, envy, jealousy, greed, and resentment. One should be able to recognize the existence of aggression that is part of the normal ambivalence toward those one loves most. This recognition of one's own aggression should be expressed in the normal capacity for guilt and remorse, for mourning processes, and reparative strivings that also include a realistic awareness of the reality of ultimate destruction in the form of death.

Elliott Jaques (1981), in rewriting his classical study of the mid-life crisis, stressed the relation between normal mourning, the integration of aggression, the acceptance of death, and creativity as a reparative-sublimatory trend, on the one hand, and unintegrated aggression, inordinate fear of death, or denial of the reality of death, on the other. Normally, there is less fear of death in the middle years than in early adulthood and its "mid-life crisis."

For practical purposes, the exploration of this area of conflicts includes the patient's attitude toward his or her own body, mentioned at the beginning of this presentation (self-neglect and the denial of physical fragility); how the patient expresses envy, greed, and sadism in striving for power and prestige; and whether the patient uses money to exploit others or squanders money self-destructively. Dissociated aggression is most frequently manifested by sadistic personality traits together with paranoid trends and hypochondriases. Predominance of these characteristics in the form of perversions with manifest aggression, aggressive infiltration of the pathological grandiose self in narcissistic personalities (malignant narcissism), and severe, chronic sadomasochistic patterns are also typical expressions of intense, predominant, nonintegrated aggression that may have already affected the patient's life and that add prognostically negative features to the treatment. In contrast, aggression acknowledged and integrated in the normal ambivalence of object relations, expressed in the acceptance of, yet concern over, its effects on self and others, reflects healthy elaborations of oedipal and pre-oedipal conflicts.

The Predominant Type of Character Pathology

Regardless of a patient's predominant type of character pathology, its severity is reflected in failure to achieve the developmental tasks of middle age, as evident in the following: (1) the inability to enjoy sexuality; (2) the incapacity to relate in depth to other human beings, with lack of awareness of ambivalence and a lack of the capacity for mourning over the aggression toward those who are loved; (3) a denial of aggression in self and others, expressed in naïveté, dissociated expression of aggression, and trivialization; and (4) the lack of a satisfactory, effective, and potentially creative work situation.

The evaluation of the patient's personality in all areas of functioning should provide the data required to make a diagnosis of the predominant type of character pathology and of the presence of neurotic or borderline personality organization.

Patients with neurotic personality organization whose predominant characterological constellation is hysterical, depressive-masochistic, or obsessive-compulsive have an excellent prognosis for psychoanalytic treatment in this age group. In fact, if the destructive consequences of their pathology have not limited the potential achievements in treatment for any of the reasons stated before, all these patients have definite indications for psychoanalytic treatment and a significant life span ahead of them to benefit from the consequences of treatment.

Hysterical personalities often present spontaneous improvement over the years of early adulthood, so that, if at this stage of middle age their character difficulties persist in a significant way, there is a definite indication for treatment. In patients with depressive-masochistic pathology, particularly women, self-destructive behaviors may have affected their choices because of the biological clock and the decreasing availability of partners; but this should be discussed realistically as part of the decision-making process for treatment. Obsessive-compulsive personalities may have achieved important secondary gain from their pathology in terms of professional success, but now their personal life may become more threatened as their work situation stabilizes and long-term neurotic patterns in intimate relations may bring about marital failure. Middle age is therefore a good time for them to be treated.

For those with borderline personality organization, the prognosis for psychoanalytic treatment and psychoanalytic psychotherapy is poorer at this time than if they had sought treatment in early adulthood. The destructive effects of their character pathology often have had a cumulative impact on their psychological malfunctioning, and severe limitations in their life situation as well as in their potential for therapeutic work on their difficulties make psychoanalytic treatment questionable. Nevertheless, these patients may benefit from supportive psychotherapy, and some of them may thereby develop a better capacity for an expressive modality of treatment. One additional risk, however, for these patients with severe personality disorders is the secondary gain of treatment itself. The supportive aspects of a psychotherapeutic relationship may become a safe haven which militates against further change and must become a major focus in the treatment itself. The one important exception to the rule that patients with borderline personality organization have a grave prognosis at this time is the narcissistic personality, particularly those with this disorder who do not present the syndrome of malignant narcissism or severely antisocial features and who have a sufficient degree of anxiety tolerance and impulse control to tolerate long-term psychotherapeutic treatment or psychoanalysis. These cases have a much better prognosis now than they would have had when they were in their twenties and thirties (see Kernberg, 1975, 1980, 1984). Perhaps the crucial prognostic factor is these patients' capacity to tolerate, in the transference, their envy of the psychoanalyst and to mourn constructively over the self-destructive effects of envy in their past life.

In conclusion, my clinical experience points to a definite broadening of the indications for psychoanalytic modalities of treatment for character pathology in middle adulthood, with significant prognostic improvement for some types of characterological illness that respond less well to treatment in earlier years of life.

REFERENCES

Baranger, W., and Baranger, M. 1966. Insight in the analytic situation. In *Psychoanalysis in the Americas*. Ed. Robert Lipton, 56–72. New York: International Universities Press.

Fenichel, O. 1945. *The psychoanalytic theory of neurosis*. New York: W. W. Norton.

Jaques, E. 1981. The mid-life crisis. In *The course of life*. Vol. 3, *Adulthood and the aging process*. Ed. S. J. Greenspan and G. H. Pollock. Washington, D.C.: U.S. Department of Health and Human Services.

Kernberg, O. 1975. *Borderline conditions and pathological narcissism*. New York: Aronson.

————. 1980. *Internal world and external reality*. New York: Aronson.

————. 1984. *Severe personality disorders*. New Haven: Yale University Press.

Levinson, D.; with Darrow, C.; Klein, E.; Levinson, M.; and McKee, B. 1978. *The seasons of a man's life*. New York: Knopf.

Ticho, E. 1972. Termination of psychoanalysis: Treatment goals, life goals. *Psychoanalytic Quarterly* 41:315–333.

· 16 ·

MIDDLE LIFE AS A PERIOD
OF MUTATIVE CHANGE

MILTON VIEDERMAN, M.D.

This chapter will focus on hidden aspects of a gain that accrues during middle age, a mutative effect of experience that decreases vulnerability in the system of self-esteem regulation and increases resilience to narcissistic injury. When this mutative effect is prematurely interrupted, as in the case of physical illness during middle life, latent areas of vulnerability are exposed that would otherwise have softened with time. Kernberg (1980) has commented on how features of normal and narcissistic personalities become tempered in the context of modification and reworking of earlier conflicts during middle life. This exposition examines disruptions in this mutative effect by physical illness. In healthy individuals, the inevitable small hurts garnered in the years of middle life ultimately lead to more subtle and malleable ideal self-representations. One comes more readily to accept one's limitations. Even structures that have been built on the fragile edifice of defense against unresolved conflict become more firmly rooted and autonomous. Defensive constellations take on secondary autonomy. This gradual process is preparation for the confrontation with greater decline in old age. It does not have the negative connotation of "coming to terms"; ultimately it is highly adaptive and eases one through life.

The process may be revealed when reasonably healthy and well-adapted individuals are confronted with major crises that reveal a discrepancy between their ideal self-representation and their actual representation as modified by the crisis itself. Under these circumstances, a critical alteration of the life trajectory occurs, and there is a premature confrontation with areas of vulnerability that were quiescent and unrevealed and under other circumstances would have gradually been modified. I will illustrate this process with case histories.

Mourning for a Lost Self-Representation in a
Well-Integrated Woman

The sudden onset of physical illness frequently causes a dramatic change in the self-representation. In some situations, this leads to de-

224

pression as the patient experiences a marked discordance between self and ideal self-representations (Joffe and Sandler, 1965). In other situations, where only an aspect of the self-representation is modified and other aspects rest on a solid base unaffected by the physical illness, the patient undergoes a mourning response for the aspect that has changed. This is the case with the patient described below.

CASE HISTORY

The patient was a forty-year-old married executive with three adolescent children. She presented with what appeared to be a mixture of intense grief and some depression six months after the discovery of an extensive breast carcinoma followed by chemotherapy and radiation treatment. Her diagnosis was made during the same month that her closest friend died of a breast carcinoma after three years of illness. Two other young friends and colleagues had died of the disease within the same year.

The patient was a very intelligent, engaging, and spontaneous woman who cried profusely throughout the early interviews. Her spontaneity and relatedness, charm, and capacity to laugh even through her tears coupled with a pervasive sadness suggested a mourning response rather than a true depression although there were elements of depression as well.

She described a happy early life with an attentive, maternal mother, a more distant father, and an older brother with whom she had a close relationship. The description of her early life conveyed a sense that there had been much nurturance and a solid foundation for adult life. This was echoed by her description of a happy marriage to a sensitive and supportive man and a rich and engaged relationship with her children, who were developing normally. In spite of her illness she felt lovable and never doubted the authenticity of the love she received from husband, children, friends, and parents.

The treatment of this patient was an active supportive and interpretive biweekly therapy with a focus on the present. Her emotional availability permitted easy empathic communication, and clarifications and interpretations had an immediate and powerful impact upon her, rapidly relieving distress. This evoked a strong idealized transference wherein she delegated authority to me and experienced an umbrella of safety, a holding environment. This did not prevent her from expressing hostility to me at times—for example, when she resented my having seen her vulnerability and loss of control. She compared this therapeutic experience positively with the negative experiences she had had with two other psychiatrists after the diagnosis. The first had frightened her by stating that she would have to reexamine her problems and her life. The second evoked a panic when he diagnosed a major depression.

Our first contact had been reassuring, as I immediately interpreted the inevitability of her panic about loss of control, given her previous gratifying sense of control. In this first session I went further to comment on her manner of speaking as if she were preparing to die. She revealed in the second session that she had felt enormously relieved. She felt quite well during two weeks of absence when I left for vacation. Upon my return I pointed out how her hypervigilance, highly adaptive in a business situation, was a source of great anxiety when focused on bodily illness. Moreover, the anxiety that arose when she "caught herself feeling good" represented another manifestation of her attempt to control, to avoid being caught off guard. Again she experienced relief even as she talked about her rage toward her body, which had betrayed her.

Previously she had been a confident person, inclined to minor worries about the future, but an optimistic planner and a person with a sense of control over her life as she acted in her multiple roles as mother, wife, lover, and professional. When younger she had experienced some anxiety about the future to which she had responded with a somewhat compulsive need to plan. This had been muted over the years, and by the time her children were born, the anxious compulsive component had disappeared. After six years at home with the children she had returned to work, but her planning now was an adaptive and necessary part of her work and the requirements of running a household.

The experience of the neoplasm had shaken her badly. Periodically she moved into a state in which she would compulsively plan her own course of illness and death, deciding not to enter the hospital, to refuse chemotherapy, and ultimately to commit suicide although she was clearly not suicidal. This compulsive fantasy reflected her desire to control her situation and to eliminate uncertainty, with the sense of choice implicit in the fearful alternatives she was considering. During the period that she was having these fantasies, she was unable to plan projects for months in advance as they pertained to her professional work since her longevity was not under her control. At the same time, she enjoyed making defined and time-limited plans to do "trivia" at home, tasks that were under her control and that she could confidently complete.

A fundamental aspect of her self-representation had changed and no longer approximated her ideal self-representation in this respect (Sandler and Rosenblatt, 1962). She saw herself as uncertain, out of control of her feelings and her future, even unable to control her thoughts as she recurrently experienced gloomily fearful ideas about her future. She was not the person she had been. When it was pointed out to her that she was struggling with a discrepancy between her old self, which had become increasingly confident, and her current self, she revealed that she was grieving over the person she had been and no longer was. Every experience that reminded her of the old self evoked intense sadness.

Her family had had an extremely close relationship with the family of her friend who had died at the time of her own diagnosis. The two families regularly had spent weekends together in their respective country houses, sharing impromptu meals and living closely and intimately. The husband of her dead friend continued to initiate contacts and make plans for family weekends as if to deny the reality of the loss and act as if nothing had changed. These encounters, which he so desired and saw as so useful for his children, were a source of great pain to the patient. Contact with the other family was a reminder of "what had been" and of the loss of her old confident self and her old life. The widower's wish that they spend a weekend at his seaside house, something they had not done since the death of her friend, filled her with dread and dismay. When it was pointed out that his needs and hers were dissynchronous and that she did not have to be so self-sacrificing, so "frugal," as her own mother had been, she was able to speak to this friend, who understood the nature of her distress. An anticipated visit to her own country house for the first time since her diagnosis was also experienced as threatening until it was pointed out that she was revisiting a past that was no longer the same (at least at this time). This tempered the fear, permitted a satisfying weekend, and left her with the feeling that she had worked something through. This was true in her professional life as well. The initial encounter with colleagues whom she had not seen since her illness was always painful. As she worked through this reentry into the world, each time confronting the loss of her old self, she became more comfortable and more of her time could be devoted to engagement in the world. Each newly experienced reminder of her past self and life evoked similar pain and grief, exactly as is the case with the grieving person who reworks a loss through reminders of past experience with the lost loved one. After about a month of this process, her daughter commented, "You seem much better. You cry only half the time."

As the patient began to improve, an interesting phenomenon evolved. She began to use her illness in the service of defense against antecedent minor conflicts. On one occasion she entered the room quite depressed, concerned that her illness had prevented her from attending a conference that under normal circumstances she would have partici- pated in, though reluctantly. She laughed as it became apparent that this was a competitive situation that had evoked anxiety in the past, and that the illness had permitted her to avoid what was otherwise a conflictual situation.

The patient continued to work through these problems, though there were moments of considerable pain, such as occurred on the first anniversary of the diagnosis.

DISCUSSION

This vigorous, intelligent, successful woman had been generally com- fortable in life and experienced great pleasure in her personal relation- ships and her professional activities. Her initial inclination as a young adult to worry and plan compulsively for the future had become muted, and she had found herself much less apprehensive as she discovered herself capable of handling the difficulties that confronted her before she became physically ill. She had had a sense of herself as competent and able to cope. Another aspect of change that had been occurring over the previous twenty years had had to do with a diminishing iden- tification with her mother's self-sacrificing frugality and an increasing willingness on her part to "pleasurably indulge" herself on occasion and respond to her own needs even when they were in opposition to those of others.

That her illness had occurred under unfortunate circumstances—at the time of her closest friend's death of breast cancer and after the loss of two other friends to the disease over the previous year—was an important contributing factor to the pessimistic, worrisome view of the future she developed about her own illness. This led to an inten- sified perception of herself as pessimistic, fearful, and out of control of her feelings.[1] The illness undermined the gains she had made as a

1. The patient confirmed the interpretation of the importance of the context of her illness as it augmented a pessimistic outlook. A relative she disliked because of her self-

young adult in overcoming her tendency to worry about the future. The gains had been facilitated by having to come to terms with her father's chronic illness, which had taught her that she could master pain.

It was clear that a mutative process had been occurring over the years before she became ill. During this period her strength was apparent as it was reflected in her professional life, in her marriage, and in her relationships with her friends and her family. Her general optimism and the joy she experienced in life were highly adaptive. These traits deeply rooted in her personality and did not in themselves seem substantially defensive against other more fearful concerns. It is likely that if the illness had not occurred and shaken her equilibrium, the inevitable hurts that life brings would have tempered her optimism and made her aware of the incompleteness of her control. Even her apparently excellent marital relationship, with its free communication and intimacy, would have been subject to the vicissitudes of inevitable conflict to which she would have accommodated. These experiences in a fundamentally healthy personality structure would have softened the outlines of her self-representation, her ideal self-representation, and the tension between them. There is every reason to expect that these modifications would have permitted her to weather the experience of old age and illness in old age in a gentler way.

The confrontation with physical illness before the mutative change could be consolidated left her with a strong sense of loss, as it pertained to an aspect of her self-representation that she had highly valued—the sense of control and increasing optimism. The goal of psychotherapy was in part to mute the traumatic aspect of the experience and to facilitate a change that would have been accomplished over time had she not become ill. The therapy was facilitated by her trusting attitude and conviction of the commitment of other people to her. She viewed herself as loving and worthy of love, an aspect of the self-representation that had not changed and that had protected her against severe depression. Under usual and felicitous circumstances life experience offers the opportunity for gradual accommodation to loss and low-grade mourning (Pollock, 1978).

---

centered loquacity had called her after she, the cousin, had had a lumpectomy. The relative described an array of women who had had positive outcomes with breast cancer. The patient felt relieved as this woman described her "research," and later she attempted to conjure up images of this conversation when she had negative thoughts about her own illness. She was spontaneously attempting a type of cognitive reframing. This patient illustrates the inadequate attention we pay to the context in which a negative experience occurs and how much it influences optimistic or pessimistic attitudes.

Unmasking: Global Regression

The phenomenon that I call unmasking is readily observed in certain individuals subjected to the psychological injury of sudden and severe physical illness before old age. The psychoanalytic genetic hypothesis (Rapaport, 1960) is a hierarchical systems model that had its prototype in Hughling Jackson's description of the nervous system. Jackson (1969) described development as the progressive organization and integration of successively higher and more complex organizations of behavior reflective of brain development. As higher and more complex forms evolve, they inhibit the more primitive forms, which, however, maintain latent potential and emerge in manifest behavior when the higher inhibiting structures are dissolved. Freud translated this into a dynamic psychological theory of fixation and regression.

Although latent intrapsychic conflict underlies all mature behavior to a greater or lesser degree, the resilience of adult behavior varies to the extent that it represents a more or less stable compromise formation with adaptive ego components—that is, autonomy from conflict (Hartmann, 1954). Independence with a capacity for mature dependency is a valued and adaptive adult trait. But individuals who appear on the surface to be independent may be defending themselves against profound dependency needs. Such a situation becomes evident when an apparently independent adult experiences serious physical illness that interferes with activities that previously acted as tonic supports for the patient's view of himself as independent. Under these circumstances, the underlying conflictual organization is unmasked. Such was the case with the patient presented below.

CASE HISTORY

The patient was a forty-eight-year-old married father of two adopted children. He had had a kidney transplant for six years after undergoing dialysis for three years. In spite of the well-functioning transplant, he experienced chronic fatigue, dissatisfaction, and a general disillusionment that was manifested in depression.

The patient had prided himself on his success as a tugboat captain until nine years earlier, when his illness had forced him to relinquish his job. He presented himself as an embittered, grudgingly compliant, defeated, resigned, and disabled shadow of a man. He angrily complained of the indifference of the world and particularly of the doctors, who, in fact, had been quite attentive to him. He viewed himself as a have-not dominated by those with position and material comfort. He revealed marked distress: he slept poorly, lacked energy and initiative, and wondered whether it would have been better to die. There was considerable guilt about not having properly provided for his family during his illness. Most striking was his description of the dramatic change in his personality that had occurred when he became ill and his sense of betrayal because the transplant had not made him the man he had been.

The patient was the third child in a lower-class family of five brothers and one sister. He described an early life of marked deprivation with much suppression and stated, "There's no point in digging up old graves; you're not going to seek vengeance." He remembered little of his mother who had been an alcoholic. His last contact with her occurred when he was six years of age and his parents separated. He lived with his father, who worked at two jobs and was rarely at home. He rapidly developed a self-reliant stance as an adolescent, although he experienced some support from a brother two years his senior, a somewhat idealized and powerful figure who "looked out" for him.

The patient left school to work at a number of jobs, each time rapidly advancing, until he began to work on the tugboat, which he loved. At twenty-two he married his first girlfriend, who has remained a supportive, responsive wife, tolerant of his current irascible and disgruntled nature. Because his wife was unable to conceive, they adopted two children. He became captain of the boat in his early thirties. This was a heavy responsibility, for these boats were valued in the millions, and although he was never entirely comfortable with his work, he prided himself on his skillful and competent management of it. These had been happy years for the patient. He described himself as having a devil-may-care attitude, emphasizing his freedom from anxiety, his activity, independence, self-reliance, and particularly his satisfaction at being the undisputed provider for his family (he had insisted that his wife give up her job when the children came). Thus, during this period and until his illness, he was a man of high self-esteem based on his feeling that he was meeting his responsibilities, working productively, and giving his family what he had never had. The onset of illness and the disruption of work led to marked changes in his view of himself and in his relationship to the world.

DISCUSSION

This patient had successfully coped with early emotional deprivation by becoming independent and self-reliant. His success in life before his illness was admirable, but it is clear that his self-confidence and self-esteem were contingent on his working at a responsible job and particularly on his caring for himself, his wife, and the children as he had not been cared for. His model for this ideal was a nurturant older brother. The independence generated by the patient's successful professional life and his experience of himself as nurturing his family was a real and gratifying experience which tended to solidify a view of himself as far removed from the needy child he had been. The onset of illness evoked a regressive return of anger, a reevocation of his early response to maternal deprivation, now expressed as a bitter complaint about the failure of society and the physicians to rehabilitate him, a state of mind that persisted for six years despite the successful transplant.

Before he became ill, this man had been in the process of reworking and undoing an early experience. Had his illness not occurred and had he continued to live out his successful professional life as a tugboat captain, to act as the provider for his still dependent children, and to be a mentor to others as his brother had been to him, there is every reason to believe that he would never have experienced the disruptive dissolution of what at the time of his illness had remained an unstable structure. Had the solidity of his independent adaptation come to a gentle and natural end through ultimate retirement and with the maturation and growth of his children to adulthood, it is likely that in old age his "life review" (Butler, 1963; Erikson, 1963) would have been permeated with a sense of contentment and accomplishment and that he would have vanquished the phantom of inner neediness.

The Disruption of the Life Trajectory

Individuals vary in the degree to which they develop defined perspectives on their lives and expectations of themselves. It is generally considered that an internal focus of control, a vigorous response to challenge as an opportunity for growth, and a sense of commitment to what one does with a high valuation of it are healthy and adaptive traits that protect individuals from the potential harm of stressful experiences (Kobasa, 1982). Individuals who have defined plans and expectations for the trajectory of their lives also vary in the degree to which these schema represent primarily nonconflictual motivations or defenses against unconscious fears of weakness, inadequacy, lack of masculinity, and so on. Realistic goal setting as it relates to long-term objectives is a highly adaptive tool for interacting with the world. But when these goals, adaptive though they might be, become central to the psychic equilibrium of an individual and a major interruption occurs that prevents their implementation, there are serious psychic consequences. Such was the case with the patient described below.

CASE HISTORY

The patient was a thirty-three-year-old married father of one. He was referred for evaluation of depression, which had developed eight months before when a diagnosis of progressive renal failure had been made, although hemodialysis was not required immediately. He was an intelligent, articulate man who when first seen was moderately to severely depressed. He described his life history coherently, but with resignation. He displayed a wide range of feeling, although his personality style was obsessional.

The patient was the older of two children born to a middle-class family. Father was described as a passive man, trained as an engineer, who had suffered a depression when he lost his job. Mother was described as an independent, strong woman, somewhat indifferent to the social pressures existing in the community. In spite of economic difficulties in the family, the patient described his childhood as happy. Delayed puberty and small stature as an early adolescent had contributed to a feeling of insecurity for which he had compensated effectively in adolescence and adult life through athletic activities. His excellent physical condition was a source of particular pride. A lifelong anxiety about death was related to early experiences. His grandfather had died a lingering death of cancer in the patient's home when the patient was three to four years of age. The sudden death of his grandmother when he was nine, of a coronary, was extremely disturbing to his mother, who became hysterical "for two days," although ordinarily she was under good control.

Very striking in his description of his early adult life was a remarkably defined life plan that he had been implementing before he became ill. He was an extremely competent and industrious man who saw himself as moving up the corporate ladder according to a precise schedule. In addition, he had plans to participate in an Olympic sailing competition and was making "the necessary preparations."

The first evidence of illness occurred about a year and a half before he was first seen, when he developed edema while sailing. He initially minimized the threat by focusing on ambiguity about the etiology of the disease. He convinced an otherwise responsible physician that he should be treated with Cytozan, a toxic drug, in the hope and expectation that it would reverse the disease, although he was not clearly in the category of patients who usually profit from such treatment. It was with the failure of this treatment, and at the time of a second biopsy, when he could no longer deny the progressive and irreversible nature of his disease, that he became despondent. Each deterioration of the laboratory values related to kidney functions led to increasing depression and irritability. In the context of a diminution of his physical prowess, he indicated that a life not controlled by him was "a life not worth living." He particularly resented the increasing strength and assertiveness of his wife, who had been quite dependent on him at the time they married. Her independence coupled with his fear of his own dependency needs aroused by the illness were extremely demoralizing.

A crisis intervention (a Psychodynamic Life Narrative; Viederman, 1983)[2] provided understanding to the patient of how his current depression was a logical and inevitable product of his life experience. It rapidly relieved his depression, led to a changed perspective on himself, and helped him accept a transplant from his sister, which resulted in marked improvement in his physical status.

DISCUSSION

This intelligent and vigorous man had developed a somewhat brittle but energetic life-style characterized by action and expectation of achievement. This was in part a defense against identification with a passive father and doubts about masculinity generated by his small stature and the stresses of delayed puberty. A conflicted identification with a powerful mother also increased his doubts about his masculinity. His defensive, competitive coping style, abetted by his talent, energy,

2. A Psychodynamic Life Narrative is a construct offered by a therapist to a patient in crisis which demonstrates to the patient that his emotional reaction to a particular event is a logical product of his life experience and not a direct reaction to the event itself.

strong motivation, and willingness to work, enabled him to solidify his image as a powerful man capable of implementing his professional and athletic goals. This thrust was interrupted by his physical illness which left him depressed and without purpose.

Had he not become ill, it is certain that life events would have periodically interfered with his plans. Nevertheless, given his life trajectory, this man probably would have achieved at least some of his more reasonable goals. He would have gradually moved into old age with the sense of satisfaction that accompanies achievement of purpose and with the realization that he had lived a life different from his father's.

It is to be noted that after initial resistance to consultation with a psychiatrist, he eventually accepted a crisis intervention with follow-up treatment. This led to a considerable change in his perception of himself and the underlying motivations for his driven behavior.

General Discussion

Psychoanalytic theory is derived from work with psychoanalytic patients. In enriching the concept of ego and giving it new status in psychoanalytic theory, Hartmann (1954) had as his purpose the development of a general psychology of human behavior. Although psychoanalysis as a treatment modality and by extension as a research tool is especially useful in elaborating the nuances of intrapsychic conflict, its limits as a general psychology relate to its dependence on the psychoanalytic situation except as extended to applied psychoanalysis. Often, however, there is a suspicion of data not generated in the psychoanalytic situation. But how are we to examine our theory as it applies to the vast population of individuals who neither require nor are suitable for psychoanalysis? Psychoanalysts have manifested an interest in the life cycle (Erikson, 1963; Vaillant, 1977; Levinson, 1978; Gould, 1972; Colarusso and Nemiroff, 1981) and normative behavior, but, except for Erikson's, this work has been seen as peripheral to analytic thinking and not as important to the main corpus of psychoanalytic thinking and theory, although the child development literature is rich in this regard (Emde, 1984; Kagan, 1984). This volume reflects the increasing interest of psychoanalysts in behavior and the process of normative change throughout the life cycle.

There is however, a theoretical problem implicit in the psychoanalytic consideration of change over the course of the life cycle. When the primary thrust of psychoanalysis shifted from symptom resolution to the treatment of personality disorder, it was natural and proper to be impressed by the fixity of behavior and its resistance to change. This is central in the work of any practicing psychoanalyst and is implicit in the theoretical notion of structure. Interest naturally is focused on the genetic hypothesis and the relentless and often self-defeating repetition of the past. Under these circumstances, little attention has been directed to the ways in which people change significantly throughout their life cycles. Moreover, the very individuals who do develop adaptive modes of dealing with internal conflict are excluded from formal psychoanalytic scrutiny. To those analysts working in settings separate from the psychoanalytic situation, it has become apparent that individuals change through life experiences, particularly in the context of crisis which under felicitous circumstances facilitates conflict resolution, repair of damaged self-representations, and so on (Viederman, 1986; 1988; in press).

One might examine the experiences of the patients described above from the point of view of the nature of the disruption that occurred in their life trajectory. Generally, dramatically altered behaviors in response to physical illness are viewed as manifestations of disruption of psychic structure with regression related to crises. Schwartz (1987), in a recent effort to integrate neurobiological findings with psychoanalytic theory, proposes a theory of motivation that relates to the activation of hedonically regulated states that have their substrate in neurological networks. Thus, positive and negative affective states are activated in part by external stimuli and then, by virtue of their relationships to memory systems, set in motion behaviors that may include defense. Clearly the substrate for behavior rests upon memories of previous experience and the persistence of behavioral patterns reflected in the expectation that past experience will act as a guide for adaptive future behavior. When a dramatically new situation such as physical illness imposes itself, however, strikingly altered behavior results because previous experience no longer acts as a useful predictive guide for future expectation. In the absence of a reliable schema that reasonably predicts the future, the system becomes disorganized and old behavioral patterns reemerge. From this point of view one might consider that a traumatic situation, one that evokes crisis, can be defined as a situation in which previous sets of expectations that lead to predictions of what one can reasonably expect in the future are no longer to be relied upon.

The inverse is also true. Schwartz emphasizes the increasing awareness of a continuing plasticity of the nervous system which earlier had been thought to be almost irreversibly fixed in defined patterns before adulthood. The solid accretions of success encoded in memory become predictors of the response of the individual to new situations. This includes resilient responses in the face of injuries to self-esteem and failure. From this point of view, therefore, long-enduring patterns of adaptive behavior lead to structural change in the representational world.

A related issue touches on the degree to which individuals can escape from severe early deprivations and trauma to develop highly adaptive modes of engaging the world as adults. There is a bias in psychoanalytic thinking that suggests that radical escape from one's past is impossible and that the secure foundations in adult life are inevitably linked to "good-enough early experience" (borrowed from Winnicott's "good-enough mothering" [1965]). Kernberg (1980) discusses the process of maturation from this point of view: "The repeated work of recreating and consolidating the world of one's parents also increases the tolerance for the ambivalence of and toward one's children, and the freedom for maintaining, increasing, and deepening the interest in their now independently growing world" (p. 133). This process occurs in "reasonably healthy" and mature individuals. Although it is certainly true that early trauma is a frequent harbinger of adult neurosis and maladaptation, there are individuals who win the battle against their past in developing adaptive modes. Although initially defensive against intrapsychic conflict, adaptive behaviors in engagement with the world over the course of time may lead to the consolidation of new self-representations that are reasonable approximations to ideal self-representations.

The examination of some normal processes of change in nonpatients can only be inferred in the context of the examination of disrupted life trajectories that before had appeared to be following a smooth course. Although one can never be certain of what the future will hold in the face of the inevitable changes in life, many individuals become more supple as life proceeds (Neugarten, 1979). There is no proof, of course, that the individuals described above would have continued in the path they seemed to be following, yet common sense suggests that continuing positive experience would mute the pain and conflict generated in their early lives. Only the intrusion of a traumatic situation exposed the faults and fissures in their adaptations. In the case of the first woman discussed above, in spite of minor areas of vulnerability and conflict that were already in the process of change, she would have been viewed as "healthy" by any criteria before she was afflicted with cancer. Her investment in the successful, confident image of herself as she approached the middle years, however, was not rooted adequately enough to weather the disruption caused by the new circumstance. Such was the case with the other two patients as well. The crisis of physical illness intervened to disrupt the consolidation of these new representations and interfered with the mutative effect of time and the achievement of a more comfortable and gratifying old age.

REFERENCES

Butler, R. N. 1963. The life review: An interpretation of reminiscence in the aged. *Psychiatry* 26:65.

Colarusso, C., and Nemiroff, R. A. 1981. *Adult development*. New York: Plenum Press.

Emde, R. 1984. *Continuities and discontinuities in development*. Ed. R. Emde and R. Harmon. New York: Plenum Press.

Erikson, E. 1963. *Childhood and society*. 2nd ed. New York: W. W. Norton.

Freud, S. 1926. Inhibitions, symptoms and anxiety. In *Standard edition*, 20: 77–178.

———. 1937. Analysis terminable and interminable. In *Standard edition*, 23: 211.

Gould, R. L. 1972. The phases of adult life: A study in developmental psychology. *American Journal of Psychiatry*, 129:521.

Hartmann, H. 1954. *The ego and the problem of adaptation*. New York: International Universities Press.

Jackson, S. 1969. The history of Freud's concept of regression. *Journal of the American Psychoanalytic Association* 17:743–784.

Joffe, W. G., and Sandler, J. 1965. Notes of pain, depression and individuation. In *The psychoanalytic study of the child*, 20:394–424. New York: International Universities Press.

Kagan, J. 1984. *The nature of the child*. New York: Basic Books.

Kernberg, O. 1980. *Normal narcissism in middle age: Internal world and external reality*. New York: Aronson.

Kobasa, S. 1982. The hardy personality: Toward a social psychology of stress and health. In *Social psychology of health and illness*. Ed. G. S. Sanders and J. Sulx, 3–32. New York: Erlbaum Associates.

Levinson, D. 1978. *The seasons of a man's life*. New York: Alfred Knopf.

Neugarten, B. 1979. Time, age and the life cycle. *American Journal of Psychiatry* 136:887–893.

Pollock, G. H. 1978. Process and affect: Mourning and grief. *International Journal of Psychoanalysis* 59:225–276.

Rapaport, D. 1960. *The structure of psychoanalytic theory: A systematizing attempt.* Psychological Issues, Monograph no. 6, vol. 2. New York: International Universities Press.

Sandler, J., and Rosenblatt, B. 1962. The concept of the representational world. In *The psychoanalytic study of the child*, 17:128–145. New York: International Universities Press.

Schwartz, A. 1987. Drives, affects, behavior, and learning. *Journal of the American Psychoanalytic Association* 35:467–506.

Vaillant, G. 1977. *Adaptation to life.* Boston: Little, Brown.

Viederman, M. 1983. The psychodynamic life narrative: A psychotherapeutic intervention useful in crisis situations. *Psychiatry* 46:236–246.

———. 1986. Personality change through life experience I. *Psychiatry* 49:204–217.

———. 1988. Personality change through life experience III: The role of object loss. In *The problem of loss and mourning: Psychoanalytic perspectives.* Ed. D. Dietrich and P. Shabad. New York: International Universities Press.

———. In press. Personality change through life experience II: The role of ego ideal, personality. In *Psychoanalysis: The second century.* Ed. A. Cooper. New Haven: Yale University Press.

Winnicott, D. W. 1965. Ego distortion in terms of true or false self. In *The maturational process and the facilitating environment.* New York: International Universities Press.

· 17 ·

DEBATE
As One Gets Older, Brief Therapy Is More Often Indicated than Psychoanalysis

ALLEN FRANCES, M. D. *Affirmative*

CHARLES BRENNER, M. D. *Negative*

GERALD I. FOGEL, M. D. *Moderator*

GERALD I. FOGEL: I suspect that the provocative title and the debate format of this portion of the book may lead some readers to anticipate sharply drawn battle lines between our two distinguished participants. The major characterological goals of psychoanalysis and the time it takes to accomplish these goals make that treatment less often indicated for older patients than treatments that are more focal, take less time, and allow people to do the things they want while they still have the capacity to do so: true or false? Dr. Frances is a knowledgeable analyst but also an articulate spokesman for the efficacy of briefer, focal treatments; Dr. Brenner believes that psychoanalysis offers greater therapeutic power and potential than other therapies and that it is therefore the treatment of choice for the patient who can use it. In practice, however, each of these seasoned analytic thinkers and clinicians has his own conception of the strengths and limits of analytic work, and their approaches to a particular clinical situation may therefore be expected sometimes to overlap.

There are also larger questions embedded in our topic which our participants must almost inevitably address. What, in general, are the indications and contraindications for psychoanalytic treatment? Is psychoanalysis the treatment of choice in every instance where it might be beneficial? When psychoanalysis is not indicated, what are the alternatives, and what are the criteria for choosing appropriately among them? Are alternative treatments inevitably less complete in their therapeutic benefits, or may such therapies sometimes be merely different from and even more effective than psychoanalysis? What are some of the special considerations in the middle years that may or should affect such clinical judgments? In specific clinical instances, might there be differences of degree and emphasis, which, though they can and must be more sharply conceptualized, may not be as black and white as we have framed them in our title?

Each participant will give an opening statement, followed by response from the other. Then will come a dialogue between the two, as well as some comments by others.

ALLEN FRANCES: Let me start with my summary. Freud developed two types of psychotherapy. The second type chronologically, and the one I suspect he practiced less often, was a treatment that made use of a regressive transference neurosis. The first type of psychotherapy, the one I suspect he practiced much more often than we think, did not depend on a regressive transference neurosis. Unfortunately, a kind of family feud has evolved between these two types of psychodynamic treatment that probably reflects a narcissism of small differences. Perhaps we could afford this feud previously, but not any more. We should instead be very happy to have a variety of psychodynamic treatments available, ranging from those that are quite brief and intentionally nonregressive to those that are more expressive and include some regression, and on to psychoanalysis, with its encouragement of the transference neurosis. The major task is not to find out which of these is better in some overall sense but rather to try to determine which to use in a given situation.

The subject of this discussion is the question of the differential indications for brief treatments as opposed to more regressive psychoanalytic treatment as these are applied to the middle years. Because I do not see mid-life crises as one generic construct, I won't argue that "time is running out" for everyone in mid-life. Instead, I will focus on a few developmental crises that occur with special frequency during mid-life and for which I think brief therapy is indicated in preference to psychoanalysis.

Freud was an unsung but remarkably effective brief therapist. This comes through most clearly in "Studies in Hysteria." Everything that has ever been said since about brief therapy he actually practiced quite clearly, and documented in case studies. Throughout his career many of Freud's treatments were quite brief. At times it was not unusual for most of his practice to be conducted in English with people who spent relatively short amounts of time in Vienna. Freud is always described by those he treated as an active and focusing therapist who talked a great deal and had decisive opinions. He was anything but an anonymous figure to his patients—indeed, he may have been in many ways the least anonymous person to live in our century. It is my guess that most of Freud's actual treatments were not characterized by the same interest in regressive transference neurosis that became characteristic of classical psychoanalysis. This is not to say that he never did such treatments, but I think we should not ignore that he fathered two different psychodynamic approaches.

Given that the early psychoanalytic treatments were usually brief, why did they get longer? One major reason was an increasing interest in the analysis of resistance, character, and transference. Furthermore, analysis came to rely more and more only on free association as a technical device and became less active and less interpretive. Analysts tried to create a lack of structure and ambiguity in the analytic situation in order to promote a regressive transference experience in the patient. Psychoanalysis caused a kind of artificial developmental crisis in the transference neurosis that could then be analyzed.

Very quickly, there was a reaction against the increasing length of analysis. The first people to write explicitly what was essentially a brief-therapy manual were Ferenczi and Rank. They produced an absolutely brilliant piece of work which follows from the early Freud and provides us with all the essentials that have since been described for focal therapy. Essentially their recommendations include therapist activity and the rapid formulation of the central conflict that ties together the chief complaint, the patient's early transferences, and patterns of behavior going back to early important object relations. Ferenczi and Rank suggested that early interpretations connecting these three spheres would create the conditions for a circumscribed characterological change. They involved an essentially nonregressive treatment. Although they borrowed heavily from Freud, Ferenczi and Rank were not at this point highly regarded by their psychoanalytic colleagues, who did not accept the suggested clinical innovations in a kind and fraternal way. Partly, this was because of the way these suggestions were offered. It was feared that psychoanalysis would be replaced by this other form of treatment rather than being complemented and thus enhanced. And so brief therapy in its first official manifestation, in the mid-1920s, was not accepted within the corpus of "official" psychodynamic psychotherapy.

In the 1930s and 1940s, Alexander and French made the second major attempt to alert clinicians to the usefulness of the suggestions originally made by Freud and then taken up by Ferenczi and Rank. Their writings are clinically brilliant but did not add very much that was new except the term *corrective emotional experience.* The unfortunate thing about this term was that it became associated in people's minds with a manipulative transference, an association that is not really inherent or necessary. The work of Alexander and French also was received with severe condemnation and disregarded by many people within the psychoanalytic movement.

There is a perhaps apocryphal story that Alexander visited Freud shortly after his migration to London in 1938. Freud is reported to have said, "Franz, I like your work on the brief treatments very much and would like to write about it, but those people at the New York Psychoanalytic would give me too much trouble."

During the past twenty-five years many centers have become involved in developing focal therapy. Malan has been the most important contributor, especially in his ability to do psychotherapy research in the clinical setting in a way that does justice both to research needs and to the clinical setting. Sifneos, Mann, Davanloo, Marmor, and the sex therapists who have a psychodynamic orientation have also been important in developing focal therapy techniques. This has become a more and more substantial body of therapeutic innovation.

The basic question for us here is when do we conduct a nonregressive treatment and when do we conduct a treatment that encourages regression within the therapeutic relationship for purposes of a more ambitious kind of character change? For heuristic purposes we are artificially dichotomizing brief treatment versus psychoanalysis and leaving out of the discussion long-term exploratory psychotherapies which can have aspects of each, depending on the length of the treatment, its intensity, the kind of patient, and the kind of therapist. We will leave out the middle ground between focal therapy and analysis for purposes of clarity.

One rule of thumb is that a focal therapy is most useful for those who have considerable ability as patients, so that they do not require a long induction before productive work can be done. The therapist and patient together are able to establish a focal unconscious conflict that ties together surface symptomatology with early transference and past experience. The goals of treatment do not include a thoroughgoing characterological change, and there is a willingness to accept less ambitious results. Perhaps most important and pertinent to this debate, focal therapy is especially indicated when there is a need for rapid change. It seems quite likely that brief treatments produce quicker results.

How do these indications for focal therapy stack up with the situation in mid-life? In this volume, Dr. Kernberg, Dr. Nadelson, and Dr. Kalinich emphasize an issue that I think is pertinent in this regard— the biological clock. The statistics predicting marriage and childbearing opportunities are alarming for women entering their thirties. For many people, the decision to remain single and/or childless may reflect a conscious choice and one that should be accepted. For others, it is certainly not a result achieved by their own design. Although the demographic obstacles may play a large role in women's remaining single, my experience is that intrapsychic factors can be quite important. It seems to me that for women in this situation, it makes great sense to conduct a treatment that is likely to move the patient quickly forward to face the specific personal inhibitions and conflicts that might otherwise reduce opportunities for marriage and/or childbearing. The major relationship that should be analyzed probably will *not* include that between the patient and the therapist. The transference analysis will be part of the treatment and an important illustration of conflicts, but the relationships the patient is having or avoiding with other people outside of treatment will be central and the important focus for interpretation. This is not to say that all women in mid-life should receive brief treatment rather than analysis. I am suggesting, however, that in many instances it makes sense for the treatment to be directed early and in a focused way to inhibitions that can be rapidly mobilized, analyzed, and addressed.

This contradicts the assumption that the patient must undergo the tribulations and time involved in the regressive transference experience and that the only way she will be able to rework internal conflicts so that a love relationship and childbearing are possible is through the reexperience and resolution of that regressive transference experience with the analyst. I don't think that transference neurosis is the most efficient way of working when time is of the essence. It is time-consuming, and for certain people opportunities may be missed that won't come back again. The biological clock creates situations that must be addressed quickly because there may not be a second chance.

There are many other similar situations that occur in the middle years both with men and with women—the Ph.D. candidate who spends twelve years on a doctorate, or the person possibly in line for an important new job. In my experience, mid-life is a particularly crucial time for some people either to succeed or not, depending on concrete actions and decisions that often must be made in the short run. Opportunities often knock but once. In these situations, it may make great sense to aim for a more limited and circumscribed characterological treatment. For people who are already in a developmental crisis, intra-psychic change can be much more rapid.

Other developmental issues that often call for focal therapy include problems with parenting, with dealing with one's own parents, and with job loss and retirement. When there is a developmental crisis and an interaction between character and the crisis, it may be more efficient to deal with that interaction "on the hoof," as it were, rather than attempt to re-create a developmentally regressed transference neurosis. Admit-tedly, psychoanalysis may in many instances result in more profound change if the treatment works, but sometimes the changes may come too slowly for the patient to reap available rewards.

When is psychoanalysis indicated during the middle years? I have highlighted several developmental issues that happen not infrequently among people in their middle years. But one also sees many patients in mid-life who are pretty much stuck intrapsychically and in a very stable external situation in their lives, and who don't have a developmental crisis. For them time is not particularly "running out" any more than it is "running out" for all of us. It is not running out in the same especially poignant way as it is for those in the developmental crises of middle age. For these people, analysis is still a very sensible treatment, if that is what they want and what the therapist thinks is best, and they are capable of doing it together. This is what I meant when I said earlier that I don't see mid-life as a generic time of developmental crisis. I think, therefore, that I am redefining the terms of the discussion a bit. I am focusing on time as "running out" only for those people during the middle years who have one of the developmental crises that we have mentioned.

CHARLES BRENNER: I agree essentially with Dr. Frances about indica-tions for analysis and indications for brief psychotherapy in mid-life, in the later years, or in earlier years. When there are indications for analy-sis, practical as well as clinical, then that's the treatment of choice. Dr. Frances referred some to the history of the development of psychoana-lytically based forms of treatment. One of the things Freud said back in the 1920s was that people are eager for a quick, inexpensive, and afford-able form of treatment for their psychoneuroses. He said he shared that desire and wished he could satisfy it. And he reminded his readers that it would be nice to have a similarly brief form of treatment, for example, for tuberculosis and cancer. Well, we're on our way as far as cancer is concerned—whether we will ever arrive there we don't know. As for tuberculosis, certainly, to a large extent that wish has been satisfied. Maybe the same will be true someday for psychological illness, but we are not there yet.

If a person comes to your office and consults you for psychological symptoms that are caused by a recent upset or crisis or problem in his external life situation, whether it is a question of losing a job, as Dr. Francis said, or a question of some other crisis that has arisen, then you'd be very wary, or I would be, about recommending analysis for that patient under those circumstances. On the other hand, if a patient comes who's had problems of the sort that Dr. Kernberg has referred to in his chapter, which seem likely to be amenable to psychoanalysis, then if it is practically possible to do so, I think you would advise that person to undergo analysis. And that's independent of how old or how young the person is.

Since Dr. Frances spoke some about the history of psychoanalysis, it may be interesting to spend a few minutes on that subject. I would go even further than he did and say that *all* psychoanalysis before, let's say, 1930 was by our standards very brief. At the beginning Freud saw patients for only a few weeks in what he called analysis at that time. According to what I have been told, the first really long analysis he undertook was of the patient we refer to as the "Wolf-Man."

That was the very first. And if you read that article, you'll come across an interesting thing. He didn't call the first three and a half years of that four-year treatment "analysis." He called that part "preparatory to analysis." What seemed to him, on the basis of his experience with other patients, to be analysis was what happened in the last six months of the treatment. That gives you an idea of what was understood to be analysis at that time, before the First World War, and for a number of years after. A patient would come in, would be instructed in the technique of free association, would lie down on the couch, and would start talking. On the basis of a few weeks of association and the careful analysis of the dreams the patient brought, the analyst would arrive at a formulation of the core conflict and its relation to the present symptoms. The rest of the time that was available was devoted in those early years to showing the patient, by analyzing the transference, when possible, that in fact the interpretation was correct and that, despite his or her resistance to accepting it, the way to help lay in overcoming resistances and accepting the interpretation. The idea of analyzing defenses really began only with the Wolf-Man. So much for history.

Now clearly, if you have a patient whose life expectancy is a week, you are not going to start the patient in analysis. If time really is running out, obviously you don't try analysis; you try whatever form of psychotherapy you can reasonably undertake. I would think it's important to realize, in addition to what I have said about the history of analysis as a form of therapy, that even so recently as the beginning of my own analytic career, people thought rather hard before they would recommend accepting somebody over the age of thirty or at the most thirty-five in psychoanalysis. Analysis was, we were taught, a form of therapy for young adults. Today I don't think anybody would consider it unusual or unorthodox to accept into treatment somebody, indications being favorable, who was close to the age of fifty. The question now is—should you take somebody in the middle or late fifties or perhaps early sixties? And there I would echo what Dr. Frances said toward the end of his remarks—namely, that other things being equal, a patient should be given an opportunity to try the most effective form of psychotherapy we have at the present time, which is analysis. If that's practically impossible or if the indications for analysis are not as clear as we would like them to be, then you don't recommend analysis.

Incidentally, it's been my experience that patients occasionally ask for psychotherapy in order to deny physical illness. If a person has adjusted well for sixty-five years or so and comes and asks for analysis at that time, and there's no external situation that can account for the person's being upset, it's wise to bear in mind the possibility that the patient may be anxious about and denying the fact of some symptoms that may be of physical origin. But that's more or less beside the point of the main topic for this discussion. In any given case, I would probably lean more in the direction of preferring analysis for a patient than Dr. Frances might counsel you to do. But this difference would be a matter only of degree, and the considerations that would determine my choice, I believe, would be exactly the same as those he says would determine his.

DR. FRANCES: I think we may have smoked out a few differences in emphasis although perhaps not any great differences in kind. I think Dr. Brenner tends to see psychoanalysis more as the general treatment of choice whenever it can be done, and will allow for a brief, less ambitious treatment only if there is a real crisis, or the person is about to die, or there isn't sufficient time and money. I see us as benefiting from the availability of a menu of psychodynamic treatments. Psychoanalysis is just one treatment within that menu and probably not the one that is going to be used most. I like the other psychodynamic treatments more than Dr. Brenner does. There is no research evidence that psychoanalysis is the most effective treatment and there never will be. It is impossible to do controlled studies comparing psychoanalysis and brief treatment because patients would be crazy to sign informed consent. We all, therefore, base our opinions regarding the choice of briefer treatment versus psychoanalysis on our own experience. I believe that psychoanalysis is certainly the more ambitious treatment and, in selected individuals, promotes a deeper change. But that does not make it more effective and certainly not more efficient. And so I would be more conservative about the recommendation of psychoanalysis.

There is evidence that even brief treatments can promote characterological changes in some patients and that these changes endure on follow-up ten to fifteen years after the treatments are completed. Brief treatments do not concern just symptoms. They aim at circumscribed characterological change. It would be interesting if we were discussing given specific situations to determine how Dr. Brenner and I might differently define *quick, crisis,* and *goal direction.* He and I, in any given situation, would likely have the same general way of looking at patient problems, but we might emphasize different parts of the presentation in recommending and conducting treatment.

The other point to emphasize about focal therapy is that it does indeed include the analysis of defense, of character, of transference, and genetic interpretations. It includes all the essentials of psychodynamic psychoanalysis except that these are not done within the context of a regressive transference neurosis.

The differences between Dr. Brenner and me are perhaps less in theory than in practice. I would see psychoanalysis as a very valued part of the psychodynamic treatment repertoire but not the treatment of choice to be given whenever you can, with other treatments regarded as second-rate substitutes. I think we are lucky to have a variety of psychodynamic treatments. They are all useful, and we should attempt to pick the best treatment method for the given situation.

One last thought: I think patients should learn a lot about the goals, expectations, rationales, techniques, and contexts of the different choices and often should make up their own minds in choosing among them. We usually lack clear grounds for knowing which treatment is best in most of the instances we are discussing. It is usually the patient's decision from among the possible alternatives that determines what follows.

DR. BRENNER: If *we* don't know how to choose, surely the patients are not likely to know how to choose. We certainly have to advise them, right?

DR. FRANCES: Precisely because we don't know how to choose, their own inclinations and preferences should be greatly respected.

DR. BRENNER: Their inclinations should be respected—there's no doubt about that—but I think we are obligated to give them some advice. That's what they come for, and however you phrase it, your description of the various forms of treatment you think are available (and the way in which you present it to them) is, I think, going to contain some kernel of advice, isn't it?

DR. FRANCES: It depends on how you do it.

DR. BRENNER: I suppose so. Perhaps so. That would be a real poker face.

DR. FRANCES: It is only a poker face if you're sure you know what's right and you have trouble presenting the others as being possibly correct. For me, in many instances, I think that several different treatments are quite rational, and the choice is largely a matter of taste and goals. Under those circumstances, I don't have a favorite. I think it's really up to the patient to decide what he thinks best meets his needs.

DR. FOGEL: In a discussion of this kind it is difficult to formulate sharp conceptual differences in the absence of a specific case example. This may be difficult to supply, but I wonder, Dr. Frances, if you could give us an example of a situation of that kind—a patient for whom you see possible indications for psychoanalytic treatment if the patient so desires, but you also see significant possible contraindications.

DR. FRANCES: Yes. It's not a bit hard. The typical person among the healthier patients who present for consultation is generally doing well in life, is often analyzable, and has the potential to be a gifted patient. The question is—does such an individual want it and need it? The issue is the difference between suitability for analysis, which is widely present among healthier patients, versus indications and desire for it. The typical situation is someone who is doing quite well in many areas of life who has the talent to be in focal therapy but also the talent to be in psychoanalysis. I think that for such an individual one can fairly lay out the advantages and disadvantages of both, what's expected in each, and give the patient a choice. Moreover, the best trial for psychoanalysis is a focal treatment, and for many people it may serve as an induction. The therapist and patient can see how far they get in brief treatment and at the end of the three months or so, a more ambitious treatment may make sense to both.

DR. BRENNER: Inching closer, Allen!

DR. FRANCES: For a percentage of the people. Lots of people get better during the three months—well enough to meet their own goals. With them, it's a real question whether we should be deciding what's well enough or they should be deciding for themselves what's well enough.

DR. BRENNER: I agree. I think that analysis is to be recommended only in cases where a person is sufficiently disabled in one way or another to warrant the investment of time, energy, and money that analysis requires. I don't think it's a recommendation to be given lightly to somebody who's doing quite well in life and who's faced by some problem or crisis situation that doesn't seem to be serious enough to warrant analysis. Now you notice that when Dr. Frances was describing brief therapy he said, "It does indeed include the analysis of defense, of character, of transference, and genetic interpretations." Right? Well, to me that's analysis.

DR. FRANCES: No regressive transferences?

DR. BRENNER: No regressive transferences.

DR. FRANCES: Actually I should say *you're* inching closer.

DR. BRENNER: But you see I don't believe that the phenomena referred to by the conventional term *regressive transference* are best understood by the concept of a regressive transference. I think that what distinguishes transference in analysis or analytic therapy from the transference elements of any other object relationship is one thing only: the analyst does not respond to the patient's expressed wishes derived from childhood conflicts in any way except to try to understand them and help the patient understand them. In other words, in analysis the transference is analyzed. It is not responded to in any other way.

In this connection, let me say a few words about the people to whom Dr. Frances referred specifically—Ferenczi and Rank. Ferenczi was treated in brief-term analytic therapy by Freud, with good result. He was able to overcome his inhibition about getting married, and he married the woman he had been unable to bring himself to marry until that time. Now this was a therapy of a few periods of two or three weeks during which Ferenczi came from Budapest to Vienna and spent time with Freud. In his later years Ferenczi developed what at least some of those who knew him well considered to be a psychosis. In any case, the forms of therapy he later developed would strike us as rather peculiar. He would take a patient on his lap if he thought that was necessary with a very infantile schizoid patient. That's not, I think, what Dr. Frances would include under brief therapy as something he would recommend. Rank decided at about the same time that everything was due to birth trauma and that all neurosis could be treated within a period of a few weeks by focusing on the universal focal conflict. There again, I don't think Dr. Frances would go along with that at all. So while they both wrote a very fine and brilliant paper for that time, a monograph really on psychoanalytically oriented brief therapy, their own subsequent development doesn't so highly recommend what they recommended to us. To be sure, that doesn't invalidate their conclusions. It's only that I think it would probably be better to refer to people other than Ferenczi and Rank in recommending brief therapy by analysts.

DR. FOGEL: Dr. Brenner agrees with Dr. Frances in theory that not every patient who seeks help and who is analyzable should be analyzed, but in practice he believes it is important who presents these choices and how they are presented. I hate to interrupt the dialogue, but it is time to open the discussion to others.

DR. PAUL ORNSTEIN: I find myself in a very awkward position because earlier I thought that I agreed with both of you. Now I find myself still agreeing with some things you have said but somehow taking a third position. Let me just briefly state that third position. But first I would like to make a comment about Ferenczi and Rank because I have felt that the major emphasis of their particular monograph had nothing to do with what they subsequently developed but rather with the recognition that the transference as lived experience in the analytic situation was not sufficiently recognized. Their argument was that what had become abstract and highly cognitive and intellectual ought to be more related to experience. What happened to them subsequently is a different issue. I am not arguing that it didn't have any roots earlier, but Ferenczi recognized that taking his patients on his lap was a mistake. With respect to the argument that he was psychotic at the end, the psychosis may have been related to pernicious anemia, and Balint insists that until the very last days of his life he knew what was what. But that's another point.

The point about the issue at hand that I would like to comment on briefly has to do with the sharp differentiation that Dr. Frances makes about psychotherapy versus analysis and the less sharp differentiation that Dr. Brenner makes. I happen to side with Dr. Brenner, and I have the feeling that it makes a difference how we think about psychoanalysis versus psychotherapy, and the issue of the regressive transference. I wonder if we could look at brief therapy still as something that could be effective and intense, and that has transference elements, yet we do not thoroughly explore all the roots of the transference that are visible at the moment. Nevertheless, it still could be transference-oriented, and the transference becomes an obstacle in need of being interpretively responded to. So I don't see the two issues as sharply divergent, but here I side with Dr. Brenner. Although he didn't spell it out in that way, I don't see psychotherapy as being related to a menu. If we look at the process of treatment, the question for me would be, what particular brief or prolonged process is evoked by the encounter between patient and therapist, and how can that evoked process be dealt with interpretively? If it is dealt with interpretively, it can be short and it can be analytic. If it is dealt with in other ways, it's manipulative. I don't want to use prejudicial terms, but it's not psychotherapy in the sense in which we analysts conceive of psychotherapy.

The last brief point is, how do we make a choice? Do we make a choice? Does the patient make a choice? And here I am more tempted to agree with Dr. Frances, although I have a different view of it. The patient does not make a conscious choice. We are not offering the patient two or three alternatives from which to choose. That would not make much sense as far as I am concerned, although it's done. What we are listening for is the patient's unconscious curative fantasy, with which he or she comes to us. Then the question is, can we understand from that fantasy whether the patient is committed to something brief or something more prolonged, more intensive, and more reconstructive? So that's where my position would be, slightly different, but in great agreement with a lot of what has been said.

DR. FRANCES: I think Dr. Ornstein makes a number of important points in his refinement of our discussion.

DR. WAYNE MYERS: Allen, I would like to address these questions to you mostly. You mention that in the brief-therapy issue, the doctor and the patient established the nature of the conflict in advance. Then the therapy proceeds. How do you establish the nature of the conflict without setting up an inexact interpretation that may go nowhere? Frequently we see in treatment centers or in our private consultations people who have had a number of focal treatments in the past for particular issues. At what point do you decide that analysis, which really might be indicated, should be undertaken with such a patient? I think that the nature of the inexact interpretation offered to the patient, which may certainly fit his conscious needs, but not his unconscious ones, is a very important issue.

DR. FRANCES: I think all interpretations are inexact. One hopes they become more exact the better one knows the patient and the patient knows himself. I think the issue you raise is an interesting one. What happens is that people who have brief treatments that aren't enough often go to a more ambitious treatment. I think this is a very reasonable progression. Psychoanalysis is a difficult, time-consuming, expensive treatment and should be reserved for people who haven't gotten sufficient gains from a less expensive approach. This is part of what I meant by the notion that a brief trial of treatment should often precede psychoanalysis.

Wayne also implies that when a patient is disappointed and fails in brief treatment, this may sour him on trying other treatments. Again I should point out that this may be a selection bias. Working at the Admissions Office of the Psychoanalytic Center, one may often see people with failed treatments who have therefore come to the Psychoanalytic Center for more ambitious and difficult treatment. If you are doing brief treatments in practice, you see many people who get very satisfying results. What literature is available also suggests that some people really do have quite gratifying results. Also, there is the other side of the picture. Not everyone does well in psychoanalysis, and for many people—I thought Dr. Brenner was going to say this and then he switched the sentence a bit—many people may start in psychoanalysis as a way of avoiding changes in life. It is therefore not a completely safe and benign choice when someone enters into psychoanalysis. For some people, particularly people at these mid-life developmental crises, it can sometimes be a choice between "I'll enter psychoanalysis" or "I'll begin trying harder to change my position in life," and this risk has to be addressed in the equation.

DR. BRENNER: I think you are absolutely right, but if a person enters analysis in order to avoid making a choice in a life situation, that's very important for the analyst to understand and to interpret to the patient. That should be part of the analytic work. The time has long since gone by when any analyst would say to a patient, "Well, now you are coming into analysis and for the next five years you can't make any choices in your life."

DR. SIMON GROLNICK: What I want to ask about is what at the last minute is a little bit of theoretical difference. Let's say theoretically there was a patient who had some avoidant difficulties and a crisis situation and, at the same time, had some rather deep characterological problems that were self-evident. How would both of the panelists feel about the possibility of simultaneous treatment—let's say three months of short term with one therapist and then going into analysis or possibly a behavioral type of treatment at the same time that an induction into analysis was going on?

DR. BRENNER: I haven't had any experience with that type of conjoint therapy. I would feel a little shaky about it, I am afraid.

DR. FRANCES: I have considerable experience with conjoint behavioral and psychoanalytic therapy. I am usually against starting multiple treatment approaches at the same time whenever it can be avoided because it makes it hard to know what is happening. But in certain situations, I think it is just right.

DR. FOGEL: In some ways, we have barely scratched the many surfaces of this subject. There are many areas of agreement. It is also clear that where there is disagreement the issues are complex and multileveled. Much more discussion would be needed to develop the various considerations and points of views as they apply to particular clinical situations. Nevertheless, as brief a discussion as this was, it was illuminating and enjoyable.

Part V

Applied Psychoanalysis

·18·

MATISSE'S NICE PERIOD, 1917–1928
A Confrontation with Middle Age

MILTON VIEDERMAN, M.D.

"**D**onatello among the wild beasts": in this way the critic Louis Vauxcelles characterized the fauve painters at the Salon d'Automne in Paris in 1905. Vauxcelles spoke of an "orgy" of pure color and movement in describing a group of works by Henri Matisse, Henri Manguin, Jean Puy, Louis Valtat, Georges Rouault, and André Derain. The "wild beasts" later would include Albert Marquet, Emile-Othon Friesz, Charles Camoin, Raoul Dufy, Maurice de Vlaminck, and Kees van Dongen. The fauves were never formally described by the members as a school, although the painters influenced one another during the formative period. Each painter was destined to move in his own direction, and although friendship continued to link many through the years, fauvism as a specific style soon ceased to exist.[1] Matisse was the oldest and clearly the master.

What does one discover as one examines the evolution of these painters? Within a period of a few years, each of them, with the single exception of Matisse, tended to move into a mature style with its own individual stamp, easily recognizable as the work of the specific artist.

Much of the biographical material in this chapter is based on works by Schneider (1984), Flam (1986), and Cowart and Fourcade (1986).

I would like to thank the following for their gracious permission to reproduce the paintings in their collection: Statens Museum for Kunst, Copenhagen; The Hermitage Museum, Leningrad; Museum of Modern Art, New York; The Barnes Foundation, Pennsylvania; Mrs. John Hays-Whitney, New York; The Davlyn Gallery, New York; Philadelphia Museum of Art, Philadelphia; Musée de l'Orangerie, Paris; Georgia T. Colin, New York; Musée National d'Art Moderne, Paris; Galerie Jan Krugier, Geneva; David Rockefeller; and those private collectors who preferred to remain anonymous.

1. As is the case with most designated artistic movements, it is easier to qualify a painting as belonging to a group than to define precisely the characteristics of the movement. This is particularly true of fauvism, which had no theoretician intent on promulgating it as a movement. In general, fauvism refers to the work of painters who used "brilliant, arbitrary color, more intense than that of the neoimpressionists . . . and . . . direct, violent brushwork . . . leading to a final liberation of color. [The fauves] . . . wished to use violent color squeezed directly from the tube, not to describe objects in nature, not simply to set up retinal vibrations, not to accentuate a romantic or mystical subject, but to build new pictorial values apart from all these" (Arnason, 1977, p. 98).

Vlaminck, brilliant in this early phase, moved through a period of manifest influence by Cézanne to a static, repetitive style of gloomy, harshly painted expressionistic landscapes, which seem to reflect an inability to form new perceptions. What depressive demons possessed this man to repeat compulsively his dark and empty landscapes? Friesz and Derain, with their darkened palates, seem to have followed a similar path. Dufy, a powerful fauve, became a cheerful painter who would repeat his highly colored, exuberant, but finally superficial statements about the world with broad washes and superimposed linear designs, pretty but powerless and without surprise. Marquet and Manguin, more successful in their later work, painted rich, happy, but unchanging pictures that echoed the contentment that appears to have characterized their family lives of equilibrium and the relative absence of inner or outer challenge. The former group seems to have been deadened by a depressive mode; the latter, to have luxuriated in happiness without the need for novelty that could lead to an ever changing perception of the world.

Only Matisse appears to have been in perpetual conflict, struggling with opposites. Only he was in constant flux, seeking new styles and visions of the world as he resolved problems and undid the resolutions. Reason struggled with romance and adventure, reality with imagination, critical authority and control with sensuality and eroticism, science with fantasy (Schneider, 1984). In his constant shifts of style he resembles the other great master of the first half of the twentieth century, Picasso, although their paths were separate and opposed. A constant dialectic characterizes Matisse's painting. Objects flattened on the picture plane compete with molded statuesque forms and recessions into space. Broad application of color contrasts with linear design. Hard, straight lines exist as foils to rhythmic and curved arabesques. Confined interiors contrast with images of outer space, viewed through windows and doors. Thick impastos are juxtaposed with thin washes through which the whiteness of the canvas can be discerned.

As one examines Matisse's life and work, the complex flux can be observed both microscopically, in the form of continuous shifts at any stage in his development, and macroscopically, in the form of changes in formal style and content at various phases of his life. In this chapter I examine the shift in Matisse's life and in the style and content of his painting as he approached and weathered middle age, from the time he was forty-seven until he was sixty-one (1916–1928), before he moved to the new style ushered in by *The Dance* in 1930. I view his work during this period as an expression of antecedent conflict and the transformation and re-creation of his inner world as he struggled with the conflicts of middle age, utilizing his special creative potential to construct a visual world designed to express and resolve an inner state of conflict and depression. If creativity can be viewed as bringing something new into existence, one of the functions of the new involves a change or attempted change in the inner state.[2] One discovers in examining Matisse's work a personal iconography, a repetition of favorite themes treated differently at different periods in his long career. My method in part will be to examine the transformation in his handling of these themes as he approached and moved into middle age, with the assumption that these images represented expressions and protective modifications of changing inner states.

Of particular interest in this regard are the repeated interiors with windows and open doors, which can be seen as a metaphor for interior states and their relationship to the perception of reality. One can observe the varying relations between inner and outer space, the attention paid to each, the degrees of vigor with which they are represented, the tonality of colors, the intensity of light, all with a view to understanding Matisse's experience of self and the world, both expressively and defensively. His treatment of women, nudes in particular, also undergoes such transformations.

This is not to be understood as a reductionistic or all-encompassing view of Matisse's creative genius or his motivation as a painter, but rather as a facet of his endeavor. My intent is to make a coherent organizing statement about Matisse that increases the viewer's informed curiosity in examining his painting and thereby offers greater pleasure. Especially important are the ideas both of revelation and of transformation in the act of painting. Not only is an inner vision or experience concretized in the external form of a painting, but the process of painting itself, when successful, transforms the painful experience of inner conflict by creating an external vision that is calming, soothing, gratifying, not simply in the sense of drive gratification but in the broader sense of creating in a painting what is absent or elusive in the inner world. It also substitutes for what may not be realized directly in com-

2. Kuspit (1987) alludes to this approach in his support of the deconstructionist critics who "always look for the critical moment of rupture and regard the self-aware artist as himself in search and rupture. . . . The deconstructionist looks for instabilities, and tries to articulate the artist's development in all its instability—dialectical and otherwise (with all its dead ends, false starts, grandstanding)" (p. 124).

1. *The Green Line*, 1905. 40.5
× 32.5cm. Statens Museum
for Kunst, Copenhagen.
Photo Petersen.

merce with the world. Hence there are elements of sublimation in the
broadest sense of the term and attempts at mastery. In this endeavor
the creative artist has a special advantage, as Freud (1911) pointed out,
for he can escape through artistic creation the burden of modifying
implacable reality to suit his needs. He is capable of creating a new,
personal reality substantially under his control, although he may accomplish this more or less successfully, and part of the product may
reveal the imprint of defense and failure of resolution and integration.
On the simplest level, "if you can paint a demon, you are less afraid of
it" ("The Surreal Eye," PBS, Jan. 12, 1987). By extension, if you can
paint a demon, you can make it less demonic by concealing its fearful
countenance. Kuspit (1987) recommends an interpretive model based
on an analogy between the work and its maker: thinking of the work's
surface "as existing in relation to its 'depth' much the same way that
the exterior of the human subject is understood to relate to its internal
. . . self" (p. 126).

In some respects change in middle age may be viewed as a dialectic
between the safety accompanying wearisome and stultifying repetition
and the risks and danger of seeking new experience and perception of
the world. Matisse was unable to accept the safety and comfort that
recognition and material success had brought him in middle life and

was compelled to change the structure of his life and the form and content of his painting in a flight to the South. His initial voyages, at the turn of the century when he was thirty-six, culminated in a joyous sojourn at Collioure in 1905 with Amélie, his wife, who was his model and inspiration for some of the great works of his fauve period, *The Woman with the Hat* and *The Green Line* (fig. 1). *The Woman with the Hat* had the special distinction of being the first painting sold to Leo Stein, an event that initiated Matisse's public recognition and success. The second descent toward Nice in 1917,[3] when Matisse was forty-eight and his children were no longer at home, took place without Amélie and was a flight rather than a pilgrimage, intended to redesign a world to replace the one that had become burdensome to him and no longer offered satisfaction.

Early Life

Henri Matisse was born in 1869 in Picardy, a province of northeastern France characterized by grayness, flatness, frequent rain, and an atmosphere of darkness and gloom. There is reason to believe that his inner emotional landscape echoed the outer one. He was the elder of two sons (his brother was three years his junior), born to a middle-class family who operated a prosperous general store where grain, textiles, and paints were sold. The personality contrast between the parents has been emphasized by students of Matisse as the source of the two poles of Matisse's personality (Schneider, 1984; Flam, 1986). The mother was apparently warm, responsive, and artistically inclined. She strongly supported Matisse's effort to become an artist and became a catalyst of her son's career. Her interest in colors and father's interest in textiles would play a role in Henri's painting. Matisse père was a highly controlling, authoritarian, demanding, and critical man, very practical, rational, and insistent upon hard work. Visiting Matisse when he was a successful painter, with a large house and garden at Issy-les-Moulineaux he is said to have criticized his son for his poor utilization of the terrain.

Matisse was a somewhat passive and sickly child, not an enthusiastic student, and given to bouts of "chronic appendicitis," which it has

---

3. It is understood that Matisse made many voyages to the South, including North Africa. In speaking of his second descent, I refer to a significant change in the pattern of his life when he spent long periods without Amélie.

2. *Harmony in Red*, 1908. 180 × 200cm. The Hermitage, Leningrad.

been suggested may have been a sort of colitis. It was more likely a
manifestation of a low-grade depression. He studied law in Paris and
returned to Picardy to become a lawyer's clerk at St. Quentin. Even
during this stay in Paris, he apparently did not visit the museums. After
some months of lackluster and mediocre performance at his work, he
again fell ill of his intestinal disturbance and was nursed by his mother.
During this illness, his mother brought him a box of colors to pass the
time, and Matisse, apparently for the first time, came to life with a vigor
that was never to leave him. From this point on, painting dominated
his life. As he said in his old age, "Do you understand now why I am
never bored? For over 50 years I have not stopped work for an instant"
(Schneider, 1984, p. 716, ref. 12). His mother was not only the vehicle
for his commencement as a painter but his muse as well. He described
his sudden awareness of drawing and the power of art in this way:

> The revelation of the interest to be had in the study of portraits
> came to me when I was thinking of my mother, in a post office
> in Picardy, as I was waiting for a telephone call. To pass the time
> I picked up a telegraph form lying on a table, and used the pen

to draw on it a woman's head. I drew without thinking of what I was doing, my pen going by itself and I was surprised to recognize my mother's face with all its subtleties. My mother had a face with generous features, the highly distinctive traits of French Flanders. (Schneider, 1984, p. 716, ref. 9)

At the age of eighty he remembered that in his early years he would finish a painting, not for the salon, but as a gift to his mother, "because my mother loved everything I did. It was out of tenderness for her that I was prompted to add something I couldn't get from theory which enabled me to finish the painting" (Schneider, 1984, p. 717). Clearly, his mother was his inspiration and the initial source of passion for art. It was due to her entreaties that the father who opposed his painting acceded to their son's desire to attend the Beaux-Arts. The theme of the maternal function was especially important in some of his early paintings such as *The Breton Serving Girl*, 1896, *The Dinner Table*, and ultimately his great work *Harmony in Red*, 1908 (fig. 2).[4]

The apparently happy relationship with his mother can be contrasted with the highly conflicted and uncertain relationship with his father and paternal surrogates in his early adult life. Matisse appears to have sought father surrogates and then disengaged from them. Gustave Moreau was his first major mentor during his formative period in Paris, but Matisse broke with him over Moreau's insistence that he continue to be guided by the great masters at the Louvre. After a brief period under the tutelage of Pissarro, he followed Signac to the South, struggling to integrate the tenets of pointillism. Signac's insistence that he follow the prescriptions of divisionism led to a rupture and to the emergence of Matisse as a creative master in his own right, at the age of thirty-six. This was his symbolic emancipation from father.

Antecedents of Middle Age

Matisse was profoundly attached to his family. His daughter, Marguerite, born in 1894, the child to whom he was closest, was the product

4. Matisse's relationship with his mother may be viewed as a prototype for his relationships with women throughout his life, particularly as they influenced his creativity. Different theoretical models may be used to understand their function. Whether they are best viewed as Kohutian self objects, as the sources of a potential or transitional space in Winnicott's terms, or as catalytic objects in a passionate relationship (Viederman, 1987) will not be addressed here.

of a union with a mistress that ended in 1898. Marguerite became his charge and was lovingly adopted by Amélie, whom he married in 1898. Amélie rapidly produced two sons, Jean, born in 1899, and Pierre, in 1900. Matisse was closer to his wife and his daughter than to his sons, from whom he was separated during the periods when they were at school. Marguerite was a frequent model and the object of tender attention in his paintings. He joyfully purchased beautiful colorful dresses for her as she grew up. Amélie, to whom he was profoundly attached, was a constant inspiration who played the roles of lover, mother, supporter, encouraging partner, reassuring presence, and model during his early to middle adulthood as he achieved maturity as an artist. In this, she seems to have taken on the roles previously assumed by his mother. It was she who supported him both materially and emotionally in the first few years of their marriage, when he could sell no paintings and extreme poverty forced him to leave the children with their grandparents in Bohain and Toulouse.[5] This was a period of great despair, frustration, and a sense of competitive failure as he observed the success of his contemporaries Bonnard and Vuillard. This despair was manifested in early works, sometimes with violence and anger, as in an early sculpture of a predatory cat after Bayre, and sometimes with gloom, as in the dark interior of *Studio under the Eaves*, 1903 (fig. 3).

The period from 1905 to 1917 was one of great richness, innovation, and experimentation in Matisse's art, which reveals his full expansion as a master from the time of his travels to the South and his discovery of fauvism. Within a few years, major collectors, following the Steins, acquired or commissioned important works and major dealers began to compete for his paintings, so that by 1907 the dealer Kahnweiler found him "already too big for him." Increasing prosperity permitted Matisse in 1908 to rent a studio with a garden in Paris and in 1910 to buy a house at Issy-les-Moulineaux, which he kept for many years.

It is clear that Matisse obtained gratification and sustenance as the

5. Pleynet (1984) also emphasizes Matisse's intimate emotional life (particularly the importance of his mother) as it relates to the expressive erotic dimension of his paintings. He stresses the relationship between "the religious feeling for life" and the "revelation of life through art that he owes his mother." Pleynet also relates Matisse's conflict about sexuality to the Oedipus complex and describes it as manifested in Matisse's work as a fragmentation of top from bottom (intellect from sexuality). I view his depersonification of the erotic figure, specifically during middle age, in the same way. Pleynet approaches Matisse from the Kleinian viewpoint and, consistent with this theoretical orientation, sees Matisse's mother as a persecutory object of envy. I do not find support for this position in my own analysis of the material.

3. *Studio under the Eaves*, 1903. 55.2 × 46cm. Fitzmilliam Museum, Cambridge. By permission of Syndics of the Fitzmilliam Museum.

head of the family, and Schneider states that "the family was the guardian of meaningfulness of reality." *The Piano Lesson*, 1916 (fig. 4), has Pierre as a model playing the piano. Schneider points out that Matisse's depiction of Pierre (which appears to be highly depersonified) is the picture of a child much younger than Pierre was at that time, which Schneider interprets as reflecting Matisse's struggle against allowing his children to grow up.[6] This cubist Pierre is an unhappy lad, flanked by a rigidly vertical woman at the top and a diminutive female figure at the bottom. Do we see in this picture evidence of the impulse to fly from the isolated women who surround him and with whom he no longer has a relationship? *The Music Lesson*, 1917 (fig. 5) depicts the family as a unit, although the representations of his sons in submissive poses strangely reproduce the experience he had with his own father, unlike his treatment of Marguerite, who in this painting is seen on the balcony separate from the family. Here too there is considerable isolation. Moreover, on the other side of a pool is a nude figure remarkably like the painting *The Blue Nude*, 1906. Did this voluptuous figure tempt him in the voyage he was about to undertake?

This period from 1905 to 1916, the period of middle adulthood,

6. This interpretation is congruent with my own thinking that Matisse used his paintings to create a reality to counteract a threatening inner and outer reality that he was reluctant to admit—in short, to create a wishful world to oppose the real world.

although not without conflict was nonetheless a period of happiness, growth, and maturation in which the benefits outweighed the losses. The family appears to have acted as a base for his activities, a tonic support, a holding environment, that permitted and encouraged his exploration of the world through art. The antecedents of crisis were evident, however, as World War I led to a disruption of this structure. He spoke regretfully of the absence of the boys and "the dissolution of the family, shattered because they have their own lives to lead" when he wrote to Camoin. War led to new concerns as his mother, brother, sister-in-law, and sons found themselves in territory occupied by the Germans. His mother, seriously ill in 1914 when the Germans invaded France, promised to wait for her son and in fact died in 1918, shortly after he was able to visit her (Schneider, 1984).

In 1917, Matisse, aged forty-eight, was about to change his painting radically. In the absence of information about his inner life it is difficult to speak with assurance about what must be viewed as a crisis in his life. What I will present is a construct based on knowledge of a few concrete aspects of Matisse's life and what we know of middle age.

The war, the disruption of family, and particularly the illness and death of Matisse's mother, the person central to his artistic activity, had a profound impact on him. It confronted him not only with his own mortality but with the ultimate mortality of his wife, Amélie, who had so manifestly taken on from his mother the functions of his muse. His flight to Nice would appear to represent an attempt at mastery over death, an attempt to deny the painful intrusion of death. Confronted with his mother's mortality, Matisse ceased to find the aging Amélie a sexual, protective, or catalytic object and emotionally abandoned her. To actively abandon rather than passively experience loss is a familiar mode of coping. Only gradually could Matisse rediscover his life force and creative potential through the inspiration provided by a series of young, beautiful, and talented models who themselves took on the role of transitional objects. In this way Matisse could again enrich what had become a barren inner world, by creating a powerful new artistic style.

The Nice Period

During the period starting in 1916, Matisse's life and the form and content of his painting changed dramatically. From 1917 until 1930, he spent long periods of time in Nice, at first living in hotel rooms and

4. *The Piano Lesson*, 1916. 24.5 × 212.7cm. Museum of Modern Art, New York City. Mrs. Simon Guggenheim Fund.

5. *The Music Lesson*, 1917. 243.8 × 209.5m. The Barnes Foundation, Merion, Pa.

6. *The Open Window, Collioure,* 1905. 55.2 × 45cm. Collection of Mrs. John Hay, Whitney, N.Y.

7. *Interior at Etretat, 14 July*, 1920. 72.5 × 60cm. Courtesy of Daulyn Gallery, New York City.

8. *Landscape with Olive Trees*, 1918. 33 × 41cm. Private collection.

9. *View of Collioure*, 1905. 59.5 × 73cm. The Hermitage, Leningrad.

10. *My Room at Beau-Rivage*, 1917–18. 73.7 × 60.6cm. Philadelphia Museum of Art. The A. E. Gallatin Collection.

11 *Interior at Nice*, 1918. 65.5 × 54.5cm. Private collection.

12. *The Open Window*, 1918. 42 × 33cm. Private collection.

13. *Two Women in an Interior*, 1921. 92 × 73cm. Musée de l'Orangerie, Paris. Collection of Jean Walter and Paul Guillaume.

14. *The Interior at Nice, Woman in a Green Dress Leaning at the Window*, 1921. 65 × 55cm. Colin Collection.

15. *The Session at Three o'Clock*, 1924. 92 × 73cm. Private collection.

16. *Luxe 1*, 1907. 210 × 138cm. Musée National d'Art Moderne, Paris. Photo Flammarion.

17. *Nymph and Satyr*, 1909. 89 × 117cm. The Hermitage, Leningrad. Photo: DR.

villas, and then renting an apartment where Amélie finally came to live with him in 1928. This period involved long separations from Amélie, who ceased to be a model, and only occasional visits from Pierre and Marguerite. Marguerite remained an important model for him until 1924, when she married. His treatment of her changed from the beginning of the Nice period, however, and he paid increasing attention to other young models as subjects. His interest in young models (such as Lorette) in 1916 preceded by a year the trip to Nice and may have initiated his search for a younger woman.

In parallel with this dramatic change in his life-style, an important change in the formal characteristics of his painting became evident. The traditional view of the critics has been negative. Schneider sees this period as "a decor, a fragile thing, very beautiful but you won't find anything . . . a lowering of tension, a loss of direction, though with some melancholy. The family had been the guardian of the meaningfulness of reality; its removal led to a flattening of reality, a lack of significance, a movement toward abstraction with decoration as an end." Schneider also notes an egocentricity in Matisse's changed way of life, with decreasing contact with his friends. Moreover, he observes an underlying melancholy in spite of the color and light of these paintings, a view with which I concur. According to Schneider, Matisse himself turned his back on this period. The traditional view has been that this was a period of self-indulgence, a flight into happiness on the Riviera.

Cowart and Fourcade (1986) dispute this point of view as a cultural prejudice that denigrates the figurative (often characteristic of Matisse during this period) in favor of the abstract. Certainly, Matisse's work during the Nice period reveals his continued brilliance as a creative artist. Yet one senses a flight, an underlying melancholy, a loneliness, and an attempted resolution of conflict for the artist who has left wife, comfort, and material ease behind in Paris to search for new images in cramped hotel rooms. This flight reflected a need for change and resolution in a setting removed from wife and family.

Matisse's treatment of specific thematic content can be regarded as a reflection of his inner state, as the painter, now middle-aged, sought the light of the South in an effort to dissipate the blackness of spirit that dominated him during the early part of this period. Whether Matisse experienced manifest depression or a state of demoralization and emptiness is a matter of conjecture, but one can reasonably infer a painful disturbance of mood. This state seems to have echoed similar states in childhood and adolescence, when the gloomy landscape of the

North resonated with a cold and colorless internal one. The only formal self-portrait of this period, done in 1918, reveals a stiffness, muted tan tones, diluted and without warmth, that hardly suggest a joie de vivre.

Interiors with Open Windows and Doors

The theme of interiors with open windows and doors recurs in Matisse's work and may be seen as a metaphor for his mood, a statement about his inner world, to be compared with his view of and attention to reality. These paintings reflect disguised inner realities. As one examines the transitions in this iconography, one appreciates the power of the multiple statements they make.

Studio under the Eves, 1903 (fig. 3), was painted at a time of considerable difficulty in Matisse's life. He was aged thirty-three, with a wife and three young children, and without money, having made no significant sale and without the prospects of one. External reality was grim, and he was soon to send the boys to live with their grandparents for want of the ability to support them.[7] The painting reveals a darkness of inner space dominated by somber hues with light scarcely penetrating the interior, which has a womblike quality. An easel, symbol of the painter's métier, is lost in the gloom and enveloped by it, barely touched by the light of day. The focal point of the painting, the outer vision of beautiful trees, light, and space, is distant, inaccessible, and, though richly detailed, it is at best the light at the end of the tunnel. One is overpowered by the heavy, monotonous tonality of the interior. *The Open Window, Collioure*, 1905 (fig. 6), is in contrast a brilliant painting executed during a period of great exuberance. This was the time Matisse came into his own as a painter, having thrown off the yoke of Signac's tyranny. He was freely experimenting with a multiplicity of personal styles. His family was united and with him. Derain was painting at his side, and the painters stimulated each other. Flam's formal analysis of the painting is particularly rich:

> This painting contains what is probably the fullest range of brushwork and the most complete spatial structure of any Matisse paint-

7. It is worth noting that this early period of depression, although clearly accentuated by Matisse's desperate financial situation and his failure to achieve success, was also accompanied by the fragmentation of his young family. A second fragmentation of the family ushered in the Nice period.

ing of the period. Here, three orders of space are created, each characterized by its physical position and by the way in which the paint is applied. The space of the interior is characterized by flat, thinly brushed areas of color; the transitional space of the window area is characterized by short, curving strokes; and the space of the harbor with its rocking boats is rendered in linear strokes. Each of these areas is thus painted in a way that expresses something essential about the nature and rhythm of what that area represents: the flatness of the walls, the arabesque of the growing plant forms, the measured rocking of the boats on the rippled water. Thus the varied brush stroke contains within itself metaphors for the time frame in which each of these entities exists—the relatively static quality of architecture, the vibrant quickness of growing plants, the pulse of moving water. . . . The harbor scene has been brought forward almost to the picture plane, condensing the space of the painting in a way that parallels the condensed shorthand of the brushwork. The harbor view, in fact, is like a picture within the picture, framed by the border of vines and grillwork, which is in turn framed by the rectangle of the window, which is in turn framed by the edges of the canvas; and all three of these similarly proportioned rectangles exchange space, light, and energy through the medium of the white ground. . . . Nowhere in Matisse's oeuvre—indeed, nowhere else in all of 20th century painting—is more sheer force or denser or more complex visual thought packed into so small a picture. (Flam, 1986, pp. 132–134)

The psychological extension of this analysis becomes readily apparent when we compare this painting with *Studio under the Eves* (fig. 3) and use this comparison as a substrate for consideration of the many open window and door scenes of the Nice period. In the Collioure picture the richness of the exterior is forcibly brought indoors (inside). Here is a dynamic sky and sea with rocking boats, rich in color and movement, painted in a thick impasto, garlanded by beautiful flowers, unlike the wash of the interior, which is hardly to be noted, for the external world is so inviting. Inner space and inner world are static, thinly brushed, and of less importance, forming only a framework for the garland of growing plants, themselves in the process of expansion and renewal—as was Matisse—toward an engagement with a receptive outer world that dominates the picture. All is focused on the passionate embrace of fulfilling reality. This is a painting of exuberance, of spontaneity, of rapid and easy placement of thick and pure colors. It is a youthful painting of an outside world that offers an invitation, that dominates and distracts, mutes attention and preoccupation with the inner world. This is an explosion of color and joy.

Harmony in Red, 1908 (fig. 2), reveals another transition. Confidence and conviction as a painter are here coupled with the support of an outside world that has concretely affirmed his value. This painting was commissioned by the great Russian collector Stchoukine. It is a large, dazzling, overwhelming work that reflects an inner state of harmony. The main surface of the painting is devoted to an elegant interior with a decorative female figure standing at a table bountifully covered with food; the composition is in perfect equilibrium. Although smaller in surface area, a window looking out onto a garden is no less distinguished or important. The linear arabesques of interior and exterior echo one another, yet the colors, tones, and modes of representation of the trees and the exterior world are clearly distinguishable and of equal valence and interest, in constant and harmonious interplay. Moreover, the outside world is a whimsical fairy-tale landscape. Matisse repainted the red from its original blue to contrast the inner and outer spheres more effectively. Unlike *Studio under the Eves* (fig. 3), where the interior dominates, or the Collioure picture (fig. 6), where the outside dominates, the two are here in perfect harmony. Schneider (1984) points out that this painting has additional iconographic derivatives. Matisse painted a series of women at table. The first, *Breton Serving Girl*, has pentimenti, the head and shoulders of a little girl, his two-year-old daughter, Marguerite, and a woman leaning toward her. The echo of the child remains in the subsequent version of this painting, *The Dinner Table*, and reaches culmination in *Harmony in Red*, in which the inner world is enriched by the fantasy of a mother and child (daughter) in harmonious relationship. This painting is a perfect expression of contrasts, yet beauty, balance, and peace in inner and outer worlds dominate. All the interiors of this period are richly painted, and when a window is shown, the outside world is revealed in a contrasting but equally vibrant way.

Although no single description can encapsulate the multitude of interiors Matisse painted during his Nice period, certain characteristics distinguish them from his earlier work. None of the interiors of this period has a woman serving at table. The focus is clearly on the interior, with little attention paid to what is seen on the outside, which remains undetailed and vague, thinly painted in broad washes with few reference points, hardly very inviting initially and of little interest throughout this period. On the rare occasions when the outside does take form, it is gloomy or raining, as in *The Woman in a Spanish Shawl Standing in Front of the Window*, 1919. *Interior at Etretat, 14 July*, 1920 (fig. 7) stands in marked contrast to the Collioure window of 1905. The earlier painting reveals the experienced world boldly seen and stated with solidity of form and paint. This contrasts with the dullness of the sea, the faded deadness of the tricolored boats, and the equally life-less interior of the Etretat painting. Moreover, Bastille Day is hardly a day to be indoors. It is interesting that this dull evocation of the out-side world is encapsulated in a painting of the North, the region of his early life. One senses an older, depressed, less vigorous and hope-ful man. This painting exemplifies the extreme of Matisse's state in middle age and reflects the depressive gloom of other interiors of this period. Gradually, however, as the decade of the twenties proceeded, Matisse was more successful in overcoming the burdensome heaviness he reveals here. Yet the exteriors are less developed, and none has the vibrancy of the Collioure painting.

The few landscapes Matisse painted during this period tend to be small, confined, and claustrophobic with very little external sky and little in the way of vistas and open spaces, quite unlike the landscapes of his earlier mature period. Even when there is a broad perspective, melancholy pervades the scene, as in *Landscape with Olive Trees*, 1918 (fig. 8). They frequently are thinly painted in diluted colors or darker tones and lack the radiance and brilliance of the earlier paintings. With some exceptions they are without people. They contrast markedly with the landscapes of the fauve period, such as *View of Collioure*, 1905 (fig. 9). The inner world, the interiority of the middle-aged man (Neu-garten, 1979), is the subject of these paintings. One can discern a clear transition in the interior spaces and how they are handled from empti-ness, frugality, and blandness in 1917 through a muted peopling of the spaces in 1920 to a return to full-bodied vigor in 1924.

Three paintings of 1917 and early 1918 demonstrate Matisse's empti-ness of spirit. *My Room at Beau-Rivage*, 1917–18 (fig. 10), records Ma-tisse's arrival at Nice. The light in this painting, though intense, is diffuse and unconcentrated, and objects are not defined by shadow. The scene is painted with thin washes that cover an underlying gray-ness, unlike the robust strokes of the Collioure painting (fig. 6) and the later paintings of this period. The room is empty of people. A bed sup-porting a valise and an empty chair are the only furniture. One senses

Matisse's need to bring in light to fill the room, to undo what appears to be a terrible loneliness. The furniture is of small scale, emphasizing the space in the room, so that a visitor to Matisse's studio during these years was surprised to discover how small and cramped it actually was. It is clear that Matisse was transforming a confined inner space into something larger that he attempted to fill with light. Light and space are utilized to undo a claustrophobic confinement. The painter barely exists in this room; we see only the edge of the easel at the far left. *Interior at Nice*, 1918 (fig. 11), brings us closer to the window, which reveals an empty sea and sky. The vigorous plants of the Collioure painting have given way to vaguely painted tops of palms that are dull and lifeless. *The Open Window*, 1918 (fig. 12), offers an even closer view of the outside, now barely nuanced, with a few ill-defined black figures on the beach. There is little interest in sea and sky. This fleeting glance at the outside world is hardly rewarding, and from this point on the artist returns to the interior in a sequence of paintings. It is the internal world that must change.

The use of mirrors in these interiors follows an interesting progression of its own. Fourcade observes that the tonality of the mirrors in these early paintings is the inverse of the tonality of the picture itself (Cowart and Fourcade, 1986). Bright paintings, such as *Interior with Violin Case*, 1918–19, already more vigorous in the use of undiluted bold color, reveal a room less barren and more comfortably filled with well-arranged furniture. The mirror over the dressing table has a black surface. The reflection of bouquet and palm trees in *The Painting Session*, 1919, is framed by a black wall. The mirrors of *The Morning Tea*, 1920, and that of *Two Women in an Interior*, 1921, by these years, have taken on a bright noncontrasting tonality. Although the contrast of light and dark has important formal compositional qualities, its psychological significance is highly suggestive. As Matisse began to escape from the blackness, loneliness, and emptiness of heart that he had initially attempted to cover with the bland washes of his 1917 interiors, and as he began to reconstitute a rich inner experience, revealed in the greater exuberance of his painting, only a remnant of the blackness remained, reflected in the mirror, until it was relinquished in 1920.

Another change in the direction of a filling and enrichment of his inner space becomes apparent as the interiors themselves become more livable, attractive objects fill the space, and flowers and fruit are found on the tables. Women, the symbol and source of his inspiration, with roots in his relationship with mother and then wife, begin to inhabit his rooms, as in *Two Women in an Interior*, 1921 (fig. 13). In this painting one of the women, sketched broadly and without features, seems enveloped by the outline of the couch—one might almost imagine a coffin. Was he trying to free himself from the dead mother, or was he in the process of resurrecting her by transformation into a beautiful model? *The Interior at Nice, Woman in a Green Dress Leaning at the Window*, 1921 (fig. 14), and *The Session at Three o'Clock*, 1924 (fig. 15), reveal a transformation of the interior. The inner world is again full and rich and a nice place to live. Inner harmony has been recaptured in the context of a new creative thrust with the development of a new formal style. In *The Session at Three o'Clock* it is the woman who paints, perhaps a direct reference to the source of his inspiration. Even the exterior in this painting suggests some interest in sailboats and palm trees, and one can view the window as an invitation to the outside.

The interiors of this period reveal an artist in a period of middle-age crisis struggling, at first unsuccessfully, to overcome a desperate and painful state of emptiness and depletion. The gradual reassertion of vigor under the catalytic influence of the young models he incorporated into his paintings led to the development of a new and radically different style, equal in power to that of the past.

Women in Matisse's Paintings

Coinciding with the evolution of his paintings of interiors with windows and doors was a progressive development of important relationships with young women, beautiful models who were a source equally of inspiration and of erotic desire. Given the importance of first his mother and then his wife as catalyst and stimulant of the creative process, one may assume that these models served a similar function for this middle-aged man in crisis who was seeking renewal. This is borne out by the chronology of the Nice development. His discovery and use of Antoinette as a model began in 1919 and apparently coincided with the unfolding and development of the interiors.

Models played an important role for Matisse throughout his career. Some of his earliest nude figures were painted in Gustave Moreau's studio around 1895. These were models in public studios, unambiguously objects in a literal sense, to be studied and translated into drawings and paintings. The studios were occupied by many students, and personal relationships with the models did not exist. The figures in these paintings have volume and solidity, but they are statuesque and clearly not inviting in an erotic sense.

As Matisse developed his personal style and revealed for the first time his unique creative stamp, nude figures around 1905 became important decorative objects in his paintings, important for their linearity, for design, and for composition. Although there are exceptions, and highly erotic paintings, drawings, and lithographs punctuate Matisse's entire work, their concentration in the later Nice period is striking. During earlier periods they are often flattened against the picture plane, lack substance and volume, and are devoid of erotic qualities. *Luxe, Calm, and Voluptuousness*, 1904,[8] and *Luxe I*, 1905 (fig. 16), which portrays three nude figures as features of a landscape, are characteristic in this regard. The most defined of the women has an androgenous quality. *The Blue Nude*, 1906, has greater volume and voluptuousness, but the sensuousness of this painting is a sensuousness of line, echoed in the plants behind the woman. The figure has her legs closed in a noninviting way. *Nymph and Satyr*, 1909 (fig. 17), is a manifestly sexual scene with the figures used uniquely for design, in distinct contrast to those of the middle phases of the Nice period.

It should be noted that there were basically two lines of development in Matisse's use of models throughout his career. One involved portraits of clothed women, often reading, and the other, of nudes. Amélie had been a constant object of portraiture in the period before he went to Nice. Her figure was developed in many ways, sometimes decoratively as a woman in an interior, sometimes in the form of a psychological portrait with modeling and expression. She ceased to be used as a model during the Nice period. When one examines the portraits of Marguerite painted during her occasional visits to Nice, she appears less a psychological being than she had been and more a decorative object. Moreover, when an expression can be noted, it is often sullen and pouting, which makes her less attractive.

Parallel with Matisse's decreasing interest in his wife and his daughter as objects of psychological portraiture was the development of his relationships with models. In 1916 and 1917, as he was about to embark on trips to the South, he began to use as his prime model a young woman named Lorette. In contrast to his portraits of Marguerite at this time, Lorette is portrayed psychologically, with an extraordinary

8. Amélie was the model for the clothed figure on the left in this painting. Its title was taken from Mallariné's poem, an ode to his mistress.

diversity of moods and expressions—at times languid, sensuous, seductive, erotic, penetrating, and so on. Lorette was succeeded in Nice by
Antoinette in, for example, *Head of a Woman with Flowers in Her Hair*,
1919 (fig. 18). The richness of character portrayal and the powerful
expression of feeling in this portrait contrast with the depiction of Marguerite during this same period. Antoinette was followed by Henriette,
who figured in Matisse's paintings repeatedly from 1921 to 1927. She
has been described as a beautiful and intelligent woman who enjoyed
reading and was a talented musician. Although Matisse established
powerful emotional connections with his models, he tended to maintain
a split in his use of them as objects for portraits: they were developed
as individuals or as objects of erotic desire. The eroticism present in
the paintings and drawings of the 1920s is more intense than before,
yet the model's anonymity in the nude studies separates his emotional
connection with her from his depiction of her as a sexual object. This is
exemplified in *Nude with the Spanish Rug*, 1919 (fig. 19), which depicts a
voluminous, sensuous nude, Antoinette, who is entirely faceless. One
senses the powerful eroticism generated in Matisse, which he had to
control through depersonification of the model. The nudes are treated
in series, moving from the flattened decorative images of the models as
forms on the picture plane to the richly contoured, fleshy, erotic female
figures of the odalisques, such as *Odalisque with Magnolias*, 1923 (fig. 20).
Matisse derived the images of the odalisque from classical forms—in
particular, from Ingres—and from the tradition of the salon painters of
the preceding generation, especially Bouguereau. The transformation,
however, involved the mutation of a statuesque, idealized, and deeroti-
cized figure into a richly developed image of a sexual woman. Matisse
thereby transformed on two levels. He utilized the icon of the past to
create his own erotic world, and he transmuted his flattened decorative
figures into voluminous, erotic ones.

That this transformation should occur in a man in his fifties comes
as no surprise. His decreasing erotic interest in his aging wife, coupled
with oedipal inhibitions restimulated by his mother's death, diverted
his erotic interest to young women, with whom he became intensely
involved. Increasing stimulation and involvement with erotic objects
acted as a stimulus to the refurbishing of his inner world. Yet the
eroticism generated by his models was often defended against by a
depersonification in his representations of them as erotic figures and
his portrayals of them as exotic, oriental figures in order to maintain
distance.

18. *Head of a Woman with Flowers in Her Hair*, 1919. 35 × 27cm. Courtesy Galerie, Jan Krugier, Geneva.

19. *Nude with the Spanish Rug*, 1919. 65 × 54cm. Private collection.

20. *Odalisque with Magnolias*, 1923. 65 × 81cm. Collection of David Rockefeller.

By 1925, in *Decorative Figure on an Ornamental Background*, there was a return toward use of the nude as a decorative figure. In 1928, when Amélie came to live with him in Nice, Matisse painted his final portrait of Henriette, the lovely and talented woman who had been his inspiration for six years. *Woman with a Veil*, 1927, portrays her in a strangely distorted version of the youthful, charming, sensuous, and lovely young woman she had been. She sits pensively, in a mood of dejection, with her chin resting on her hand, the classical pose of melancholia. Her face is grotesquely deformed and asymmetrical, with one side revealing a scowl and the other side, perhaps, a smile. She is hidden behind a veil, although the eyes through the veil reveal profound sadness. She is fully clothed, her body flattened through clothes that are half light, half dark. Her molded face has a strange vertical crease in the middle of the forehead, disturbing and unpleasant. This figure is a projection of gloom. Just as Matisse had received her lightness and youth into his life, now he had to discard her with a portrait that could be judged almost hideous when compared with the previous exaltation of her beauty. In his reunion with his wife, he prepared for a new creative thrust characterized by the flattening of objects on the picture plane.

Relatively few of Matisse's paintings present man and woman together, and striking in all of them are the distance between the two, the presence of obstacles between them, and the extreme contrast between the linearity and verticality of the man and the curves and arabesques of the woman. In *The Painter and His Model*, 1916, there is a curious reversal: the flesh color of the painter suggests that *he* is unclothed and exposed. A powerful blackness separates the two. In *The Painting Seance*, 1919, the painter is but a phantom barely sketched. In *The Painter and His Model, the Interior of the Studio*, 1919, a clutter of table and easel separates the attentive painter from the object of his desire. This convention of Matisse's represents more than the contrast between the phallic male and the receptive female. It represents fear of connection with the erotic object as the painter carefully attends to his métier and stiffly, through his work, maintains distance from the curvaceous, sensuous, and inviting woman. The distance between painter and model appears great and yet indeterminate.

Conclusion

Matisse's Nice period was not a flight into happiness. The reemphasis on space and volume in many of his paintings, which was seen as a retrograde step, was an attempt to give substance to an inner world that was depleted and black. The need to represent, to fill with light, to restore volume and substance led to a reparative effort to undo the despair that had followed the loss of the tonic support of his family life during World War I. The confrontation with death, a feature of middle age accentuated by the loss of his mother, led Matisse to abandon his middle-aged wife to seek a new life and a new form in his art. His interiors initially revealed this emptiness; only gradually did he fill them with objects, plants, and particularly women. The early interiors revealed not only the emptiness of his inner world but also his loneliness during this period when the central figures in his life, Amélie and Marguerite, ceased to appear in his paintings. They were gradually replaced by youthful models who represented a life force and thereby helped him to renew his painting and to enrich his inner world once again. He began to translate powerful erotic impulses into canvases and drawings of splendid erotic nudes, yet he attempted to dissociate their eroticism from his portrayal of them as individuals. Toward the end of the 1920s his wife came to live with him, and he again transformed his art with new and great power.

REFERENCES

Arnason, H. H. 1977. *History of modern art*. New York: Harry Abrams.

Cowart, J., and Fourcade, D. 1986. *Henri Matisse: The early years in Nice 1916–1930*. New York: Harry Abrams.

Elderfield, J. 1976. *The "wild beasts": Fauvism and its affinities*. New York: Oxford University Press.

Flam, J. 1986. *Matisse: The man and his art 1869–1918*. Ithaca: Cornell University Press.

Freud, S. 1911. Formulations on two principles of mental functioning. In *Standard edition*, 12:215–226.

Kuspit, D. B. 1987. Conflicting logics: Twentieth-century studies at the crossroads. *Art Bulletin* 69:118–132.

Neugarten, B. 1979. Tune, age and the life cycles. *American Journal of Psychiatry* 136:887–893.

Pleynet, M. 1984. Matisse's system. In *Painting and System*. Chicago, n.p.

Schneider, P. 1984. *Matisse*. New York: Rizzoli International Publications.

Viederman, M. 1987. The nature of passionate love. In *Passionate attachment*. Ed. E. Person and W. Gaylin, 1–14. New York: Analytic Free Press.

CONTRIBUTORS AND EDITORS

ELIZABETH L. AUCHINCLOSS, M.D.
Faculty, Columbia University Center for Psychoanalytic Training and Research; clinical assistant professor of psychiatry, Cornell University Medical College.

CHARLES BRENNER, M.D.
Training and supervising psychoanalyst, New York Psychoanalytic Institute; clinical professor of psychiatry, State University of New York, Downstate Medical Center; author, *The Mind in Conflict*.

GERALD I. FOGEL, M.D.
Training and supervising psychoanalyst, Columbia University Center for Psychoanalytic Training and Research; assistant clinical professor of psychiatry, College of Physicians and Surgeons, Columbia University; coeditor, *The Psychology of Men: New Psychoanalytic Perspectives*.

ALLEN FRANCES, M.D.
Faculty, Columbia University Center for Psychoanalytic Training and Research; professor of psychiatry, Cornell University Medical College; coauthor, *Differential Therapeutics in Psychiatry*.

ROBERT A. GLICK, M.D.
Associate director and training and supervising psychoanalyst, Columbia University Center for Psychoanalytic Training and Research; associate clinical professor of psychiatry, College of Physicians and Surgeons, Columbia University.

MILTON H. HOROWITZ, M.D.
Training and supervising psychoanalyst, New York Psychoanalytic Institute; clinical professor of psychiatry, New York University School of Medicine.

LILA J. KALINICH, M.D.
Training and supervising psychoanalyst, Columbia University Center for Psychoanalytic Training and Research; associate clinical professor of psychiatry, College of Physicians and Surgeons, Columbia University; consultant to liaison psychiatry in obstetrics and gynecology, Presbyterian Hospital.

OTTO F. KERNBERG, M.D.
Associate chairman and medical director, New York Hospital–Cornell Medical Center, Westchester Division; professor of psychiatry, Cornell University Medical College; training and supervising psychoanalyst,

287

Columbia University Center for Psychoanalytic Training and Research; author, *Severe Personality Disorders: Psychotherapeutic Strategies*.

MARTHA KIRKPATRICK, M.D.
Faculty, Los Angeles Psychoanalytic Institute; clinical professor, Department of Psychiatry, University of California, Los Angeles; editor, *Women's Sexual Experience* and *Women's Sexual Development*.

ROBERT S. LIEBERT, M.D. (1930–1988)
Training and supervising psychoanalyst, Columbia University Center for Psychoanalytic Training and Research; clinical professor of psychiatry, College of Physicians and Surgeons, Columbia University; author, *Michelangelo: A Study of the Man and His Images*.

HELEN MEYERS, M.D.
Assistant director and training and supervising psychoanalyst, Columbia University Center for Psychoanalytic Training and Research; clinical professor of psychiatry, College of Physicians and Surgeons, Columbia University; editor, *Between Analyst and Patient: New Dimensions in Countertransference and Transference*.

ROBERT MICHELS, M.D.
Barklie McKee Henry Professor and chairman, Department of Psychiatry, Cornell University Medical College; training and supervising psychoanalyst, Columbia University Center for Psychoanalytic Training and Research; chairman, editorial board, *Psychiatry*.

ARNOLD H. MODELL, M.D.
Training and supervising psychoanalyst, Boston Psychoanalytic Institute; clinical professor of psychiatry, Harvard Medical School at the Beth Israel Hospital; author, *Psychoanalysis in a New Context*.

CAROL C. NADELSON, M.D.
Professor and vice-chairman of academic affairs, Department of Psychiatry, Tufts University School of Medicine; director of training and education, Department of Psychiatry, New England Medical Center Hospitals; past president, American Psychiatric Association; coeditor, *Women Physicians in Leadership Roles*.

JOHN M. OLDHAM, M.D.
Training and supervising psychoanalyst, Columbia University Center for Psychoanalytic Training and Research; professor and associate chairman, Department of Psychiatry, College of Physicians and Surgeons, Columbia University; coauthor, *Dynamic Therapy in Brief Hospitalization*.

PAUL H. ORNSTEIN, M.D.
Professor of psychiatry, University of Cincinnati Medical School; co-director, International Center for the Study of Psychoanalytic Self Psychology; editor, *The Search for the Self: Selected Writings of Heinz Kohut*, Vols. 1–4.

HERBERT PARDES, M.D.
Lawrence C. Kolb Professor and chairman, Department of Psychiatry; Vice President for Health Sciences and Dean, College of Physicians and Surgeons, Columbia University; coeditor, *Understanding Human Behavior in Health and Illness*.

SAMUEL W. PERRY, M.D.
Professor of clinical psychiatry, Cornell University Medical College; training and supervising psychoanalyst, Columbia University Center for Psychoanalytic Training and Research; author, *The DSM III Casebook of Differential Therapeutics*.

STEVEN P. ROOSE, M.D.
Faculty, Columbia University Center for Psychoanalytic Training and Research; associate professor of clinical psychiatry, College of Physicians and Surgeons, Columbia University; research psychiatrist, New York State Psychiatric Institute.

FRED M. SANDER, M.D.
Trustee, New York Psychoanalytic Institute; author, *Individual and Family Therapy*.

GEORGE E. VAILLANT, M.D.
Faculty, Boston Psychoanalytic Institute; Raymond Sobel Professor of Psychiatry, Dartmouth Medical School; author, *Adaptation to Life*.

MILTON VIEDERMAN, M.D.
Training and supervising psychoanalyst, Columbia University Center for Psychoanalytic Training and Research; professor of clinical psychiatry, Cornell University Medical College; director, Consultation-Liaison Service, New York Hospital.

INDEX